ENCYCLOPEDIA OF THE
Animal World

Vol 20   Tits—Water deer

Bay Books Sydney

TITS, term normally used to cover the small birds of the family Paridae of which there are some 50–60 species distributed throughout the world with the exception of the land masses in the southern hemisphere—Australia, New Zealand, Madagascar and South America. The word has been misleadingly used in different parts of the world as a name for birds in many different families, for example Bearded tit, Tree tits, Wren tits, Shrike tit, etc. The word 'tit' is an abbreviation of the earlier 'titmouse', though the latter is still used to describe one group of these birds in North America, while 'chickadee' is used for the others, on that continent.

All the birds are small, only the Sultan tit *Melanochlora sultanea* weighing much over $\frac{3}{4}$ oz (20 gm). While the North American and European species include some that are well known (indeed the Great tit must be amongst the most studied of all wild birds), the tits of Central Asia and the tropics are not well known, being small and rather inconspicuous members of large avifaunas. However, the great majority of the species are resident, or undergo only short migratory movements. All nest either in holes or in domed nests that they build themselves. They have large clutches, often of eight or more eggs, which are white with red spots.

The family is currently divided into three subfamilies, the Parinae or true tits, the Aegithalinae or Long-tailed tits and the Remizinae or Penduline tits. There is some doubt as to whether all these families are really closely related and some taxonomists divide them into three separate families. It has been suggested that the Parinae are more closely related to the Sittidae (nuthatches) than to the other 'tits'. It is only recently that the Bearded tit *Panurus biarmicus*, now sometimes called the reedling, was removed from this family and put with a family of the flycatcher group (Muscicapidae). Even if the three families are related it is likely that one or two of the species still included in them will be shown eventually to be more closely related to birds of other families.

The Penduline tits fall into three groups. The Penduline tit *Remiz pendulinus* is patchily distributed throughout southern Asia and its range extends into southern and eastern Europe, where it has been increasing in recent years. Tit-like in behaviour, it has a longish tail, is reddish chestnut above and buff beneath and the pale grey head and neck with the big black mask is diagnostic. It is a bird of marshy scrub and reeds. In the summer it feeds itself (and its chicks) on tiny insects which it collects off the herbage with its needle-shaped bill. In the winter it supplements its insect diet with small seeds from reeds etc. One of the most striking features of this species is its nest, which is a very soft

The Crested tit of Europe.

pouch-like structure with a small tubular entrance at the top. The nest is suspended from small twigs in a bush (hence the name of the species) and when it is built of the down from the seeds of the reed-mace, or similar material, it is strikingly soft and pliable.

There are six species of Penduline tit in Africa, all occurring south of the Sahara and all being placed in the genus *Anthoscopus*. They are birds of semi-open country with thin scrub, but are not so dependent on the proximity of water as is the European and Asian species. They also build domed nests, often less soft than those of the previous species. They are, however, probably tougher since they are used locally as purses.

The last species put in this family is the verdin *Auriparus flaviceps,* from the arid areas of southern United States and Mexico. It is quite different from the others in appearance being greyish above and white below with a chestnut shoulder and a yellow face and throat. The verdin builds the poorest nest in the group; although still domed it is a stiffer structure and less finely finished.

There are also some eight species of Long-tailed tits. The best known of these is again the one that occurs in Europe, *Aegithalos caudatus.* This species has a very wide distribution through Europe and Asia. It is striking in appearance with a pinkish and whitish body with black wings and a black tail with white edgings to the feathers. One of the smallest of the family, it weighs only about $\frac{1}{4}$ oz (6–8 gm), but has a tail of about $3\frac{1}{2}$ in (9 cm)—hence its name. Long-tailed tits are usually seen in small parties of six to ten birds. They feed on insects collected from the thin outer twigs of trees and tall bushes. They join with mixed parties of other tits.

Like the Penduline tits, the Long-tailed tits build a complex and striking domed nest and, although not suspended, it is woven into the branches of a gorse bush or bramble clump, or built into the fork of a tree high off the ground. The nest is made mainly of feathers and moss which are woven together with cobwebs—over 2,000 feathers have been counted in a single nest. The outside is usually camouflaged with a covering of lichens. Eight to twelve eggs are laid in the frail structure and when the young are large the nest expands to hold them all and bulges when they move.

Another striking feature of this species is its roosting habit. Each party roosts together in a little ball. At dusk they fly onto a selected small branch and cluster together, tails outwards. Doubtless this helps them to keep warm during the long winter nights.

There are four other species in the genus *Aegithalos*, which are similar to the European species in general appearance and are found in the Himalayas and China. They have more restricted ranges than the Euro-

pean one. The one other Old World species, *Psaltria exilis*, only occurs in Java. The two other species in this subfamily are bush-tits of the genus *Psaltriparus*. These are rather nondescript, greyish birds about the size of the other Long-tailed tits and with long tails. The Black-eared bush-tit *Psaltriparus melanotis* has a black mask reminiscent of the Penduline tit. It occurs on high ground in Mexico and extends just into the southern USA. The Common bush-tit *Psaltriparus minimus* is found mainly in the southwestern part of the USA and is common in rather arid scrubby country and open woodland. Like the Long-tailed tit, it lives in parties, but in this species the parties are much bigger, sometimes several hundred may be seen together. The bush-tits have sometimes been put in a separate family to the Long-tailed tits, but they are very similar in many ways: in their general appearance, calls and behaviour, their nests and in the habit of roosting communally.

The true tits of the subfamily Parinae include the best known species. They are small, active, arboreal birds, usually fairly tame and easy to see, often quite noisy. The great majority of them have the same general appearance and are easily recognized as tits, once the observer is familiar with one or two of the species. The majority have a 'capped' appearance. Usually the cap is black or brown and this is enhanced by white or pale cheeks. A black or dark brown bib is also often present, though not in most of the titmice of North America. Some, including this last group and the European Crested tit *Parus cristatus,* have quite conspicuous crests. The sexes are always similar and, in most species, cannot be distinguished in the field. However, in the two most common European species, the Great tit *Parus major* and the Blue tit *Parus caeruleus,* the males are generally brighter in colour. In the Great tit the male has a broader, blacker and shinier band down the centre of the yellow underparts.

There are some 40 or more species and they range over the whole of the area described above for the family. 11 of these are found in North America and nine in Europe. However, the ranges of many of these species do not overlap one another at all. Only in Britain (and some other parts of Europe) can one see feeding parties in winter which include five species of tits (six if one includes the Long-tailed). Some of the species are confined to relatively small areas of the world such as the Mexican chickadee *Parus sclatieri* from the mountains of Central America, while others, such as the Willow tit *Parus atricapillus,* spread the whole way across the Palearctic from Britain to Japan. The Great tit also does this but in addition extends southwards through the Middle East, much of India, China and Java. In

some of these areas it seems to be main confined to mangrove swamps. Througho this area there is great variation in t colours of the birds and many subspeci have been recognized.

These tits are predominantly woodlar dwellers, but they are very agile and versati and one of the reasons why they have bee popular with people is that they have foun it easy to live in garden habitats and to tak food from bird-tables in winter. They a relatively intelligent (by human standard and can be taught tricks, for example the are quick to learn to pull up pieces of strir to reach food on the end. In Japan t Varied tit *Parus varius* has been trained b fortune-tellers to carry small pieces of pap to people wishing to have their fortune told.

As far as is known they are all omni orous taking a mixed diet of insects, oth small animals and seeds. Their short, sto bills are very strong and a Blue tit can brea open the scales of pine cones to remove t insects inside, while the larger Great tit w hold down an acorn or a hazel nut with i feet and hack it open with woodpecker-lil blows. The Great tit has also been recorde killing young birds and adults of some of t smaller species such as goldcrests. It is pro ably a fair generalization to say that mo species feed on seeds and a few insects in t winter and almost exclusively on insects i the summer. Most of the European speci feed their young on caterpillars off trees.

Although most species are resident son of the northernmost tits may migrate sou for the winter and some of the Russian Grea tits have been recovered up to 1,240 mile (2,000 km) from the place of ringing, on even being recorded in Portugal. This i however, unusual and many of the bird remain for the winter at surprisingly hig latitudes. At least some of these seem to b dependent on man for their food at suc times. Great tits in northern Scandinavi have been recorded hopping around on on leg with the other tucked up inside the bel plumage to get warm. When this is warm the other leg is put up into the plumag and the warmed leg used for hopping.

To aid survival in such cold climate most tit species store considerable amount of seed in the autumn, jamming them int crevices in tree trunks for future consump tion. They may store large amounts of foo in this way. The habit does not seem to be s common in Britain, but Coal tits *Parus ate* may be observed doing this with peanut taken from bird tables. The seed supply i the autumn is very important to the tits as good crop of seeds is essential if the birds ar to survive the winter easily. Several specie among them the very common Blue an

A Blue tit at the entrance to its nest in a hollov in a tree trunk.

Great tits need a good crop of beech seed (mast) and the numbers of birds surviving the winter fluctuate according to the crop, being low when there is no crop and high when there is a rich crop. In years when there is a failure of many of the seed crops in northern Europe and Russia many tits may leave these areas and fly south and west to places where the winter weather is milder. These irruptive movements occur irregularly since they are dependent on seed-crop failure and, also to some extent, on there being large populations of tits. Occasionally these ir-rupting birds reach Britain in large numbers. However, the effect of the seed supply in Britain is more commonly noticed since the tits are well known for their tendency to feed at bird tables and they come to these most frequently when natural foods are short. Many of the birds that come to the bird tables are ones that normally live in wood-land. These will 'commute' to bird tables during the day and return to roost in the woods. Journeys of up to 3 miles (5 km) each way seem to be quite regular under such conditions.

All species are hole-nesters—unlike the species in the other two subfamilies. Many species need to find a ready-made hole, though they may enlarge it slightly; usually this is in a tree, but some species will nest in holes in the ground, the Coal tit doing this quite frequently. Nesting boxes are readily used and this habit, together with the abun-dance of some of the species, is the main reason why some of these species have proved so convenient for study and hence are so well known. A few species, such as the Willow tit and the Black-capped chickadee of North America (those two are considered by most authorities as the same species), normally excavate their own hole from a rotten stump of wood just prior to breeding. This appears to be part of a very rigid behaviour pattern, necessary before breeding can start, since they will not normally use a nesting box or even a hole that they made the previous year. Recently it has been shown that they will use a nesting box—if it is filled with wood shavings that they can excavate.

Both sexes help to build the nest which is basically of moss and may be lined with grass, feathers, hair, fur etc. During the laying period the eggs are kept covered with a wad of nesting material, but once incu-bation is properly under way the eggs are left uncovered when the bird is off the nest. The clutches are large, usually of seven to twelve eggs, though some of the tropical species may have smaller ones. The Blue tit not infrequently lays more eggs than this, clutch-es of 18 and 19 being recorded and, although

The Penduline tit *Remiz pendulinus* of Asia and Europe at its bag-like nest.

the young from such broods are usually very light in weight, the parents may well succeed in raising most of them to the point of leaving the nest. The total weight of clutches of this size may be of the order of $1\frac{1}{2}$ times the weight of the female and since the eggs are laid at the rate of one a day the strain of getting enough food to do this is considerable. It is not surprising that the male brings food to the female through much of the laying period. The male also feeds the female during incubation since the female alone incubates the eggs. He does not normally come to the nest, but approaches to within a few yards and quietly calls her off the nest and gives her the food.

The young usually hatch in about 13 days from the start of incubation. Normally most young hatch within a 24 hour period, though in some late broods hatching may be staggered over several days (in these broods the female starts to incubate some eggs before she has finished laying the others). The large number of young need a lot of food and the parents have to work hard to collect it. At the point in the nestling period when the young are needing the most food, the parents not infrequently bring a caterpillar a minute to the nest for 14 or 16 hours a day. A brood not infrequently receives 10,000 caterpillars during the time that it is in the nest.

The nestling period is about 18–21 days and this, together with a longish incubation period and the 10–14 days taken to lay the eggs, means that it takes some six or seven weeks to raise a brood, not counting the post-fledging care usually given to the young. This is longer than for many other birds of similar size (a European robin might complete a brood in about four weeks) but larger broods, longer incubation and longer fledging periods are characteristic of birds that nest in holes. Presumably this reflects the relative safety of the nest-site as contrasted with the normal 'open' nest which is so vulnerable to predation. The disadvantage of nesting in holes is that such sites are not always easy to find. Tits frequently fight over nesting sites and these fights take place not only between pairs of the same species, but also between different species. In Europe when such fights occur, the Great tit, being the largest, usually wins and the Blue tit wins in competition with the other smaller tits. Fights for nest-sites also occur between tits and other species such as nuthatch, Tree sparrow and Pied flycatcher. When these occur the tit usually loses against the first two and wins against the last.

In the case of the Blue and Great tits, the clutch size has been shown to vary under different conditions. Clutches laid by birds that are one year old are smaller than those laid by older birds, which is as well because they are less experienced in raising young. Clutches are smaller if the bird breeds late in

A male Bearded tit among the reeds, its usual habitat. The tendency today is to classify this species with the flycatchers, family Muscicapidae.

the season, because only those birds that lay early are able to make full use of the very abundant supply of caterpillars, present for a short time only. Clutches are smaller in gardens than in woodland because there is a much richer supply of caterpillars in the latter habitat and they are also smaller when there are many birds in the breeding area, as presumably there is less food for each bird when the population is high. Hence the birds are able to adjust their clutch-size somehow in relation to what the feeding conditions are likely to be. A similar situation has been noted with respect to second broods. Many tit species are usually single-brooded, partly because it takes so long to raise a brood and partly because their main food, the woodland caterpillars, are available for so brief a period. However, in the case of the Great tit second clutches are laid by the older birds and those that breed early. Second clutches are also laid when the population density is low. FAMILY: Paridae, ORDER: Passeriformes, CLASS: Aves.   C.M.P.

TOAD, a name referring strictly only to members of the family Bufonidae, but the terms 'frog' and 'toad' are the only common names available to describe the 2,000 species of the order Anura. Frog is used for those which have smooth skin and live in or near water while toad is used for those which have a warty skin or live in drier habitats. The terms are used independently of the actual relationships of the animals involved. For example, *Bombina bombina* of Europe is known as the Fire-bellied toad, but belongs to the family Discoglossidae, while *Scaphiopus holbrooki*, the Eastern spadefoot toad of America, is a member of the Pelobatidae. The term 'toad' was originally used for the genus *Bufo* which comprises the Common European toad *Bufo bufo* and the American toad *Bufo americanus* so the family Bufonidae can be referred to as the 'true toads'. The other toads are dealt with under their appropriate families while frogs and toads in general are dealt with under Anura.

In their internal structure members of the

When confronted by a Grass snake its natural enemy, the European Common toad blows itself up and rises high on stiff legs, making it difficult for the snake to swallow it.

toad can jump fairly well while others, such as the natterjack *B. calamita,* of Europe, have even shorter legs and only walk or run.

Toads are generally considered to be more intelligent than frogs although this is partly because, not relying on sudden leaps for their defence, they are slower and more predictable in their movements. While a frog will leap blindly off a table regardless of its height above the ground a toad will walk to the edge and look over. Toads learn fairly quickly (after about six attempts) not to eat bees and the lesson is remembered for about two weeks.

Toads have a marked homing instinct. Many species rest each day in a particular spot and, if taken and liberated as much as 1 ml (1·6 km) away, rapidly return to it. The mechanism by which they are able to do this is not fully understood although during the breeding season the calling of other toads certainly guides them back to their pond from a considerable distance.

Bufo bufo is the Common toad of Great Britain and Europe. It is usually brown in colour, sometimes spotted with dark brown, black or red, and females reach a length of about $3\frac{1}{2}$ in (8·7 cm) and males $2\frac{1}{2}$ in (6·2 cm) although in some warmer areas, probably because of the greater abundance of insect food, larger specimens are found, sometimes reaching a length of about $5\frac{1}{2}$ in (13·7 cm). Largely on the basis of such size differences the species is divided into several subspecies.

Toads are nocturnal, spending the day concealed in holes in walls, drainpipes or similar places. They emerge at night and feed on any small animal which moves. They are sometimes found sitting near a lighted window or lamp snapping up the insects attracted by the light. Like other anurans they are only able to recognize food if it moves but the feeding action of a toad is more deliberate than that of some anurans. If a worm is placed a few inches away from a toad, for example, it walks rapidly up to it and looks down at it for several seconds, its nervous energy being shown by a twitching of its toes. The worm is then snapped up, the toad's tongue flicking rapidly out and dragging the worm into the mouth.

Toads hibernate on land, burying themselves in loose soil, either alone or in groups. On emerging from hibernation, usually in March, they migrate to the breeding pond where the males attract the females to them by their calling. They usually call while raising themselves on their front legs in shallow water. The male clasps the female behind the arms and the pair swim about in amplexus until the female comes into contact with some waterweed. Oviposition then commences. The female extrudes the eggs in the form of a long string while the male ejects

Bufonidae are characterized by having an arciferal shoulder girdle (one in which the two ventral halves overlap in the mid-line) and procoelous vertebrae (this refers to the shape of the centra—the spool-shaped bones in the vertebral column). They are distinguished from the Atelopodidae and the Leptodactylidae, which also have these characters, in having a sternum or breastbone (it is absent in the Atelopodidae) and in not having an episternum, a bone on the front of the sternum (it is present in the Leptodactylidae).

There are 17 genera and the family is represented throughout the world except in Madagascar and Australasia.

The genus *Bufo* is the largest and most widespread, more than 200 species occurring throughout the world. Members of the genus are easily distinguished from other anurans. They have a short squat body and short legs and their skin is dry and covered with tubercles or warts. These warts are in fact collections of poison glands. Such glands are

present in most anurans but are most prominent in toads. When a toad is attacked it does not rely on long rapid jumps for defence but on these glands. Each wart exudes a milky fluid which acts as an irritant to the mucous membranes of the attacker. A dog, for example, which has picked up a toad in its mouth quickly drops it. It then shows signs of distress and copious saliva flows from its mouth. If larger doses of the fluid are injected into laboratory animals it acts as a cardiotoxin, slowing and eventually stopping the heart. The poison glands do not protect the toad against all predators; most snakes and birds are apparently unaffected by it. Two concentrations of these poison glands form a conspicuous oval ridge behind each eye known as *parotid glands.

The hindlegs of toads are relatively shorter than those of some other anurans such as the true frogs *(Rana)* and in general they crawl or progress in short hopping movements. This is not universal however and some species of

The natterjack, the European Toad that runs.

sperm over them. This continues at intervals for several hours, the female swimming round so that the long string of eggs, about 7–10 ft (2·1–3·0 m) long, is wrapped around waterweed. A total of about 4,000–5,000 eggs is laid. The tadpoles hatch after about 12 days but the time taken to develop into the adult varies considerably, depending on the temperature. About three months is an average period although in warm areas it may be two months while in some cold areas the tadpoles have been known to hibernate and metamorphose the next year.

This description of the habits of *B. bufo* is applicable in general to all the 150 species of the genus *Bufo*. They are all similar in appearance and habits and are not highly specialized for a particular habitat. It is probably this general adaptability which has enabled the genus to become world-wide in distribution. In general toads are found in open country rather than in wooded parts. The skin is thick and resists desiccation and several species are found in desert areas.

The American toad *B. americanus* is found throughout the eastern half of North America in almost any habitat, from gardens to mountains, the only requisites being shallow breeding pools and moist hiding places. It is 3–5 in (7·5–12·5 cm) in length and usually a reddish brown although there is a great variation in the markings. Like several species of *Bufo* the American toad has a pattern of bony crests on the head.

The Southern toad *B. terrestris* is more restricted in its range occurring in the southeast coastal plain from North Carolina to the Mississippi River. It is $1\frac{1}{2}$–$3\frac{1}{2}$ in (3·7–8·7 cm) long and the bony crests have two pronounced knobs behind the eyes which give the toad a 'horned' appearance. It is found in most open situations but is particularly abundant in sandy areas. There are about 16 species of *Bufo* in North America although the number of subspecies is uncertain.

It is a characteristic of the genus *Bufo* that because the species are all so similar the taxonomy is not fully worked out. For example, hybrids between some species have been found and some forms which were thought to be a single species are found to be two which can only be distinguished by the call of the male. In southern Africa 21 forms of *Bufo* are found and these can be grouped into five distinct groups but what taxonomic status these groups should be given is uncertain.

The Common or Square-marked toad *B. regularis* is the commonest toad in Africa and is found from the Cape to Egypt. It is up to 4 in (10 cm) in length with a pattern of dark brown blotches on a light background. These are so arranged that there is a conspicuous light-coloured cross between the eyes which is distinctive of the species. It spends the day

hiding under logs and stones and emerges to feed at night. It breeds from August to late summer, as many as 24,000 eggs being laid by each female. The tadpoles hatch after four days and change into toads after about one month.

B. anotis is the only toad in southern Africa which is forest-dwelling. Nothing is known of its breeding habits but it is found a long way from water and its eggs are large which may indicate that the development occurs on land. Further investigation may show that it does not in fact belong to the genus *Bufo*.

Some of the smallest members of the genus are found in South Africa. The Striped mountain toad *B. rosei* is an agile little toad about $1\frac{1}{2}$ in (3·7 cm) in length and dark brown with three light stripes running along the body. It is found in marshy areas on open mountain slopes. The Pigmy toad *B. vertebralis* is even smaller, females being about 1 in (2·5 cm) long. They are light brown with dark brown patches and the parotid glands

are very indistinct. They are found in open sandy and grassy areas and the development is very rapid, small toads, about $\frac{1}{4}$ in (6 mm) long, emerging from the water about 16 days after the eggs are laid.

Another small toad is the Oak toad *B. quercicus* of North America. The adults are $\frac{3}{4}$–$1\frac{1}{4}$ in (20–32 mm) long with a short fat body. They are dusky brown, with black and white patches and a light stripe down the middle of the back. They are common in the pinewoods of the southeast, preferring sandy areas. They spend some time buried under leaves or in the sand but are more active during the day than other species of toad.

For a long time toads have been generally regarded with loathing as poisonous or evil creatures. They are, of course, completely harmless and are in fact beneficial to man in the enormous numbers of insects which they eat in gardens and farms. This feature has been made use of in the Marine toad *B. marinus*, one of the largest species of toad reaching a length of 9 in (22·5 cm) and found

Spawn of the European Common toad consists of strings of eggs.

from Patagonia to southern Texas. It has been introduced into several parts of the world such as Puerto Rica, Haiti and Hawaii to control the beetles which cause considerable damage to the sugar cane crops. Following such successes it was introduced into Australia in 1935 to combat the beetle *Dermolepida albohirtum.* This has not been very successful and in the absence of many natural predators the toads, which are known as Cane toads in Australia, are multiplying rapidly and increasing their range.

Other genera of Bufonidae are more restricted in their range. Species of *Pseudobufo* are found in the Malay peninsula and Borneo. Although their skin is rough like that of *Bufo* their toes are completely webbed and they are aquatic. The tip of the snout is turned up so that the nostrils protrude above the surface as they lie in the water.

Nectophryne is another genus which has habits different from those of *Bufo.* Species of this genus are found in southern Asia and have small discs on the tips of their digits which help them to climb bushes and trees.

Species of *Ansonia* from the Philippines breed in fast-flowing mountain streams and the tadpoles have flattened bodies and sucker-like mouths to cling to rocks.

Two species of *Nectophrynoides* are found in Africa and are unique among anurans in that the female gives birth to fully metamorphosed toads. The eggs, about 100 in number in *N. vivipara,* are retained in the oviducts where the tadpole stage is passed through. How the sperms are transmitted from the male is not known as no copulatory organs have been seen. FAMILY: Bufonidae, ORDER: Anura, CLASS: Amphibia.   M.E.D.

TOADSTONE. A common legend about toads was that there lay in their heads a precious stone called toadstone, noset or crapaudina.

'The toad, ugly and venomous,
Wears yet a precious jewel in his head.'
As you like it

The value of toadstone lay in its ability to cure the poisonous bites of snakes, spiders, wasps and other animals merely by touching the affected part with it. It also changed colour or became warm in the presence of venom. There were several ways of obtaining toadstone. One was to put a toad in an earthenware pot and bury it in an ant hill. The ants removed the flesh leaving only the bones and the stone. Another method was to place a live toad on a scarlet cloth. The toad would stretch itself with delight and cast out the stone which had to be quickly removed before the toad swallowed it again. One could tell that a toadstone was genuine by showing it to a toad who would leap at it and try to snatch it away.

TOAD BUGS, a small family of bugs distributed through the warmer parts of the Americas. In the United States, they are not uncommon in damp vegetation bordering streams and rivers, particularly in the southern States. Their common name aptly describes their appearance, for the small, squat, brown body is surmounted by a pair of prominent, bulging eyes. They are predatory, feeding on other small insects. FAMILY: Gelastocoridae, ORDER: Hemiptera, CLASS: Insecta, PHYLUM: Arthropoda.

TOADFISHES, sluggish, heavily-built, bottom-living fishes found in all tropical seas. They are distantly related to both the cod-like fishes (Gadiformes) and the angler-fishes (Lophiiformes). Most are marine, but a few enter estuaries. Toadfishes have broad, slightly flattened heads, their skin is naked or has very tiny smooth scales. Some have small teeth, while others have a few large and pointed ones. These fishes appear to be willing to eat almost anything and some have strong jaws able to crush shellfish. Two dorsal fins are present, the first small and spiny and quite separate from a longer soft-rayed fin. Both dorsal fins are covered in skin, the fin-rays being apparent only when the fin is pinched between the fingers.

Toadfishes of the genus *Thalassophryne,* from the Pacific coast of Panama, have poisonous spines. One spine is located on the upper edge of the gill cover (operculum) and there are two more in the spiny dorsal fin. The spines are hollow, with a poison gland at the base of each spine. Pressure on the spine releases the poison, which flows along the spine and into the wound. The poison is not lethal to man but can cause a most painful wound.

Certain toadfishes, such as the midshipman *Porichthys porosissimus* from the Atlantic and *P. notatus* from the Pacific, are equipped with several hundred small luminous organs along the underside of the body, the arrangement of these organs being specific and presumably an aid to recognition by members of the same species.

In Australia, the toadfishes are referred to as frogfishes. The genus *Batrachoemus* contains species which reach 14 in (35 cm) in length, lack poison glands and have scaleless bodies. These are egg-layers, the female often depositing the eggs inside such man-made objects as tin cans. This habit presumably arose because toadfishes frequently congregate in areas where refuse is dumped. Normally, however, the eggs are deposited in crevices in rocks. During the incubation period the male actively guards the eggs, an important precaution when a single predator could easily snap up an entire brood. Toadfishes can happily live in foul water and they can also survive for a surprising length of time out of water. Many toadfishes make

grunting noises with their swimbladder. FAMILY: Batrachidae, ORDER: Batrachoidiformes, CLASS: Pisces.

TODIES, five very similar species of tiny, kingfisher-like birds. Four of these are lowland forest birds occurring on different islands of the Caribbean—Cuba, Jamaica, Hispaniola and Puerto Rico. They closely resemble each other and may be regarded as island representatives of the same superspecies. Their long bills are relatively broad. The fifth species the Narrow-billed tody *Todus augustirostris,* occurs in the mountain forests of Hispaniola and has, as the name implies, a more slender bill. Todies are small plump birds, 3–4 in ($7\frac{1}{2}$–10 cm) long, with short legs and long, straight and somewhat flattened bills. They inhabit forests where they keep to shady areas among the foliage, squatting on small twigs, usually with the bill tilted up at a sharp angle. They are green above and white, sometimes tinted with green, yellow or pink below. They have varying amounts of bright red on the throat. The young are similar in appearance to the adults but lack the red throat, having a pale grey one until after the first moult.

Their principal food is insects. A tody sits and waits until it sees an insect, then rises suddenly from the perch with a buzzing sound, flying out and seizing the insect with a snap of the bill, then returning to the perch again. It will also take other small moving creatures such as tiny lizards. The buzzing or whirring sound of the wings is produced by the narrow tapering outer primary feather of each wing. This noise appears to be, to some degree, under the conscious control of the bird. It is made by both sexes and is most often heard during the breeding season and probably has some function in display.

The tody nests in a tunnel in a bank in the forest, excavating its own hole with its bill. The bank need be of no great height, and may be very small indeed, for example the side of a cart-rut. The tunnel is anything from a few inches to 2 ft (up to 60 cm) in length. The diameter of it is small, about the size of the bird, but it opens out at the end into an enlarged nest-chamber. No nest material is used and the eggs are laid on the floor of the chamber itself. There are from two to five small round eggs in a clutch and they are relatively large in relation to the body size of the bird. They are white at first, becoming gradually discoloured by the soil on which they lie. Both parents take part in the incubation.

Todies are sedentary, rarely travelling far, and usually associating in pairs. The short rounded wings, while satisfactory for short, fly-catching flights, are not used for long sustained flights. The voice consists of sharp chipping notes and, although all todies are rather similar in other respects, the voice differs from one species to another. The Narrow-billed tody has a sharp chattering call. FAMILY: Todidae, ORDER: Coraciiformes, CLASS: Aves.

TOKAY Gekko gecko, a small common *gecko of the tropics of southeastern Asia. Its common name is derived from its loud call of to kay.

TOLERANCE RANGE, range of physical factors in the environment of animals, such as temperature, light or humidity, with upper and lower limits beyond which the species cannot survive. The House fly Musca domestica for instance, has a tolerance range for temperature of 42·8–111·2°F (6–44°C), though it can survive colder or hotter conditions for a few minutes. Near the centre of its tolerance range to a particular factor the species has an optimum range in which the physiology of the animal seems to function best; in the House fly this range is 59–73°F (15–23°C). Outside the optimum range, but within the tolerance range, are conditions in which the animal suffers various forms of physiological stress.

The prefixes eury– and steno– are used to indicate a wide or narrow tolerance range for an environmental factor, e.g. a eurythermal species has a wide tolerance range for temperature and a stenothermal species a narrow one. The Common frog Rana temporaria has eggs which are eurythermal and can develop over the temperature range 32–86°F (0°–30°C). This tolerance range is necessary for the survival of the frog as the spawn is laid in spring when the nights are cold, but when a warm spring day may cause a quite considerable temperature increase in the shallow ponds and ditches where frogs breed. Most trout eggs, however, are relatively stenothermal and cannot develop outside the temperature range 32–52°F (0°–12°C); since trout breed in mountain streams and lakes which are cool at all times of the year, these temperatures are rarely exceeded. Cold- and warm-bloodedness (poikilothermy and homoiothermy) are special aspects of stenothermy and eurythermy. Warm-blooded animals regulate their body temperature so that they are to some extent independent of climatic conditions. They can, however, tolerate only small changes in their internal body temperature and in this respect are strongly stenothermal. The human body temperature of 98·4°F (36·9°C) need vary by only half a degree centigrade for us to feel unwell. Cold-blooded animals have a body temperature close to that of their surroundings; they have a greater tolerance to variations in their body temperature than do warm-blooded animals, but this has the disadvantage that they become inactive during cold spells and overactive when the temperature is high.

Some insects, however, particularly social Hymenoptera (ants, bees and wasps), have behaviour-patterns which allow them to exert some control over their body temperature. Among ants this may consist only of opening up or closing the entrance to the nest according to the temperature of the air, but in the honeybee the temperature in the hive is maintained during the summer around 93–95°F (34–35°C) by complex social behaviour. If the temperature rises slightly above the optimum level the nest is cooled by wing fanning; at higher temperatures the bees spread water over the surface of the comb. When the temperature of the nest falls below 86°F (30°C) they cluster tightly together and are able in winter to maintain a minimum temperature of 55·4°F (13°C). Honeybees are able to act collectively as a 'homoiotherm' in maintaining a nest temperature within the optimum range of the species during periods when temperature conditions outside the nest are unfavourable for the survival of the individual.

The tolerance and optimum ranges of a species are closely related to its choice of habitat and its geographical distribution. Animals with a limited tolerance range to most environmental factors (stenokic) are restricted to stable environments and may consequently be limited in their geographical distribution (stenotopic). Other species which are tolerant to fluctuations in many physical and biotic factors (eurokic) are likely to be represented in more varied and variable habitats. Since this high degree of tolerance breaks down many physiological barriers to distribution, eurokic animals tend to have a wider geographical distribution (eurytopic) than stenokic species. Animals frequently vary in their susceptibility to environmental fluctuations at different stages of their life-cycle. Many insects are able to survive, as eggs or pupae, winter conditions which would kill the adults; alternatively breeding may be linked to the seasonal cycle so that the young are produced during periods most favourable to their survival. Most animals have a restricted tolerance range for one physical factor or combination of factors. Mammals are tolerant of high temperatures only if sufficient water is available. Some marine animals, which can survive wide variations in the salt content of the water (euryhaline), can live in the brackish upper reaches of estuaries and even freshwater only when the temperature, and consequently their metabolic activity, is high, but are restricted to the lower, more saline reaches of the estuary and the open sea in winter. The physical factor which limits the distribution of an animal species, even when it is tolerant of other environmental conditions, for example water and temperature respectively in the examples given above, is known as a limiting factor.

Many species can become acclimatized to a different tolerance range if the change is made sufficiently slowly; however, the characteristic tolerance ranges to environmental factors are inheritable by the next generation. J.M.A.

TOMMYGOFF, vernacular name used in Panama for the snake also known as *fer-de-lance.

TOMOPTERIS, one of the few polychaete worms that are completely pelagic. The whole life-cycle is spent in the open water, often far from land or at great depths. The large number of species are all very similar in appearance. Their bodies are long, transparent, tapering at the end, with a row of paddle-like parapodia along each side. From the head on either side trails backwards what looks like a long slender tentacle. It is, in fact, a drawn-out parapodium supported by a long bristle. Most tomopterids are small, especially those in tropical waters but in colder waters and greater depths or in polar waters, they may be up to 4 in (100 mm) long. The great majority are only up to 1 in (10–25 mm) or so in length. The paddle-like parapodia contain various glands, some of which act as luminescent organs. The sexes are separate, the eggs or sperm maturing within the body cavity to be eventually shed into the sea where development takes place. The gut is a simple tube and there is a muscular proboscis which can be protruded to grasp the prey. The delicate appearance of tomopterids belies their voracious nature: they prey greedily on other planktonic organisms such as copepods. FAMILY: Tomopteridae, CLASS: Polychaeta, PHYLUM: Annelida. R.P.D.

TONGUE SOLES, a family of elongated, tongue-shaped flatfishes from warm seas. The dorsal, anal and caudal fins coalesce to form a single fin round the body; the pelvic fins are absent. These fishes lie on their right side, the eyes being on the left. The head somewhat resembles that in the true soles (family Soleidae) in that the snout projects well beyond the mouth. Ribs are absent. The Tongue soles are found in warm waters but Cynoglossus brownii has once been recorded from the North Sea, some thousands of miles from its usual habitat off the west coast of Africa. This species is also one of the few that is large enough to be of any great commercial importance although some Indo-Pacific species attain 15 in (38 cm) and are caught for food. FAMILY: Cynoglossidae, ORDER: Pleuronectiformes, CLASS: Pisces.

TOOL USING, the manipulation by an animal of an inanimate object with a resulting increase in efficiency in the behaviour pattern of which it is a part. A number of animals manipulate such objects during play: young hawks play with fir cones and cats play with a wide variety of materials. This is different from tool-using in which the object manipulated acts as an intermediary between the animal and some observable goal.

The prime tool-user is man, whose use of tools has reached a very high level of development. Other primates also use tools. The chimpanzees' tea party at the London Zoo is an outstanding example of such tool-using and of its popular appeal. Chimpanzees in the wild regularly use sticks deliberately for obtaining food, as well as throwing sticks, stones, and vegetation in both playful and aggressive encounters. Their most advanced tool-usage is in their manipulation of sticks or grass stems for feeding on termites. In Tanzania termites build large mounds up to 4 ft (1·2 m) high and very hard. The chimpanzees locate the mounds more efficiently than can a human and then apparently test them by smell for their suitability as a source of termites. When a mound has been chosen the ape selects a thin twig or grass stem, holds it in its mouth while opening up a hole in the mound by digging with a finger, and then deftly inserts the twig, held in the hand. The twig is withdrawn again almost immediately and, if all goes well, will have a number of large termites attached to it by their jaws. These are quickly taken off, by the animal passing the twig through its mouth, and crunched up. If the probe is unsuccessful the ape is likely to take another tool or try another hole. One old experienced male chimpanzee watched feeding in this way caught and ate over a thousand large termites and many smaller ones in 75 minutes. A competent human observer attempting to copy the process could only catch 60 termites in an hour. The apes commonly carry out running repairs on their probes by biting off the bent end with their teeth, and will carry really good probes 50 yd or more between mounds.

The only other mammal that regularly uses a tool is the Sea otter *Enhydra lutris*. After diving for food it habitually surfaces with a stone, turns onto its back, places the stone on its chest, and pounds hard food such as mussels, crabs and Sea urchins against it. The prey is held with both forepaws together and brought down sharply on the stone, many rapid blows being struck, at a rate of about 2 per sec, breaking the hard shells so that the otter can remove the flesh. Sometimes the otter will retain the same stone for a considerable time, diving and resurfacing with it again and again. This indicates that the otter is fully aware of what it is doing. There is even evidence that it carries the stone in the armpit when it has its hands full.

The fact that the prey is banged against the stone and not vice versa simply means that this is the best way to do it. The alternative would be to bang the prey on a stone on the seabed, in which case the otter would run out

of air and would have to resurface repeatedly while dealing with one prey animal. This clearly would be inefficient.

The use of an anvil for smashing mollusc shells is also seen in some birds, particularly well known in the European Song thrush *Turdus philomelos*. Snails, and in some areas even winkles from the sea-shore, are picked up in the bill and struck against stones or other hard objects. Such anvils, with a surrounding litter of broken shells, are familiar sights in certain areas. A number of birds drop prey from a height. Crows and gulls drop shellfish and eggs to break them. Gulls, at least, not uncommonly drop such prey onto ground which is too soft to do much damage, but the Bearded vulture or lammergeier *Gypaetus barbatus*, which drops bones or tortoises to break them open, carefully selects suitable rocks on which to let them fall.

A different example of tool-using is that of the Egyptian vulture *Neophron percnopterus*, which in many parts of its range in Africa breaks open ostrich eggs by throwing stones at them. The bird takes a stone in its bill and with a forward and downward movement propels it at the egg. Here again there seems not always to be a conscious connection between cause and effect, for some individuals will continue throwing stones in the direction of broken egg shells.

The most highly developed example of tool-using in birds is in the Galapagos Woodpecker finch *Camarhynchus pallidus*. It will probe and dig in trees with its bill, but it will also take a cactus spine or fine twig in its bill and poke in crevices, including those it has itself dug, to drive out the insect or other invertebrate. The tool may even be retained in the foot while the bird is feeding on animals it has disturbed, and taken up again for

further use. As in the chimpanzees, this is an example of tool-using in the strictest sense of the term.

Another form of tool-using is seen in the bowerbirds, some of which decorate the walls of their bowers with the juices of coloured berries or charcoal from a bush fire made into a paste with saliva. They use a piece of fibrous bark to apply the colours. This behaviour recalls the paintings produced by chimpanzees in captivity, and also by Capuchin monkeys of South America. In their intelligence the capuchins are the equivalent in the New World of the apes in the Old World. In problem-solving tests capuchins have shown themselves as capable as chimpanzees, able to use sticks to draw food towards the bars of their cages or to pile boxes in order to reach fruit suspended from the ceiling. They also throw things at people and one seems to have realized that throwing missiles at people's feet had little effect so it stood on a chair to be able to aim higher. This same capuchin also used a hammer in the correct manner and when too old to crack Brazil nuts with its teeth it smashed them with a marrow bone.

Among invertebrates there is at least one that shows signs of being a genuine tool-user. This is the Digger wasp *Ammophila* which digs shafts in sandy ground in which to lay its eggs. It kills caterpillars and spiders to place in the shaft for its larvae to eat and then plugs the shaft with sand. Finally it selects a grain of sand slightly larger than the rest and holding this in its jaws tamps firm the sand filling the entrance to the shaft.   P.M.D.

TOOTHCARPS, small, basically freshwater, fishes related to the Flying fishes, half-beaks and silversides. They are also known as top-minnows or killifishes (although the latter

Chriopeops goodei, the Blue-fin top minnow, one of the egg-laying toothcarps of North America.

One of the order of Toothed whales, the familiar Bottlenosed dolphin *Tursiops truncatus*, often called a porpoise, in a seaquarium.

term is one usually employed by aquarists to refer only to the egg-laying members of this suborder). The toothcarps are not related to the true carps. The group can be divided into the egg-layers (principal family Cyprinodontidae) and the live-bearers (principal family Poeciliidae).

The cyprinodonts or killifishes include the remarkable *Annual fishes whose whole life-span is confined to the rainy season, the eggs only surviving through to the next season. Probably the most beautiful member of this group is the Argentine pearlfish. The pan-chaxes are typical cyprinodonts from Asia while the lyre-tails (genus *Aphyosemion*) are rather similar fishes from Africa. The cyprinodonts are, however, most common in the Americas. The genus *Fundulus* contains many species in North and Central America as well as some of the offshore islands. These are usually cylindrical fishes with flat heads, the mouth directed upwards and the dorsal and anal fins short-based. Some species, such as *Fundulus notatus* live and feed at the surface, while others like the golden-ear *F. chrysotus* may lie in the mud. The surface-living forms have a light golden mark on the top head. Certain of the species of *Fundulus* can tolerate salt water and *F. parvipinnis* of California is found in tide-pools while the Zebra killifish *F. heteroclitus* of eastern USA is found in brackish water. Some of the killifishes are very beautifully coloured, par-ticularly those from Florida. The killifishes

are so popular amongst aquarists that societies have been formed solely for the appreciation of this group of fishes.

One highly unusual cyprinodont is *Pantanodon podoxys*, a small species from Kenya and Tanzania which reaches 1–1½ in (2·5–4 cm) in length. Unlike other toothcarps, it has no teeth in the jaws and has become adapted to filter-feeding on micro-organisms in the water. The tiny gillrakers are lined with very minute fans which can be opened or closed. This species has been successfully bred in aquaria.

The live-bearing poeciliids include such species as the guppy, the mollies, the sword-tails, the Four-eyed fishes and the mosquito-fishes. These are all confined to the New World and are discussed generally under live-bearing fishes. FAMILIES: Cyprinodontidae, Poeciliidae etc, ORDER: Atheriniformes, CLASS: Pisces.

TOOTHED WHALES, the largest and most abundant of the two main suborders of living Cetacea. As their name implies Toothed whales have teeth instead of the whalebone of the other group. They range widely in size, from small porpoises and dolphins of 4–5 ft (1½ m) in length to the huge Sperm whale *Physeter catodon* of 60 ft (20 m). Only a small proportion of the Toothed whales are whales in the generally accepted sense, that is, having a length of 20 ft (7 m) or over. The majority are the smaller porpoises and dolphins.

The exact number of species is unknown for some may still be undescribed and others only tentatively described on the basis of the one or a few skulls, the living animal never having been seen. Recently a school of the Slender blackfish *Feresa* were caught off Japan; previously they had been known from four specimens only from various parts of the world. It may be that the genus is quite plentiful and widespread and may be well known to fishing communities if not to scientists.

Although they are called Toothed whales, not all species show teeth, though even the apparently toothless ones may have teeth present in rudimentary form below the gum surface. In one species, the narwhal *Monodon monoceros*, the female has no teeth whilst the male normally possesses only a single tusk which is a modified left incisor. In the other species, the teeth where present are usually simple conical structures, but those of the porpoises are spade-like. In general, the possession of teeth indicates a need to catch prey such as fish whereas those species with few or rudimentary teeth feed on cuttlefish and similar food for which a firm mouth alone gives sufficient grip.

The blowhole is single in the Toothed whales and may even be to one side. This tendency to asymmetry is always present in the skulls of cetaceans and may be consider-able. Much of the skull asymmetry is associ-ated with the nasal passages where, in some species, one side of the internal nares is a wide channel used for the main air transit whilst the other side consists of a larger series of sac and valve mechanisms, probably associated with sound production for echolocation or sonar.

There are five living superfamilies in the order. The River dolphins Platanistoidea are in many ways the nearest to the ancestral forms. There are four genera, each living in a large freshwater inland waterway. Some of the Beaked whales (Ziphiidae) are very rare, if only to science. Most have only rudimentary teeth in the lower jaw and showing only in the male. The two species of Sperm whale (Physeteridae) are the best known Toothed whales with a large head-case and having teeth in the lower jaw only. The Monodontidae consists of two species, the narwhal and the White whale *Delphinapterus leucas.* The Delphinoidea is by the far the largest superfamily consisting of three families, the little-known Long-beaked or Rough-toothed dolphins (Stenidae), the porpoises (Phocaenidae), and the dolphins proper (Delphinidae). See Beaked whales, Cetacea, dolphins, narwhal, Pilot whale, porpoises, River dolphins, Sperm whales, whales, White whale. SUBORDER: Odonticeti, ORDER: Cetacea, CLASS: Mammalia. K.M.B.

TOPI *Damaliscus lunatus,* one of the 'bastard' *hartebeest, closely related to the bontebok and blesbok.

TOPKNOTS, small flatfishes from the North Atlantic. The name refers to the fact that the dorsal fin begins over the snout. The Common topknot *Zeugopterus punctatus* lies on its right side and reaches 10 in (25 cm) in length. It has an almost circular body, brownish in colour with dark bars just behind the eyes that resemble eyebrows and give the fish a rather quizzical look. The Norwegian topknot *Phrynorhombus norvegicus* has a longer body and black blotches. It grows to 5 in (13 cm) and is found northwards from the British Isles. Ekstrom's topknot *P. regius* is the rarest of the three, and little is known of its habits. It grows to 8 in (20 cm) and is found off the west coasts of England and France. Its rarity may be apparent rather than actual as it is small, hides in the sand and under rocks and lives in rocky areas offshore which are not fished. FAMILY: Bothidae, ORDER: Pleuronectiformes, CLASS: Pisces.

TOPMINNOWS, yet another name for the *toothcarps or killifishes.

TOP SHELL, marine snails, related to *periwinkles and named for their resemblance to the children's whip top of the 19th century. They belong to the most primitive

The Painted top shell of the coasts of Europe on a rock at low-tide.

Tortoises

group of prosobranch gastropods, having two auricles to the heart, two kidneys and only one gill. The head of the snail bears a pair of sensory tentacles for touch and taste and each has an eye near its base. Along the sides of the foot are 3–6 pairs of longer tentacles and at the rear of the foot is a circular cover, or operculum, which closes the entrance to the shell when the mollusc withdraws into it.

There are over 50 genera of Top shells ranging from $\frac{1}{25}$–6 in (1–150 mm) across the base, with the lower part of the shell usually marked with distinct spiral ridges or oblique bands of colour. The Painted top shell *Calliostoma zizyphinus,* of Europe, is pink or yellow, flecked with crimson or red-brown. It is 1 in (26 mm) high and slightly less across the base. The Brick-red top shell *Astraea inaequalis* is found on the Pacific coast of North America. One of the largest Top shells measuring up to 5–6 in (13–15 cm) across the base is the Button shell of the shallow waters of the Great Barrier Reef, the northern Australian coasts and the Indo-Pacific. Its shell is white marked with wavy red-brown bands and, because of its mother-of-pearl interior, it is collected for the manufacture of buttons, and a thriving button export industry has been built up in Australia.

Many species of Top shell are found between tidemarks but most of them live offshore and down to depths of 600 ft (182 m) being most numerous in tropical and sub-tropical seas. Most of the species feed by rasping off minute particles from very small seaweeds by means of a ribbon-like radula which has many rows of unspecialized teeth.

In the primitive Grey top shell *Gibbula cineraria* the eggs are shed into the water and a ciliated planktonic trochophore larva hatches. This stage is omitted in most Top shells which produce gelatinous egg masses from which a later stage planktonic veliger larva emerges. FAMILY: Trochidae, ORDER: Archaeogastropoda, SUBCLASS: Proso-branchia, CLASS: Gastropoda, PHYLUM: Mollusca.   R.C.N.

TORTOISES, slow-moving, heavily ar-moured reptiles which first appeared some 200 million years ago and have remained relatively unchanged for 150 million years. The body is enclosed in a box or shell which in many species is rigid and into which the head, tail and limbs can in many instances be withdrawn. The top of the shell, known as the *carapace, is formed from overgrown, widened ribs. The lower part of the shell, called the *plastron, is also made up of bony plates. Both carapace and plastron are covered with horny plates or shields known as scutes. The males are usually smaller than the females and often have a longer tail and the plastron may be concave.

The order to which tortoises belong used to

be called the *Chelonia but is now known as the *Testudines. The order includes tortoises, turtles and terrapins, three names which tend to be given different meanings in different parts of the English-speaking world, but all have certain fundamental features in com-mon.

For example, they have no teeth, but the jaws are covered with a horny bill which can be used for tearing food apart. They have moveable eyelids which are closed in sleep. Their external ear openings are covered with a membrane and it is doubtful if the Tes-tudines can hear airborne sounds but like snakes they probably can pick up vibrations through ground or through water. They all lay eggs and the aquatic species must come ashore to lay them. In temperate climates land tortoises hibernate in the ground and freshwater species under mud at the bottoms of ponds. As a group they are noted for their long life-spans, the longest recorded being in excess of 158 years, for one of the Giant tortoises, but even the Garden tortoise has been recorded as living 50 years or more.

Tortoises form one family, the Tes-tudinidae of the suborder Cryptodira or Snake-necked tortoises. The carapace is usually rigidly ossified and domed. The only substantial difference from the closely related Pond tortoises, family Emydidae, is in the structure of the feet. Whereas in the Pond

tortoises the legs end in free fingers and toes, which are more or less firmly connected with each other by webs, in the tortoises the toes are incorporated in the structure of their club-feet, so that only the horny claws can be seen. Many investigators therefore regard tortoises and Pond tortoises as two sub-families of a single family, Testudinidae.

In some types of tortoises the outsides of the forelegs and hindlegs are sometimes covered with large, strong scutes, which are partly ossified even at the base. As these parts remain visible when the creature is retracting under the carapace, the large scutes represent a special protection.

The structural arrangement of the carapace or shield of the tortoise is not basically different from that of the other neck-hiding tortoises, but the bony plates are always covered with horny epidermal plates; there is never a thick leathery epidermis such as that of the Mud turtles Trionychidae, the Papua turtle (*Carettochelys*) or the Leathery turtle (*Dermochelys*). On the other hand, in the Flexible-shelled or Tornier's tortoise *Malacochersus tornieri* the horny part of the shield has almost completely degenerated and therefore appears soft, since the creature is covered by practically no more than the horny epidermal plates. The shells of the Giant tortoises of the Galapagos and Sey-chelles Islands are also quite thin.

Above: Aldabra giant tortoises on the island of that name in the Indian Ocean.

Skeleton of a tortoise. Top: with the plastron separated and laid to one side the skeleton is exposed showing backbone, pectoral and pelvic girdles and limbs; bottom: longitudinal section showing integration of backbone carapace.

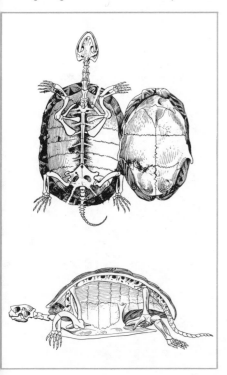

In the Pond tortoises, as in some other types of tortoises part of the plastron is hinged. The hinge is usually in the posterior part of the plastron and is found in particular in older females as in the case of the Algerian tortoise *Testudo graeca*; it probably makes its egg-laying easier. In the Spider tortoise *Pyxis arachnoides* of Madagascar, however, the fore portion of the plastron is articulated. As an exception to all other types, in the Flexible tortoises of the African genus *Kinixys* there is a transverse hinge at the posterior part of the dorsal carapace, which can be drawn down like the visor of a helmet.

Nearly all tortoises move very slowly, and therefore they feed chiefly upon vegetable matter. However, many types are also carnivorous, eating such small animals as worms and slugs. The Wood tortoise *Testudo denticulata* and the Coal tortoise *T. carbonaria* feed mostly upon carrion. The predilection of nearly all tortoises for animal or human excrement is remarkable.

Tortoises mate in the spring; the male usually makes squeaking noises during copulation, which often takes hours. The females lay spherical eggs with calcareous shells in holes in the ground which they dig themselves and then cover them again. There is no record of brood care of any kind.

Tortoises live in areas which extend from dry, hot desert regions to the humid jungles;

this includes the tropics, subtropics and warmer temperate regions in all the continents except Australia. There are about 35 species and about 30 subspecies, divided among six genera.

The four species (or subspecies?) of the Gopher tortoises *Gopherus* are found only in desert regions in the southwest of North America.

During the intolerable heat of the day they hide in holes which they dig in the ground and which consist of a long passage and a terminal, spacious living chamber. They come out at dusk when the air has cooled down and usually eat cacti. The epiglottal shields on the underside in the male are extended very much forward and are used, when fighting for the female, to lever the rival onto his back and put him out of action. It is questionable whether these extensions are also used as spades when digging the burrow.

The four species of Flat tortoises *Homopus* in southern Africa are characterized by a relatively flat carapace, the short, powerfully distributed epiglottal scutes of the dorsal shield and by the hooked horny beak of the upper jaw. Their dorsal shield shows beautiful yellow, red and even green shades. They seem to live mainly on grass roots or other unusual foods; they can rarely be kept in captivity.

The Flexible tortoises *Kinixys,* already mentioned, which are able to lower the posterior part of their carapace, live in Africa, south of the Sahara. There are three species. When resting they shelter the front part of their shield between stones and protect the posterior soft parts by lowering the rear part of the carapace. These tortoises seem to like to be near water and are even said to be able to hunt swimming fish with skill.

In the East African Tornier's tortoise *Malacochersus tornieri* the bony scutes of the extremely flat carapace have degenerated to such an extent that practically only the flexible horny scutes remain. The animals can run relatively fast and when danger threatens they shelter between clefts in rocks. They then blow up the body and the flexible shell by breathing in, so much that they are firmly clamped and cannot be drawn out of their hiding places.

The relatively small Spider tortoises *Pyxis arachnoides* live in western Madagascar. They have a transverse hinge in the plastron, but in contrast to all other tortoises, this is in the front part of the plastron.

There are about 27 species of the genus *Testudo,* and they make up by far the largest proportion of tortoises. In order to classify the multiplicity of types, many investigators distinguish between several genera including *Testudo, Agrionemys, Chersine, Geochelone* and *Psammobates*. However, until it can be proved to what extent these groups are related to each other and to other tortoises, it would

seem more suitable to allow them to be considered merely as subgenera of *Testudo*.

There are three *Testudo* species in southern Europe: the Greek tortoise *T. hermanni*, the Algerian or Iberian tortoise *T. graeca* and the Margined tortoise *T. marginata*. Of these *T. marginata* is found only in the south of Greece and on the island of Sardinia where it was introduced by soldiers during World War II. There are two subspecies of *T. hermanni* ranging from Spain and the south of France as far as Greece and Rumania. *T. graeca* looks quite similar, and there are four subspecies from northwest Africa through southern Europe to southwest Asia. It can be clearly distinguished from *T. hermanni* by the following features: the tail does not end in a horny spine; on the back, next to the root of the tail on either side, there is only a large, wide horny scute at the posterior edge of the dorsal carapace (in *T. hermanni* there is a pair of these).

Southwest and Central Asia is the home of the Four-toed tortoise *T. horsfieldii* in which, in contrast to all other tortoises, the forelegs and hindlegs each have only four claws. This tortoise is not active for more than three months of the year. It spends the remaining time in a dormant state, for which it burrows into the ground.

Some African and Asiatic *Testudo* species have more or less clearly developed radial yellow streaks on a dark background on the

shields of the carapace (sometimes also on the plastron) which can also be seen on the Madagascar Spider tortoise. In generalizing the types coloured in this way are called 'radiating tortoises' although they do not form a group of related species. Among the representatives of this species in Africa are the actual Radiated tortoises *T. radiata* of Madagascar and the Roofed tortoise *T. tentoria* in the south of the continent. In these types there is nearly always an uneven cervical scute on the anterior edge of the dorsal carapace over the neck. On the other hand, it is lacking in the Asiatic species of this pattern type, such as the Star tortoise *T. elegans* and its relatives.

In the New World, the genus *Testudo* is found only in South America; to the north of this the only tortoises are the species of *Gopherus*. The Wood tortoise *Testudo denticulata* and the Coal tortoise *T. carbonaria* inhabit the humid, tropical rain-forest. *T. chilensis* is found only in Argentina and despite its scientific name is not found in Chile.

The carapace of the Giant tortoises *T. elephantopus* of the Galapagos Islands and *T. gigantea* of the Seychelles is up to 4 ft (1·2 m) long. The Galapagos types lack the uneven nape scute on the front margin of the carapace, which is developed in the Seychelles species. Several strains of both species inhabit the small islands of the two archi-

pelagos, but some have died out or are threatened with extinction. In some of their subspecies the front part of the carapace curves upwards in the shape of a saddle. This enables the animals to stretch the head and neck up farther than other tortoises and thus to feed on plants higher up. These island tortoises originally had no natural enemies and their shield has become relatively thin.

Many people keep tortoises in captivity, but unfortunately often in unsuitable conditions. These animals should in no circumstances be allowed to run around freely on the floor of a room, since it is too cold and draughty there. It is far better to give them a roomy, light and sufficiently warm terrarium, with a drinking vessel and hiding places, and which is always kept clean. Lettuce (well-washed!), dandelion, fruit, tomatoes, bananas and sometimes a little meat or fish are suitable food. To prevent the tortoises from becoming rickety lime and vitamin preparations are added to their food (bread, macaroni or cake soaked in milk). Take care! they eat it with relish, but it causes digestive trouble. At least once a week the tortoises should be bathed in shallow warm water at 77–80°F (25–27°C), so that they can drink and evacuate therein. In summer it is essential for them to spend some time regularly in a well fenced-in open space, so that they get unfiltered sunlight; together with the lime in their food they need it to build the bones of their skeleton and of

The Greek or Hermann's tortoise is a popular Garden tortoise . . .

. . . and so is the Algerian tortoise (below) named *Testudo graeca*!

Not a prehistoric monster in an antediluvian forest but one of its surviving descendants, a Giant tortoise.

Malacochersus tornieri, of North America, differs from other land tortoises in having a flat carapace. It also is peculiar in laying only one egg at a time.

the carapace. This applies also to the tropical types; they should enjoy direct sunlight at least during the midday hours.

Only those species coming from the far north (but not the south!) of the tortoises range of distribution should be allowed to hibernate cold. If they have thoroughly evacuated in the autumn and have become comatose at temperatures around 50–47°F (10–8°C) put them in a well ventilated box with peat moss (not peat mull) and transfer them to a dark cellar which must, of course, be free of rats or mice. The temperature should not be more than 40–47°F (4–8°C) so that they will neither freeze nor become lively. The moss must be slightly moistened now and again so that the tortoises do not dry up. In March or April gradually move the tortoise to warmer, lighter rooms, so that they awaken from their winter sleep. If they have become lively, after two or three days bathe them in moderately warm water, to compensate for the loss of fluid and to help them evacuate. Only then must they be given food again.

It may be mentioned that probably only the Four-toed tortoises *Testudo horsfieldi* actually need such hibernation. All other species can or even should be kept fully active during the winter in suitably equipped containers. SUBORDER: Cryptodira, ORDER: Testudines, CLASS: Reptilia.   H.W

TORTOISE LONGEVITY. The longevity of tortoises is much disputed but there are three candidates for life-spans of 150–200 years. These are Giant tortoises known as the St. Helena tortoise, the Tonga tortoise and Marion's tortoise. The St Helena tortoise, Jonathan, was imported to St Helena, with two companions before Napoleon started his exile there. It is supposed to be 300 years old but there are no definite records of its arrival on the island. The Tonga tortoise, named Tu'imalila and accorded the rank of chief, was presented to the King of Tonga by Captain Cook in 1774. It was no doubt well grown then and was still alive in 1949. Doubt has, however, been cast by experts who suggest that the original could have been replaced by a substitute when it died. Marion's tortoise was taken to Mauritius in 1766 by Marion de Fresne. It lived in the grounds of an artillery barracks until accidentally killed in 1918.

A common Garden tortoise is said to have lived in the garden of Lambeth Palace for 120 years, dying through neglect in 1753.

TORTOISESHELL, the name given to the horny scutes on the shell of Sea turtles, especially to those of the Hawksbill turtle *Eretmochelys imbricata,* which are renowned for their vivid pattern of amber, reddish-brown, blackish brown and yellow.

One of the idiosyncrasies of the English language is that we call a land chelonian a tortoise and a marine chelonian a turtle, but we call the shell from a turtle 'tortoiseshell'. The word 'turtle' is from a corruption by English sailors in the 16th and 17th centuries of either the French *tortue* or Spanish *tortuga,* meaning in both cases tortoise, the animal with the tortuous or twisted feet. More confusing still, in North America the name tortoiseshell is used although practically all chelonians are called turtles. Paradoxically, the flippers (or feet) of turtles are anything but twisted.

When taken from the turtle the scutes can be welded together by applying heat and pressure and thus thicker pieces of tortoiseshell can be made, which can be used to make combs, tortoiseshell boxes and trinkets. The horny scutes of the hawksbill overlap like the tiles of a roof and they are thicker than the scutes of other species.

To strip the scutes from the turtle, heat has to be applied and in some areas the turtle used to be held over glowing embers or hot water was poured onto it. Of course, the scutes can also be removed from a freshly killed turtle, but it used to be said that the quality was superior if the scutes were taken from the living animal. Moreover, it is be-

lieved that if the turtle, after careful stripping, is put back into the sea it will develop a new set of scutes. Indeed, Deraniyagala did show that in a young hawksbill which had lost a scute, this was replaced by a new one in about eight months. There is no proof, however, that if all scutes are stripped from the turtle it will survive and form a completely new set of scutes.

The tortoiseshell from various parts of the world differs in colour and quality. That from the West Indies is usually more reddish, that from the Indian Ocean more dark in colour. A large hawksbill with the carapace 30 in (75 cm) long will yield 8 lb (3·6 kg) of tortoiseshell. The trade in tortoise-shell has declined through the years being partly replaced by synthetic materials, but is still exported from the Caribbean.

The scutes of the Green turtle and those of the Loggerhead turtle are too thin to be of much use and they do not show the vivid pattern that makes real tortoiseshell so attractive. Still it seems that in the past even the scutes of the Green turtle and of the Loggerhead turtle were used to some extent. 18th century authors mention them as being used for panes of lanterns and for inlay. L.D.B.

TOUCANS, a family of about 37 species of South American birds, with heavy bodies and long and often bulky bills. They vary

A typical South American toucan *Rhamphastos sulfuratus.*

from 12–24 in (30–60 cm) in length, most species having a bold pattern of black, yellow, orange, red, green, blue or white plumage, in one combination or another. The most arresting feature of the larger species of toucans is the huge bill. This may be 6 in (15 cm) long, 2 in (5 cm) deep and coloured in gaudy patterns, often of orange, red or yellow. The smaller species tend to have duller plumage-patterns and smaller bills. The sexes are alike in plumage in nearly all species and both sexes of most of them have a patch of bare skin round the eye. All toucans are heavy-bodied birds with rounded wings, a rather long graduated tail and short strong legs, with stout feet of the zygodactyl pattern—that is with two toes pointing forwards and two back.

They are birds of the woodlands and forests of Central and South America, found from Vera Cruz southward to Paraguay and northern Argentina. All of them are primarily fruit-eaters, though some species have been recorded taking large insects, small snakes and the nestlings of other birds. The huge bill may serve one or more functions: it is probably used to reach fruit that is far out on thin twigs; it may help in intimidating other birds that might rob toucans' nests were it not for this defence; and it may be used in display.

Nests are in tree holes, either natural ones caused by decay, or those excavated by other birds. Two to four white eggs are laid and incubated by both the male and female. Incubating toucans are very restless for birds of their size, seldom staying on the eggs for more than an hour at a time. The incubation period is known only for one of the smaller species, the Blue-throated toucanet *Aulacorhynchus caeruleogularis* in which it is 16 days. Young toucans hatch without a covering of down and develop very slowly. They are fed by both parents, mainly on food regurgitated from the crop and throat of the parents, though some food items are carried in the bill.

Some of the smaller toucans roost in tree holes throughout the year, a small group roosting together in one of a number of old woodpecker holes or similar sites between which they intermittently move. Captive individuals of some of the larger species roost with the long bill in the plumage of the back and the tail folded over the bill, so that they became formless balls of feathers. In some of these larger toucans newly fledged young return to roost in the nest with their parents for some time after fledging, these family parties perhaps persisting for some months.

All toucans have a very limited vocabulary, some giving mewing and barking calls, though the majority give low frog-like croaks and high pitched rattles. FAMILY: Ramphastidae, ORDER: Piciformes, CLASS: Aves.   D.H.

TOUCH, one of the five primary senses. At least seven different kinds of sense organ have been described from mammalian skin, although it has recently been suggested that most of these are artifacts and that only three types of receptor are present. In either case the allocation of specific sensations to these sense organs is uncertain. In its narrow sense touch, in all animals, may be looked upon as the detection of light pressure; hairs and bristles aid in this by acting as levers and magnifying the deformation of the sense organ caused by light touch. In exploring a surface the sense of touch is closely linked with temperature and pain reception and integrated with information concerning muscle movement and tension. Skin receptors in general are not evenly distributed but are much more numerous in certain areas than others.

TOXOPLASMA, a highly dangerous protozoan species of uncertain affinities until the electron microscope showed clearly that it belongs with the class Sporozoa. *Toxoplasma gondii* is parasitic in practically all birds and mammals, including man, and there is some evidence that it can infect reptiles. The diagnostic stage is a spore which is crescentic in shape with one end more rounded than the other. Little is known of the life-cycle despite its common occurrence, but it is known that the spore stage multiplies by a process of internal budding in various cells of the host's body. Two distinct kinds of cysts are formed, pseudocysts and cysts. The former are the most dangerous for the proliferation of the spores may continue unchecked while in the cysts a thick wall limits the spread of the parasite. In herbivores such as sheep the cysts in various parts of the body serve to infect carnivores but how the herbivores become infected is obscure. In man the incidence of antibodies to this parasite is very high, but clinical symptoms are rare. The most serious form of the disease is the congenital one, and many infected children either die or are mentally and physically handicapped for life because of damage to the nervous system. In adults the most serious form is ocular toxoplasmosis, and this may cause blindness. ORDER: Toxoplasmida, CLASS: Sporozoa, PHYLUM: Protozoa.   F.E.G.C.

TRACHEA, the technical name for the windpipe of air-breathing tetrapods. It is tubular with the walls reinforced at intervals with complete, or nearly complete, rings of cartilage and lined with ciliated epithelium. Its anterior, or upper, end connects with the glottis and the entry of food is usually prevented by a flap, the epiglottis. At its lower end the trachea divides into two bronchi, one of which runs to each lung. The name is also used for tubular structures, strengthened by chitinous rings, forming part of the res-

piratory system of insects and some other arthropods. They connect to the outside by a number of small apertures, the spiracles, on each side of the body and end by division into similar but finer tubules, the tracheoles.

TRAGOPANS, five distinct species of game birds also known as Horned pheasants. They are comparatively large and colourful but extremely gentle by nature. The males are birds of rare beauty having two blue fleshy horns on the head and a large brilliantly coloured lappet or bib on the throat which are extended during display.

Tragopans live in mountain forests at altitudes of 3,000–12,000 ft (900–3,600 m), according to season. Unlike most pheasants they sometimes nest high in trees, usually taking over the disused nest of another bird such as a crow. The clutch is four, sometimes three, eggs. Incubation lasts 28–30 days and the chicks can fly up to roost on a perch within 3 days of hatching.

The Western tragopan *Tragopan melanocephalus*, as its name implies, has the most westerly distribution. It is extremely rare and inhabits high altitude forests in the western Himalayas from Hazara eastwards to Bhutan and the forests of southern Tibet. Blyth's tragopan *T. blythi* is found in the mountains of Assam and northern Burma, while Temminck's tragopan *T. temmincki* occurs in the eastern Himalayas and in the forests of southern Tibet and southern China as well as in northeastern Burma. The Satyr tragopan *T. satyra* is found in the Himalayas from Jarwhal to Bhutan and southern Tibet.

Cabot's tragopan *T. caboti* is confined to the mountains of southeast China and is considered to be in danger of extinction in the wild. So far as is known the only specimens in captivity outside China are at the Pheasant Trust in England where they breed regularly. FAMILY: Phasianidae, ORDER: Galliformes, CLASS: Aves.   P.W.

TRAPDOOR SPIDERS, members of several families of mygalomorph spiders which dig deep burrows the entrances to which are closed with a hinged door carefully camouflaged with moss or debris. This may be thin like a wafer or thick like cork and formed of earth and silk. Some burrows have a branch burrow closed by a second trapdoor. The doors serve as protection from rain and dust, from excessive heat and dryness and from the entrance of enemies (though some pompilid wasps have mastered even this defence). The spider holds the door firmly closed during the day but darts out to attack passing insects, chiefly at night.

Trapdoor spiders are found in all tropical and the warmer temperate regions including southern Europe. *Atypus affinis,* the only mygalomorph spider in Britain, has wrongly been called the Trapdoor spider. A closed silk

tube extends from its burrow, which has no lid.

Trapdoors have also been devised independently by some araneomorph spiders, especially certain species of the family Lycosidae. SUBORDER: Mygalomorphae, ORDER: Araneida, CLASS: Arachnida, PHYLUM: Arthropoda. W.S.B.

TREECREEPERS, a family of small, dull-coloured birds which obtain their food by climbing along the trunks and branches of trees, usually in an upward direction. Birds from several families show a tendency to search for food in this fashion, and those which have been grouped in the treecreeper and nuthatch families may be of differing origin and only resemble each other through having similar habits.

There are six typical treecreepers of the genus *Certhia*. Three are confined to Southeast Asia around the Himalayan region. The fourth and fifth together have a circumpolar range, the Common treecreeper *C. familiaris* through the temperate forests of Eurasia and *C. americana* replacing it in similar regions of North America; the two apparently differing only in voice. The sixth is the Short-toed treecreeper *C. brachydactyla* of southern Europe which overlaps the range of the Common treecreeper *C. familiaris*. They differ in both feet and voice and where they overlap the former tends to occupy deciduous forest, the latter conifers. The North American species occupies both habitats.

The two Spotted creepers *Salpornis,* one in Africa and the other in India, superficially resemble the typical treecreepers but have a plumage with pale spots overall and have also a short tail which is not used as a support while climbing. More recent authorities have grouped these birds with the nuthatches. Another group is the Australian treecreepers of the genus *Climacteris*. These are larger, strong-footed birds of variable feeding habits and do not appear related to the typical treecreepers. They have been variously assigned to nuthatches, Australian warblers and more recently to the honey-eaters. There are also two treecreepers *Rhabdornis* in the Philippines, sometimes placed with the Australian treecreepers or with the nuthatches. The little long-billed wallcreeper *Tichodroma muraria* appears to be a close relative of the nuthatches.

Typical treecreepers are small birds with large feet and fairly long, slender, decurved bills for probing in crevices for insects. The tail feathers have strong shafts and spiny tips and pressed against the tree, act as a prop to support the bird. The upper plumage is brown and streaky, the underside white. The tree-

The European Common treecreeper runs mouselike vertically up tree trunks searching the bark crevices for insects.

creeper moves head-upwards, backing down if it wishes to return to a spot it has passed. When it has climbed one trunk it flies to the bottom of another and spirals up it.

Treecreepers roost in hollows in the bark of tree-trunks, sometimes scraping their own hollows in the spongy bark of a Sequoia. A nest of moss, twigs and bark is built in the narrow cavity behind a loose piece of bark. The newly-emerged young climb with agility when they can barely fly. FAMILY: Certhiidae, ORDER: Passeriformes, CLASS: Aves.

TREE DUCK, term applied to certain ducks which commonly perch in trees. Two groups of ducks are involved: the Whistling ducks of the tribe Dendrocygnini and the Perching ducks of the tribe Cairinini. An alternative name for the Whistling ducks is in fact 'Tree ducks', but they perch in trees much less regularly than the Cairinini and some of them do so hardly at all.

The Whistling ducks form a distinct group of goose-like ducks which are placed with the geese and swans in the subfamily Anserinae. They have long legs and walk well and in a more upright posture than most ducks. There are eight species, covering much of the world excepting Europe.

The Perching duck tribe includes a wide variety of forms but that with which we are most concerned here is the North American wood duck or Carolina duck *Aix sponsa*. This species breeds in eastern North America, frequenting secluded woodland pools and streams where it feeds along the banks and also in the woods, taking a variety of foods including some of the hardest fruits and seeds. The male is strikingly beautiful with bold bright plumage including an iridescent green crest. Even the female is more brightly coloured than is usually the case in ducks. One of the local names for this bird is 'Tree duck' and in this case it is quite applicable for the Wood duck spends much of its time in trees and almost always nests in a natural tree cavity. See also ducks. FAMILY: Anatidae, ORDER: Anseriformes, CLASS: Aves. P.M.D.

TREEFROGS, strictly only those frogs which belong to the family Hylidae. The habit of living in trees from which they are named has in fact been adopted by many species belonging to other families of frogs, while some members of the Hylidae do not have this arboreal habit. Nevertheless the Hylidae contains the largest number of arboreal genera and the family is best dealt with on its own because, although the tree-living frogs of different families may look rather similar, details of their internal anatomy reveal that they are not closely related.

Members of the Hylidae are characterized by having a pectoral girdle in which the two ventral halves overlap in the mid-line (the arciferal condition) and an extra disc-shaped element of cartilage in each finger and toe. Two other small families, the *Pseudidae and *Centrolenidae, also have these characters and are sometimes included in the Hylidae. The Hylidae differ from them in having the extra element disc-shaped (it is rod-shaped in the Pseudidae) and in having the end-bone in each digit claw-shaped (it is T-shaped in the Centrolenidae).

The extra element in each digit is found also in the treefrogs of other families and is an adaptation to their arboreal habits. It occurs between the last two bones in each digit and enables the last bone to move through a large angle relative to the rest of the digit. This last bone supports an adhesive disc and its mobility means that the disc can remain pressed flat against the surface while the hand or foot is at an angle to it. The adhesive discs, formed by an expansion of the tip of each finger and toe are a distinctive feature of treefrogs and enables them to cling to vertical surfaces. In structure a disc consists of a soft pad of tissue under the curved bone. The skin of the pad is thickened and contains many modified mucous glands which secrete a sticky fluid onto the surface.

The Hylidae is a large family, containing about 34 genera, but, with two exceptions, *Nyctimystes* and *Hyla,* they are only found in the New World. *Nyctimystes* occurs in New Guinea while *Hyla* is almost world-wide, but is absent from the Arctic and Antarctic and most of Africa.

Hyla arborea is the European treefrog and is found throughout Europe and most of Asia. On the basis of differences in colour pattern and the length of limbs it is divided into several subspecies. The typical form is a small frog, about $1\frac{3}{4}$ in (43 mm) long, bright green with a dark stripe, edged with yellow, running

One of nature's paradoxes is that tropical treefrogs are pale or cryptically-coloured when resting by day, but become marvellously coloured when active – by night.

along the side of the body; a small branch of the stripe projects forwards over the back from just in front of the hindlimb. It spends the day sitting on the leaves of trees and bushes and relies on its colouration for protection. If approached it does not jump away but crouches lower onto the leaf. It leaps at any insect which flies within reach, catching it in its mouth. In jumping it takes no account of its height above the ground or the position of other leaves and depends on its outstretched hands and feet catching onto a leaf or twig to break its fall. Most of its hunting, however, is done at night when it is more active.

During the last century European treefrogs were thought to be useful weather prophets and were often kept in small jars with a pool of water in the bottom and a small ladder. At the approach of fine weather the frog was supposed to sit at the top of the ladder while, when rain was imminent, it moved to the bottom. Experiments have shown that this is unreliable although, like most frogs, it will call more readily in dark rainy weather than on sunny days.

It hibernates in the mud at the bottom of ponds and breeds in April and May. About 800–1,000 eggs are laid in several lumps attached to water plants below the surface of the water. The tadpoles reach a length of about 2 in (5 cm) and change into frogs after about three months.

There are several hundred species of *Hyla* but they are all rather similar in habits to the European treefrog. There is, however, considerable variation in the general shape and colour. *H. versicolor,* the Common or Gray treefrog of North America, is a short squat frog about 2 in (5 cm) long, with a rough warty skin. Although, like most treefrogs, it is able to vary its colour quite considerably, it is usually grey or brown with irregular dark patches on its back and difficult to see when sitting on the lichen-encrusted bark of a tree.

The Green treefrog *H. cinerea,* also of North America, is also about 2 in (5 cm) long, but is a very slim, long-bodied frog with a completely smooth skin and long legs. Its colour is usually bright green but may occasionally be grey.

About 21 species of *Hyla* occur in Australia. Several of them are able to live in the hot, dry parts. *H. caerulea* for example, can tolerate a loss of water equivalent to 45% of its body weight while *H. moorei* from the more temperate areas can only tolerate a 30% loss. Some species, such as *H. rubella* and *H. aurea,* show a tendency away from an arboreal habit and spend much of the time in or near water.

Three species of *Hyla* have been introduced into New Zealand where they form the only amphibian population besides the three species of *Leiopelma* (see Amphicoela).

Although treefrogs live in trees, usually

The South American treefrog *Phyllomedusa pulcherrima* is nocturnal, as shown by its large eyes, and slow-moving, in contrast to the more typical treefrogs. Treefrogs generally are characterized by having suction discs at the tips of the toes and forwardly directed eyes.

some distance from water, most of them have to return to water to breed and have the pattern of development characteristic of most frogs, with a free-swimming tadpole stage. Some species, however, have developed breeding methods in which the vulnerable eggs and tadpoles are protected to a certain extent from predators.

The females of *Hyla rosenbergi* construct small pools of water in the shallows of ponds. They collect small quantities of mud from the bottom of the pond and build them into a wall. They continue until the wall is higher than the surface of the water and a small pool about 1 ft (30 cm) in diameter is cut off from the rest of the pond. The frog uses its hands to smooth the insides of the wall. The eggs are laid in these basins and the tadpoles hatch after

about four or five days. They have large external gills which float on the surface of the water and enable them to obtain sufficient oxygen, since there is only a limited quantity dissolved in such small bodies of water.

Hyla goeldii avoids laying the eggs in water altogether. The skin on the female's back has a fold down each side which forms a small hollow. About 25 large eggs are carried in this until hatching when the female moves to the small pools of water held in the bases of bromeliad leaves. The tadpoles complete their development in these pools.

All the species of *Hyla* which occur in Jamaica also lay their eggs in these bromeliad aquaria and the tadpoles show interesting modifications to such a habitat. They feed on the other eggs, either of their own or of other species, which are lying in the same pool and the horny teeth around their mouths are adapted to such a diet.

Other genera of treefrogs appear to have carried the adaptation shown by *H. goeldii* a stage further. In the Marsupial frogs *Gastrotheca* the brood pouch is a completely enclosed sac on the female's back and opens by a small slit-like opening over the cloaca. As the eggs are released and fertilized the female tilts her body so that they slide forward into the pouch. The pouch then seals up and the eggs are carried around and develop inside it. In some species, such as *G. marsupiata,* the young are released as tadpoles while in others, such as *G. ovifera,* the complete development takes place inside the brood pouch and the young emerge as froglets. The female uses the toes of her hindfeet to open the pouch, enabling the young to escape.

Frogs of the genus *Phyllomedusa* belong to another group of hylids that have an interesting breeding method. In this case the eggs are laid in a tube formed from leaves. The female, carrying the male on her back, selects a leaf overhanging water. She climbs onto it and both she and the male hold the two edges of the leaf together at the bottom. The eggs are released into the funnel thus formed and the jelly of the eggs holds the two leaves together. The frogs move up the leaf, laying more eggs as they go, until the whole leaf is formed into a tube containing about 100 eggs. The tadpoles hatch after about six days and drop into the water to complete their development. *Agalachnis* has similar breeding habits.

Some genera of hylids have the bones of the skull enlarged to form a bony shield covering the head. In *Hemiphractus scutatus* which occurs from Ecuador to Brazil the helmet is extended to form a triangular horn behind each eye. In some, for example, *Flectonotus,* the skin of the head fuses with the bone. The function of these bony helmets is not fully known. They are probably defensive although in some genera, such as *Diaglena,* in which the flat, bony snout protudes in front of the mouth, it has been suggested that it may be used to dig for insects in rotten wood.

Although most genera of hylids are arboreal in their habits there are exceptions. The Chorus frogs belong to the genus *Pseudacris* which is found only in North America. Most of them are small and delicate, about 1 in (2·5 cm) long, patterned with brown or green stripes or spots. They do not climb very much and the adhesive discs on their fingers and toes are small. Their toes are only slightly webbed and they are poor swimmers. They only call during the breeding season, which is in the Spring in the north but during the winter rains in the south. After that they are rarely found due to their small size and the effective camouflage of their colour-

ation among vegetation of the same colour.

The Cricket frog *Acris gryllus* is a representative of a genus which has progressed even further from the arboreal habits of most hylids. It is small, $\frac{1}{2}$–$1\frac{1}{4}$ in (13–31 mm) long, with a pointed snout. Its toe discs are very small and it resembles a true frog *(Rana)* more than a treefrog. It is very variable in colour and may be grey, brown, reddish tan or green. It never climbs but lives always on the ground among the grass bordering streams and swamps. Its name refers to its chirping call which is heard in chorus during the Spring. Unlike most frogs it is active during the day. FAMILY: Hylidae, ORDER: Anura, CLASS: Amphibia. M.E.D.

TREE HOPPERS, leaf-sucking insects related to Spittle bugs, cicadas and Leaf hoppers. The adults and nymphs are, like aphids, often attended by ants and they exude 'honey-dew'. They lay their eggs in slits which they cut in twigs and they guard their young when the eggs hatch. They are powerful jumpers. FAMILY: Membracidae, ORDER: Hemiptera, CLASS: Insecta, PHYLUM: Arthropoda.

TREE LOCUSTS, species of *Anacridium,* all of which feed on trees of many kinds. The greatest commercial damage is done to the gum arabic tree, *Acacia senegal.* See also entry on locusts.

TREE-SHREW, *Tupaia glis,* one of several small, squirrel-like mammals with a head and body length of 9 in (22 cm) and a bushy tail of 8 in (20 cm). The Malay name 'tupai' is used for both tree-shrews and squirrels, underlining their close resemblance.

The Common tree-shrew is basically an arboreal animal, constructing nests with leaves and mosses in hollow trees, but it also spends much time searching for fruit and insects in the leaf-litter of the forest floor. All members of the tree-shrew family (Tupaiidae) are restricted to the rain-forests of Southeast Asia, where they occupy different ecological niches. For example, the genera *Ptilocercus* and *Dendrogale* are completely arboreal, while *Urogale* and *Lyonogale* are completely terrestrial. Most tree-shrew species are still very common, but the crepuscular or nocturnal Pen-tailed tree-shrew *Ptilocercus lowi*—which is so different from the others that it is sometimes placed in a separate subfamily—is very rare.

The Common tree-shrew and the Indian tree-shrew *Anathana ellioti* both have a balanced diet of fruit and insects, collected by foraging. The diet is reflected in the dentition which is of small pointed teeth at the front for trapping and killing insects, and poorly developed molar teeth at the back for grinding soft fruit and insect carcasses. The arboreal Pen-tailed tree-shrew and Smooth-

tailed tree-shrew, *Dendrogale murina* and *D. melanura* are almost exclusively insectivorous, and they probably use their hands as well as their front teeth to trap their prey. The Terrestrial tree-shrew *Lyonogale* spp. and the Philippines tree-shrew *Urogale everetti,* on the other hand, are adapted for trapping larger animal prey on the ground, such as lizards and small mammals, and for digging up various items of food. This is reflected in the greater length of the snout and pronounced development of the claws.

All tree-shrews have a small number of offspring (one to three) in each litter, and birth takes place in a convenient hollow in a tree or an abandoned rodent burrow, which is lined with leaves a few days beforehand. Laboratory studies show that the Common tree-shrew female gives birth in a different nest from the one used as a refuge. This is linked with the fact that she apparently visits her young only once every two days to suckle them. Unlike most other small nest-living mammals, the female does not clean her offspring, and they are left to keep themselves warm. Nevertheless, the young keep a constant body-temperature of 99°F (37°C), undoubtedly aided by the fact that the maternal milk has a high proportion (25%) of fat. It seems likely that this unusual maternal behaviour is common to all tree-shrews.

All tree-shrews have a gestation period of about seven weeks, producing typical nest-living offspring (eyes and ears closed, teeth not yet erupted). Such information as is available indicates that there is no sharply defined breeding-season, and it is possible that at least some species can breed all the year round. Young of the Common tree-shrew are sexually mature at three to four months of age and can breed immediately.

The relationships of tree-shrews to other mammals are not yet clear. They were at first classified with the Insectivora and later with the Primates, but recent studies indicate that they should be placed in a separate order, characterized by the retention of many primitive characters. FAMILY: Tupaiidae, ORDER: Tupaioidea, CLASS: Mammalia. R.D.M.

TREE SNAKES, very slender snakes living in trees in Malaya and the East Indies. They are reputed to launch themselves and glide from trees to the lower bushes and are sometimes referred to as *flying snakes, especially the species of *Chrysopelea.* The Golden tree snake *C. ornata* can climb a tree by forcing the sides of its body against irregularities in the bark, as if crawling up a shallow trench. In this it is helped by its belly scales being keeled at their sides. Tree snakes have only a weak venom and some species at least also constrict their prey. FAMILY: Colubridae, ORDER: Squamata, CLASS: Reptilia.

Tree shrews are primitive mammals of uncertain relationship to other mammals.

TREMATODA, a term formerly used to denote a class of flukes, the members of which are now divided into the Monogenea and Digenea, each with the rank of a class. See flukes, naming of animals (classification) and evolution.

TRICERATOPS, the best known but not the largest of the horned *dinosaurs, it was 20 ft (6·2 m) long with a skull 6 ft (2 m) long bearing a short horn on the snout and a larger horn over each eye. The rear part of the skull was carried backwards in a bony frill over the neck. ORDER: Ornithischia, CLASS: Reptilia.

TRICHINIASIS, a disease caused by the Pork trichina worm *Trichinella spiralis,* a parasitic *roundworm. The trichina worm is an unusual parasite in many respects; for example, both the adult and larval forms occur in the same host animal and the worm is never exposed directly to the outside world. In addition, unlike most parasites, infection is commonest in the temperate and cold regions of the world. Man acquires the parasite as a result of eating meat from animals which have themselves experienced infection: in temperate regions the commonest source of infection is undercooked pork. The survival of the trichina worm as a species depends on infected host animals being eaten by new hosts and pigs acquire infection by eating infected scraps of meat or, less often, by eating infected rats. Man represents a blind alley for the parasite, as human meat is rarely eaten.

The adult trichina worms are very small and live in the small intestine of their host. After fertilization each mature female liberates about 1,500 live larvae in the intestinal wall and these penetrate into the tissue, enter blood vessels and are carried around the body of the host by the circulating blood. Eventually they leave the vessels and penetrate into muscle tissues and remain there, forming characteristic lemon-shaped cysts about $\frac{1}{100}$ in (0·25 mm) in length. When such infected muscle is eaten by a new host, the larvae are digested out and mature rapidly into adults to continue the life-cycle. If not eaten, the cyst eventually becomes impregnated by calcium and the larva inside dies.

The adult worms are harmless to man, even when present in number, but the migration of the larvae around the body and their invasion of muscles causes a variety of symptoms. When heavily infected meat is eaten, millions of larvae may be produced by the female worms and death may result. Cooking destroys the larvae in infected meat and thus acquisition of the disease is associated with the eating of undercooked pork, as in certain types of sausage.

TRICHOMONAS, free-living and parasitic flagellate Protozoa, the latter being the best known. They are very small and possess a

Trichomonas muris from a rat.

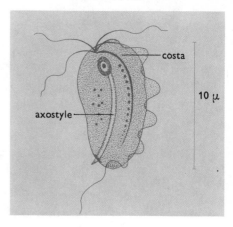

single nucleus and a supporting rod or axostyle running the length of the body. At the front end there are three, four or five free flagella and another one running backwards attached to the cell membrane in such a way that it forms an undulating membrane, which gives the flagellate a conspicuous appearance. Species of *Trichomonas* are common in the intestines of frogs and toads and also small rodents such as rats, mice and voles. Three species occur as parasites of man: *T. tenax* is found in the mouth, *T. hominis* in the intestine and *T. vaginalis* in the female vagina or the male urethra. The last of these is the only one which is pathogenic. *T. foetus*, lives in the vagina of cattle and can cause abortion. Species of *Trichomonas* are not known to form cysts and it is presumed that they must possess some other form of resistant stage in order to survive the transfer from host to host. In the case of the trichomonads living in the mouth and in the genital system transmission is by direct contact. ORDER: Trichomonadida, CLASS: Mastigophora, PHYLUM: Protozoa.

TRICHONYMPHA, the best known member of an order of flagellate protozoans all of which possess many flagella but only one nucleus. All are found in the intestines of wood-eating insects where they digest the wood by means of cellulase and other enzymes, which the insects do not possess, the flagellates then being digested by the insects. This is an example of true symbiosis. *Trichonympha* lives in the hind-gut of termites and woodroaches in the United States. When the insect host moults the flagellates begin to reproduce sexually, the process being induced by moulting hormones produced by the host. Just before the moult the nucleus of the flagellate divides and the flagellate itself becomes encysted. Then it divides so the cyst contains two individuals which have differentiated to form two sexually distinct gametes. These later escape from the cyst and pairs of unlike gametes fuse in a simple sexual reproduction. The conjugants then divide asexually, by simple fission. *Trichonympha* is always found in the termites *Zootermopsis* and in the woodroach *Cryp-*

tocercus. The flagellates are large and just visible to the naked eye. It is not necessary to kill the termite in order to find the flagellates, for they are given out from the anus when the insect is subjected to gentle pressure. In this way one termite can provide an endless supply of flagellates for study. ORDER: Hypermastigida, CLASS: Mastigophora, PHYLUM: Protozoa.   F.E.G.C.

TRIGGERFISHES, marine fishes of warm seas related to the trunkfishes and pufferfishes. The common name derives from the trigger-like action of the enlarged first dorsal spine which can be locked in the upright position by the much smaller second dorsal spine. With the spine locked, the fish is both difficult to remove from rock crevices and difficult for a predator to swallow. The body is deep and compressed, and is covered by small bony plates. The mouth is terminal and small. The triggerfishes are often brightly coloured with grotesque or even absurd colour markings that contrast with their slow and rather dignified movement around the reefs. There are about 30 species, the largest rarely exceeding 2 ft (60 cm) in length. They have powerful teeth with which they crush molluscs and crustaceans. Their flesh is reported to be poisonous but it is not yet established that this is not simply a form of ciguatera poisoning (see poisonous fishes). In Hawaii the species of *Rhinecanthus* are called humahuma and have been immortalized in song. FAMILY: Balistidae, ORDER: Tetraodontiformes, CLASS: Pisces.

TRILLERS, cuckoo-shrikes of the genus *Lalage,* and the monotypic Black-breasted triller *Chlamydochaera jeffreyi,* of Borneo. They are slender, finch- to thrush-sized songbirds of the Oriental and Australasian regions. Males are usually boldly patterned in black, white and grey, with duller, browner females sometimes finely barred. *L. aureus* of the Moluccas is chestnut on the underside. The food consists of fruit and insects. These are active birds, mainly of the tree-tops. The nest is a shallow cup, and the eggs are blue or green and patterned. See cuckoo-shrikes. FAMILY: Campephagidae, ORDER: Passeriformes, CLASS: Aves.

TRILOBITES, an extinct group of arthropods showing slight resemblance to the Crustacea although it is doubtful if this indicates a close relationship and the differences between the trilobites and other arthropods are so great that they are placed in a separate class.

The biggest species known is *Uralichas riberoi,* up to 28 in (70 cm) long, but large forms are rare and the majority were 1–4 in

The triggerfish *Rhinecanthus aculeatus* is known in Hawaii as the humuhumu-nukunuku-a-puaa.

Especially beautiful fossil, a trilobite, primitive crustacean common in Paleozoic seas.

(2·5–10 cm). The upper surface was covered by a chitinous exoskeleton impregnated with calcium salts; this turned under for a short distance around the edge forming a sort of rim, the doublure. Apart from a few chitinous plates near the mouth, nothing is known of the lower surface and it is thought to have been covered by a very thin layer of soft chitin. Appendages are very rarely preserved. The body was flattened and divided into three parts: the cephalic region or head, the thorax and the pygidial or 'tail' region. The head had a rounded outline. Its dorsal exoskeleton is called the cephalon, and this consists of a raised, central area, the glabella, with flattened cheeks on either side. Each cheek has a distinct furrow, the facial suture, separating a lateral free cheek from the fixed cheek next to the glabella and probably marking the line of splitting of the exoskeleton during moulting. In nearly all trilobites there is a compound eye on each side of the glabella. This varies a good deal in size with from 2 to 15,000 ocelli per eye. A few species appear to have been eyeless. The mouth lay on the ventral surface of the head with one or two small plates in front of it and another behind. The thorax contains from two to over 40 segments the upper surface of each being covered by a single chitinous plate movably attached to that of the neighbouring segments. The pygidial region too has a number of segments, up to 30 or more, but here the plates covering the upper surface are immovably joined together to form the pygidium. Running along the upper surface of both thorax and pygidium are a pair of longitudinal grooves, the axial furrows, which mark off each segment into three lobes—a median, axial lobe and two lateral, pleural lobes—hence the name trilobite. The appendages were attached to the ventral surface; the head bore five pairs and the rest of the body one pair per segment. The first, a pair of unbranched, jointed antennae, lay just in front of the level of the mouth. The remainder were all alike though they varied slightly and gradually in size; each had two, jointed branches; a lower, fairly stout walking leg and an upper, delicate, feathery structure used for swimming and probably for respiration as well.

At least 10,000 species are known. They appear in the Lower Cambrian (450 million years ago) and were fairly abundant from then until the end of the Devonian when the group dwindled in size, only a few lingering on until the close of the Permian Period (200 million years ago).

Trilobites seem to have been entirely marine. Most lived on the muddy bottom of shallow seas, a few with well developed spines may have been planktonic and the small, eyeless forms were probably burrowers in mud. Some were capable of rolling up like modern Pill bugs to protect the vulnerable lower surface. Like all arthropods they cast the outer layers of their exoskeletons from time to time and it is thought that most fossils consist of such cast 'skins' rather than entire animals. CLASS: Trilobita, PHYLUM: Arthropoda.   Jo.G.

TRIOPS, the name of primitive crustaceans more commonly known as *Tadpole shrimps.

TRIPLE-TAILS, heavily built perch-like fishes found in all tropical and subtropical seas. The name derives from the arrangement of the hind lobes of the dorsal and anal fins which are prolonged backwards almost as far as the caudal fin so that there appear to be three distinct tails. The front part of the long dorsal fin is spiny, the anal is fairly short-based and the pelvic fins are located immediately below the pectorals. There is a tendency for the colours of triple-tails to change during the life of the individual. In *Lobotes surinamensis* the young fishes have distinct white streaks on the body, but these become reduced as the fish ages until they eventually disappear; an occasional adult may retain the white bands on the fins. The area behind the head is blue and the scales along the back and on the flanks have green centres edged with blue. Large adults become very dark, almost black but they may later regain their juvenile colouration as a 'breeding dress'.

Triple-tails attain a weight of 30 lb (13.6 kg) and are of some commercial importance in certain fisheries. Although rather sluggish fishes, spending a lot of their time resting in the water with their bodies leaning over at an angle, triple-tails will fight furiously when hooked and are considered to be good sporting fishes. FAMILY: Lobotidae, ORDER: Perciformes, CLASS: Pisces.

TRITYLODONTA, extinct mammal-like reptiles, or 'near mammals' of the Triassic-Jurassic period. See *Oligokyphus*.

TROGONS, a family of brightly-coloured, arboreal birds of tropical forests. There are 34 species, all similar in appearance and varying from about the size of a thrush to that of a dove, about 9–13 in (23–33 cm). They are found throughout the tropics, in Africa south of the Sahara; in India, Southeast Asia and south through Malaysia and the Philippines; and in most of South America, north through Central America and the West Indies to Mexico and the southeastern United States. They are stout, heavy-bodied birds with fairly large heads and distinctive long, broad tails. Their characteristic posture is relatively upright on a perch, squatting close to it with tail hanging down vertically or at times tilted slightly forwards below the perch. The squatting appearance is due in part to the small and comparatively weak legs and feet. The foot is peculiar in that the inner toe is turned backwards to give two toes forwards and two back. In other families it is the outer toe that is moved in this way. The large dark eyes are capable of good vision in poor light. The bill is short, very broad, with serrated edges to the curved culmen. Trogons have a thick soft plumage and very thin skin.

The colouring is usually bold. The breast, belly and under-tail coverts of males are frequently bright red, pink, orange or yellow; and these areas are similar but sometimes paler or more subdued on females. On males the rest of the plumage tends to contrast with the underside; the back from head to tail, and the upper breast and head, being glossy, sometimes black, but more often glossed with purple, blue or green, the last often vivid and metallic and sometimes with gold or bronze tints. The wings tend to be black, marked with white, or so finely vermiculated as to appear grey. Females have a duller plumage with more grey, brown or buff tints. The only exceptional plumages are those of *Pharomachrus* species, the male quetzel *P. mocino*, in particular. They have spiky crown feathers forming a rounded crest and very elongated feathers of the upper-tail coverts, which are several times the bird's length, curving down to form a train of metallic green feathers.

Trogons are mainly forest birds, occurring to a limited extent in clearings, more open forest edge and plantations. They are sluggish, but feed by darting from the perch and hovering to snatch insects and other small creatures, including treefrogs, from branches or the air, while growing fruit are plucked from the stems, the serrated bill probably helping in this. They are usually solitary except when nesting. The calls are various hollow cooing, cawing or hooting notes, often difficult to locate, and a series of such notes may be run together to form a song. Brief low-pitched or squeaky notes have also been recorded. Trogons nest in unlined holes in trees. Sometimes these are natural cavities or the bird may excavate either shallow cavities or deeper cavities with entrance tunnels. The bill is not adapted for boring and soft wood is chosen and bitten away. The Gartered trogon *Trogon violaceus* utilizes papery arboreal wasp-nests into which the pair tunnel after eating the wasps. Trogons lay two to four eggs which are rounded, usually white but sometimes tinted buff or greenish. Both parents incubate the eggs and tend the young which hatch naked. FAMILY: Trogonidae, ORDER: Trogoniformes, CLASS: Aves.

TROPICBIRDS, large white seabirds belonging to the order Pelecaniformes. They differ from other species in many aspects of structure and habits and show many convergences with the terns, including size, plumage, bill and voice (which gives them the sailor's name of Boatswain birds).

All three species belong to the genus *Phaethon* and are very similar, differing mainly in size, colour of bill, tail streamers and the amount of black in the silky white plumage. They are up to 18 in (46 cm) long excluding the central tail feathers which are very elongated and double the length of the birds. Their bills are stout, razor-sharp and slightly decurved, well suited to holding the prey of fishes and squids, which are caught by diving into the sea from high in the air. The legs are very short and the birds move with an ungainly shuffle when on land. Of all the Pelecaniformes the tropicbirds are the most independent of land, only coming ashore to breed. The nest-sites are in holes in cliffs, under rocks or vegetation, where birds can come and go without having to shuffle more than a few paces.

Tropicbirds are well named as they are rarely recorded away from warm waters. The Red-billed tropicbird *P. aethereus* is widespread in the Atlantic, eastern Pacific, the Red Sea and parts of the Indian Ocean and is replaced by the Red-tailed species *P. rubricauda* in the western Pacific and southern Indian Oceans. The Yellow-billed tropicbird *P. lepturus* is common in the Pacific, Atlantic and Indian Oceans but does not occur in the eastern Pacific.

As with so many pelagic seabirds the breeding cycle is very long. When the birds first return to land to breed they spend many weeks displaying both in the air and at the nest-holes. The sight of six or eight dazzling white tropicbirds chasing each other noisily through the clear tropical air, long thin tail feathers streaming in the wind, is an unforgettable one. The single egg, white with attractive, rich brown blotchings is incubated for 40–44 days by both sexes, each sitting for about a week at a time. Unlike other Pelecaniformes the newly hatched chick is covered in long white down, but is still brooded for the first few weeks of life as a protection against other tropicbirds which would evict it while looking for nest-sites in the overcrowded colonies. Growth is slow and the young remain in the hole until fledging when about two months old.

On Ascension and Galapagos Islands, tropicbirds are found breeding throughout the year. This suggests that feeding conditions are constant so there is no advantage to be gained by birds feeding young at any particular time of year. In such colonies individual pairs lay every 8–12 months, depending on the species and whether or not they reared a chick the first season. If pairs fail to raise young they leave the colony, moult and then return to breed again as quickly as possible. FAMILY: Phaethontidae, ORDER: Pelecaniformes, CLASS: Aves. M.P.H.

Red-tailed tropicbird.

TROUGH SHELLS, marine bivalve molluscs common in muddy sand and gravel along the eastern shores of the North Atlantic. They can be easily recognized by a prominent ⌃ in the hinge of the left valve formed by the fusion of the two hinge teeth. They also have an internal hinge ligament which when decayed leaves a well defined pit. All the Trough shells have heavy durable shells.

Spawning in the Solid trough shell *Spisula solida* has been shown to be related to temperature changes in the water and, in the laboratory, solutions of potassium chloride had a similar effect. It is thought the potassium chloride stimulated the muscles of the gonad to contract and so discharge eggs or sperms.

These molluscs live buried in the sand and feed on small particles, living or dead, suspended in the water. They are all deep burrowers and so possess long fused siphons. There are light-sensitive receptors at the tips of these siphons, so these vulnerable soft parts are retracted when an approaching predator casts a shadow on them. FAMILY: Mactridae, ORDER: Eulamellibranchia, CLASS: Bivalvia, PHYLUM: Mollusca. P.F.N.

TROUPIALS, a diverse family of perching birds notable for its remarkable adaptive radiation. It includes the cowbirds, oropendolas, caciques, grackles, American blackbirds, American orioles or true troupials, meadowlarks, the bobolink *Dolichonyx oryzivorus* and, according to some authorities, the dickcissel *Spiza americana.* True troupials are colourful, small and medium-sized birds belonging to the genus *Icterus* and the name troupial is also applied without qualification to *I. icterus.* Plumages of the true troupials range from the nearly all black Epaulet oriole *I. cayensis* to the very striking yellow or orange and black of the majority of species.

Icterus species are essentially birds of the broad-leaved tropical forests of the New World but some, such as the Baltimore oriole *I. galbula,* breed as far north as southern Canada and migrate south in winter. In South America true troupials occur only as far south as northern Argentina.

Although true troupials are adapted to fruit-eating and nectar-drinking the bulk of their food is made up of insects when these are plentiful, as in the northern summer. There are two groups of true troupials. The fruit-eaters feed by thrusting the closed bill into the soft fruit then gaping and lapping up the juices released by the pressure of the opening mandibles with the brush tongue. Nectar-drinkers have thinner bills and weaker jaw muscles by comparison and their brush tongues are much better developed. They feed by probing into the open flower or by piercing its base.

The nests of the true troupials are deep, hanging cups beautifully woven from grasses and fibres but they are not as spectacular as those of the oropendolas. The two sides are completed first, hanging from adjacent twigs at the very tip of a branch, and these are then joined to form a purse-like structure narrower at the top than the bottom. The nest is well hidden by some species but daringly exposed by others. In the latter, intending nest robbers are deterred because they have to expose themselves either to the irate parents or to predators. Tropical troupials lay 2–3 eggs, the northern ones 5–6, the ground colour being pale blue or whitish with darker spots or streaking and fine scribbling. Incubation is by the female alone and both parents feed the young.

True troupials are mainly territorial unlike other members of the family which tend to be colonial or polygamous. The songs are normally very musical, that of the troupial

Common hangnest or troupial of northern South America thrusts its bill into soft fruits, prising them open by gaping. It will open a matchbox by the same method.

being exceptionally fine, and the females of some tropical species also sing. FAMILY: Icteridae, ORDER: Passeriformes, CLASS: Aves.   J.H.M.

TROUT, members of the salmon family found in the freshwaters of the northern hemisphere. There is no scientific basis for the distinction between trouts and salmons and the names are merely applied by common usage. In England, the name trout refers to the Brown trout *Salmo trutta* (a member of the same genus as the Atlantic salmon, *S. salar*), while in the United States the word trout applies to Rainbow trout *S. gairdneri*, Cutthroat trout *S. clarki* and several other species, while Brook trout, Great Lake trout and so on refer to members of the genus *Salvelinus* (otherwise termed chars).

The question of trout species has long vexed ichthyologists. In addition to the Sea trout, Lake trout and River trout, several other species were thought to occur in Great Britain. They were distinguished by colour patterns and differences in shape. The gillaroo *S. stomachius*, for example, was characterized by a very thick stomach. Other 'species' included the sewen *S. cambricus*, the Black-finned trout *S. nigripinnis*, the Great lake trout *S. ferox* and the Brook trout *S. fario*. The Sea trout was referred to as *S. eriox*. It has now been established, however, that all these forms belong to the single species *S. trutta* and that the differences are due to variations in feeding conditions and habits. The Sea trout with a partially marine habitat has developed a silvery colour; the thick stomach of the gillaroo results from its diet of shelled molluscs; the huge Lake trout enjoys the still and rich waters of lakes; dark and peaty water induces dark colour in fishes, and so on.

The Brown trout is closely related to the Atlantic salmon and the parr of the two species are very similar. The tail is less deeply forked in the Brown trout juveniles and there is always an orange or reddish tinge to the adipose fin. The natural range of the Brown trout is from England to the Pyrenees and eastwards across to the Urals, with a very small population in North Africa. Because of their sporting qualities, however, Brown trout have been introduced into the coastal regions of North America, Chile, Argentina, southern India, highland areas of East Africa, South Africa, New Zealand and Australia. In warm countries trout have been limited to the upper reaches of rivers and have not interfered with the populations of local species further down. In the Drakensberg Mountains of South Africa, however, trout with its predatory habits introduced in the last century have thrived to such an extent that a small carp-like fish *Oreodameon quathlambae,* known only from that area, is now extinct. The danger of introducing a species

The Rainbow trout, a popular sport fish of western North America, in its breeding dress, a red belly.

to a new area cannot be too highly stressed.

The Brown trout is a solid, powerful fish, usually spotted but with great variability in the number, size and colour of the spots. The mouth is large and toothed and the tail is emarginate. These are swift, active fishes that favour highly oxygenated and cool waters. In Europe they can live at sea-level but in Africa the best conditions for their survival may well lie at 5,000–6,000 ft (1,500–1,800 m) above sea-level. In small mountain streams only a few inches deep, Brown trout will thrive, feed and breed but will never reach more than a few inches in length. The Great lake trout, on the other hand, will top the scales at 30 lb (14 kg), showing that trout, like many other fishes, are extremely sensitive to the amount of food and living space available.

The breeding habits and time of spawning of Brown trout are similar to those of the Atlantic salmon. Sea trout and forms living in estuaries migrate up rivers to breed, Lake trout move into the feeder streams and riverine forms merely run further upstream. Like the salmon, the trout female constructs a shallow nest, the redd, into which the eggs are deposited and there fertilized. The young trout pass through stages similar to those of

the salmon (alevin, parr, smolt), the comparison being closer in the case of Sea trout. Throughout the whole of the northern hemisphere spawning occurs from September to April, although the actual time depends on water temperatures.

Although there is only one European species of trout, in North America there are several. One of these, the Rainbow trout, has been as widely distributed in other parts of the world as has been the Brown trout. In the Rainbow trout the flanks are pinkish and the back dark green to dark blue. Often there is a golden sheen on the flanks and the fins are always speckled (these are rarely speckled in the Brown trout). The Rainbow has a faster growth rate than the Brown trout under similar conditions and has been introduced into English trout rivers. The Rainbow has a migratory form, known as the steelhead, once thought to be a distinct species. In the United States Rainbow trouts can reach a weight of 30 lb (14 kg). The Cutthroat trout is native to the inland waters of the western part of the American continent. It derives its name from the red marking under the throat. As with all trout, the colours and markings of this species vary with the locality. The largest Cutthroat

Female Sea trout migrating up a river to breed, leaping the rapids.

recorded was 39 in (1 m) in length and weighed 41 lb (18·5 kg). The Golden trout *S. uguabonita* is confined to parts of California with an altitude of over 8,000 ft (2,400 m). It rarely exceeds 20 in (51 cm) in length although a relative giant of 11 lb (5 kg) has been recorded.

For centuries, trout have been one of the most popular of sporting fishes and more books have been devoted to trout and the techniques for catching them than to any other fishes. They are well known for their cunning and the angler may have great difficulty in deceiving a large fish with an artificial fly. FAMILY: Salmonidae, ORDER: Salmoniformes, CLASS: Pisces.

TROUT TICKLING. This is a laborious method of catching trout without any form of tackle. A trout is located near the bank of a stream and the 'angler' lies down carefully just above it. He slowly puts one hand into the water as far from the trout as possible and gently eases his hand towards it, waving the fingers gently to simulate waterweed—hence the term tickling. This must be done as quietly

as possible so that no ripple alerts the trout and it may take as much as an hour to move the hand under the trout's body so that a quick flip throws it onto the bank. The term 'tickling' is a misnomer, for the slightest touch will send the trout streaking away, a point not always appreciated, as in an old account that records 'this fish of nature loveth flattery; for, being in the water, it will suffer itself to be rubbed and clawed, and so to be taken, whose example I would wish no maids to follow'.

TROUT-PERCHES, freshwater fishes of North America with a superficial resemblance to both the trouts and the perches. There are only three species, placed in a separate order. The common name stems from the presence of a trout-like adipose fin in two of the species, combined with a spiny dorsal fin similar to that of a perch. It was long thought that the trout-perches represented an intermediate stage or missing link connecting the more primitive soft-rayed fishes with the more advanced spiny-rayed fishes. More recent studies have shown,

however, that the trout-perches are in fact an evolutionary offshoot.

The sandroller *Percopsis orniscomaycus* has an adipose fin, rough spiny scales and spines on the fins. It grows to about 6 in (15 cm) and is found in Canada and the eastern part of the United States. *Columbia transmontana* is similar in appearance and occurs in the Columbia river basin.

The pirate-perch *Aphredoderus sayanus* is placed in a separate family, partly because the adipose fin is missing. There is, however, a more remarkable feature and one which students find difficult to forget once the species name has been turned into the humerous mnemonic 'say-anus'. In the young fishes the anus is in the normal position just in front of the origin of the anal fin, but as the fish grows the anus gradually moves forward until in the adult it lies in the throat. The pirate-perch, which is confined to the eastern side of the United States, reaches about 5 in (13 cm) in length and lives on the bottom of lakes and slow moving waters where there is a thick layer of debris. FAMILIES: Percopsidae, Aphredoderidae, ORDER: Percopsiformes CLASS: Pisces.

TRUMPETERS, a family of three species of chicken-sized birds of the forests of the tropical areas of the New World. They have rather long legs, long necks, short tails, rounded wings and short, somewhat curved, bills. The plumage is mainly black with purplish reflections on the foreneck. The lower upperparts are either grey, white or brown, according to the species.

Typical forest birds, which live in flocks on the forest floor, they seldom fly but will roost in trees. Very little is known about their life in the wild but they are often kept in captivity becoming very tame. They nest in large holes in trees and lay roundish grey-white eggs. The incubation period is still unknown but the nestlings are believed to leave the hole immediately after hatching. They feed on insects and fruits. FAMILY: Psophiidae, ORDER: Gruiformes, CLASS: Aves.

TRUMPETFISHES, rather specialized warm-water fishes related to the flutemouths, pipefishes and Sea horses and placed in the single genus *Aulostoma*. There are about four species known. They have elongated bodies with long flat snouts and a series of isolated spines bearing membranes in front of the dorsal fin. The dorsal and anal fins are set far back on the body. These fishes rarely grow to more than 2 ft (60 cm). They use their long snouts to ferret out small fishes and crustaceans around coral reefs and are adept at camouflage, frequently hiding head down amongst the coral. Dr Hans Hass noticed that, when passing into open water from one

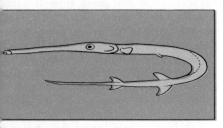

The aptly-named trumpetfish.

coral head to another, these fishes attempt to make the journey with another and larger fish. Dr Hass saw a trumpetfish shoot out of hiding to lay itself along the back of a parrotfish. The latter tried to dislodge its companion, but without success until they neared the next coral head, when the trumpetfish swam quickly to safety. Trumpetfishes usually exhibit territorial behaviour, vigorously guarding their piece of reef. FAMILY: Fistulariidae, ORDER: Gasterosteiformes, CLASS: Pisces.

TRUNKFISHES, an alternative name for *boxfishes.

TRYPANOSOMA, single-celled animals belonging to a genus of flagellates parasitizing the blood (sometimes the tissues) of vertebrates and usually the gut of a blood-sucking insect or leech which serves as vector. Characteristic of these organisms is a structure, the kinetoplast, which is a mass of cytoplasmic DNA and lies in an expansion of the single mitochondrion that passes from one end of the flagellate to the other. By light microscopy the kinetoplast is seen as a basophilic body lying apposed to the basal body of the single flagellum which emerges from a lateral pocket on the trypanosome's body and is attached to its surface as it runs forward to or beyond the flagellate's anterior end. Some trypanosomes have a very reduced kinetoplast and are termed dyskinetoplastic.

During the course of the life-cycle of the trypanosome the kinetoplast and flagellar base are seen to move from behind the nucleus to a position in front of it: trypanosomes with a posterior kinetoplast are called trypomastigote, those with an anterior one epimastigote forms, unless the body is rounded and lacks a flagellum in which case it is termed amastigote (like intracellular *Leishmania). Changes in position of the kinetoplast in cyclical development are accompanied by changes in the mitochondrion. In *Trypanosoma rhodesiense,* for example, the mitochondrion is an elaborate network of cristae-bearing canals in the epimastigote form, but is reduced to a single canal lacking cristae in the multiplicative stage in mammalian blood. These mitochondrial changes are accompanied by alterations in the respiration of the flagellate. Complete breakdown of glucose to CO_2 and water is characteristic of stages with a mitochondrial network; glycolysis to pyruvic acid which is excreted is associated with the reduced mitochondrion. Dyskinetoplastic trypanosomes are unable to activate the mitochondrion.

The trypanosomes of fishes, amphibians, reptiles and birds are non-pathogenic. Those of aquatic vertebrates are leech transmitted and undergo cyclical development in the vector's fore-gut to be injected with the leech's saliva when it feeds. Trypanosomes of mammals may be divided into two groups: the Stercoraria and the Salivaria. Stercorarian trypanosomes develop to the infective form (metacyclic) in the hind-gut of the insect vector and gain access to the mammal either by faecal contamination of the vector's bite or by the vector being crushed when it is ingested by the mammal and trypanosomes penetrating the oral mucosa: the life-cycle of the insect-borne trypanosomes of terrestrial amphibians, reptiles and birds follows a similar pattern. Salivarian trypanosomes reach the metacyclic stage in the mouthparts or salivary glands of the insect vector and from there are injected into the mammal.

Of the stercorarian trypanosomes, *Try-*

panosoma theileri is common in cattle throughout the world and is transmitted by Horse flies (Tabanidae). *T. melophagium* of sheep is transmitted by Louse flies (Hippoboscidae). Both are present in the blood in very small numbers where they divide in the epimastigote form.

Trypanosoma lewisi is a cosmopolitan parasite of wild rats and is transmitted by the fleas *Xenopsylla cheopis* and *Ceratophyllus fasciatus* in which it develops in the mid- and hind-gut. Contaminative infection of the rodent by metacyclics is followed by a multiplicative phase in which multiple fission of epimastigote forms occur in the host's visceral capillaries over a period of 4–5 days after which trypomastigote forms are found in the blood. After 7–10 days division is halted by antibody ('ablastin') production, but the non-multiplying trypomastigotes persist in the blood for a month or so until they are all eliminated by a second antibody, that is if they have not been ingested by a flea. *T. rangeli* is a non-pathogenic parasite of man in South America and is transmitted by the bug *Rhodnius prolixus* in which it may be pathogenic. In addition to contaminative transmission this species invades first the haemocoel and then the salivary glands of the vector, so that transmission can also occur by inoculation.

Trypanosoma cruzi is the causative agent of Chagas' disease in man. It occurs over South and Central America and the vectors are species of reduviid bugs, such as *Rhodnius*. Metacyclics from the insect's

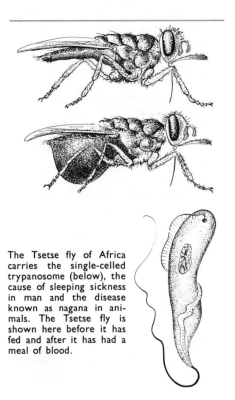

The Tsetse fly of Africa carries the single-celled trypanosome (below), the cause of sleeping sickness in man and the disease known as nagana in animals. The Tsetse fly is shown here before it has fed and after it has had a meal of blood.

faeces penetrate mucous membranes and enter a multiplicative phase in the amastigote form in heart muscle or macrophage cells. The amastigote forms metamorphose via epimastigote forms to trypomastigotes which circulate with the blood but may re-enter suitable cells to initiate another amastigote multiplicative phase.

Salivarian trypanosomes divide in the trypomastigote form in the mammalian host and relapsing bloodstream parasitaemias reflect antigenic changes of the trypanosome population in response to host antibody production: intracellular stages are not known. Many species are transmitted by *Tsetse flies (Glossina) in which they multiply first in the trypomastigote form and later in the epimastigote form. T. vivax of cattle and equines in Africa confines its development to the proboscis, metacyclics being found in the hypopharynx of the fly; but this species has spread outside Africa to Mauritius, the West Indies and South America where it is transmitted non-cyclically by biting flies acting as 'flying syringes'. T. congolense infects ungulates, pigs and dogs in Africa, has a trypomastigote phase in the mid-gut of Glossina but its epimastigote phase is in the proboscis and metacyclics in the hypopharynx.

Trypanosoma brucei of game and domestic animals is morphologically identical with the human sleeping sickness trypanosomes T. gambiense and T. rhodesiense and these two are usually regarded as variants or subspecies of T. brucei. All three variants resemble T. congolense inasmuch as they have a mid-gut trypomastigote phase in Glossina, developing first in the endotrophic and later in the peritrophic space. But from the fly mid-gut these flagellates migrate via the mouthparts to the salivary glands of the fly to multiply as epimastigotes and later produce metacyclics. T. gambiense is transmitted by riverine species of Glossina, T. rhodesiense by savannah flies. Both game animals and domestic cattle can act as a reservoir for this last species. Trypanosomes of the T. brucei complex occur as long slender, short stumpy and intermediate forms in the blood of the natural host. T. evansi of camels and horses outside the tsetse belt of Africa is morphologically similar to slender T. brucei, and is transmitted only mechanically by biting flies: T. equinum of horses in South America is a dyskinetoplastic variant of T. evansi. T. equiperdum of horses is another variant of T. evansi which tends to become localized in oedematous plaques on the skin and is transmitted from such plaques during copulation.

T. vivax, T. congolense and T. brucei are highly pathogenic in domestic animals in Africa. The presence of these trypanosomes along with their Tsetse fly vector has to a large extent prevented cattle farming in Africa and so contributed to the acute protein shortage in that continent. These trypanosomes are not usually pathogenic in native game animals, however, so while preventing the introduction of European cattle, trypanosomiasis has delayed the extermination of the game which can live with the disease. Overgrazing by cattle with consequent destruction of habitat has also been avoided, so trypanosomiasis has been an important factor in conservation in Africa. ORDER: Protomonadina, CLASS: Mastigophora, PHYLUM: Protozoa.   K.V.

TSAINE *Bos javanicus birmanicus,* the Burmese name for the *banteng.

TSETSE FLY, one of the greatest scourges of tropical Africa, the only important agent capable of transmitting human sleeping sickness from person to person. Tsetse flies are true, two-winged flies and in general appearance and in structure are very similar to House flies, except that the mouthparts are highly adapted for piercing the skin of man and other mammals and sucking blood. The mouthparts form a prominent, forward pointing proboscis consisting of a lower lip or labium with a tip for rasping and piercing, and which bears in its grooved surface the needle-like labrum-epipharynx and hypopharynx. The first conveys blood from the host animal into the insect's gut and the hypopharynx carries the saliva which, as in other blood sucking insects, is an anticoagulant which prevents clogging of the delicate mouthparts. When the tsetse is at rest the wings are folded one on top of the other over the back, whereas most other similar flies rest with the wings spread laterally. Tsetse fly species range in size from about the House fly up to larger than blowflies. They occur in Africa south of the Sahara and north of South Africa, within the Tropics of Cancer and Capricorn, except that a single species has a foothold in southwest Arabia.

Tsetse fly larvae are born fully grown and ready to change into pupae. The female ripens only a single egg at a time and after fertilization this comes to rest in the uterus. When the larva hatches it is nourished by a secretion from special nutritive glands, which it imbibes directly from a papilla or nipple. The female deposits her fully developed larva (a maggot) in the shade of a tree, shrub or log, depending on the species and the climate of the area. Immediately after this, the whitish larva burrows into dry, loose soil or under ground-litter and changes into a dark brown pupa with two prominent knobs on the posterior end. The adult flies may live for upwards of 70 days but the average length of life is only about four weeks. Although a female Tsetse fly may deposit a maximum of only twelve larvae, frequently less, in the course of her life, the task of eliminating this most harmful species has, up to the present time, proved impossible in spite of massive research over half a century.

African sleeping sickness is caused by micro-organisms known as *trypanosomes, which live as parasites in man and many big game of Africa, as well as in the Tsetse fly Glossina. The presence of trypanosomes in the bodies of man and other vertebrates is known as trypanosomiasis. Two species of trypanosome Trypanosoma gambiense and T. rhodesiense have been named as the cause of human African sleeping sickness, and both parasitize wild game and domestic animals, and domestic pigs and antelopes, especially wildebeest, are important reservoirs of trypanosomes. Other species, such as T. vivax and T. congolense, are highly pathogenic to domestic animals, especially cattle and are also transmitted by Tsetse flies. It is important to note that where trypanosome and mammalian host have long been associated, disease symptoms are either completely lacking or are very slight, whereas in new associations, the micro-organism is usually highly virulent towards its host. Thus, the native game animals of Africa harbour trypanosomes without any trace of nagana, the animal form of tsetse-borne trypanosomiasis, and in areas where human infections are of long standing the disease in indigenous populations tends to be relatively mild. On the other hand, newly exposed domestic animals and Europeans have little resistance to trypanosomiasis and effects are usually fatal if untreated.

Not all of the twenty or so species of Tsetse fly are important as transmitters of sleeping sickness to man. In many areas Glossina palpalis and G. tachinoides are the chief vectors (transmitters) of T. gambiense which occurs over a wide area of tropical West and Central Africa. Glossina morsitans is often the main vector of T. rhodesiense, but other closely related flies may be equally or more important in causing specific epidemics. Glossina palpalis and G. tachinoides are both riverine species, that is, they need shade and high humidity, which only occur along densely wooded water-courses. Spectacular control of these species may be achieved where it is possible to clear sufficient vegetation. G. morsitans is known as a non-riverine or savannah species as it frequents savannah type grassland with patches of shady bush. Control of G. morsitans and similar savannah species is difficult although several methods have been tried. The clearing of vegetation, destruction of game, insecticide spraying from aircraft and burning of grassland and bush have all offered partial solutions to the problem in certain areas. All these methods involve a drastic alteration of the natural environment which in itself is likely to create many more problems—and the Tsetse fly still remains. More recently,

Tsetse fly cleaning proboscis after feeding on the photographer.

laboratory breeding experiments have shown it may be possible to produce large enough numbers of semi-sterile Tsetse flies which if released into wild populations could cause a sharp decline in density. When the semi-sterile flies mate with normal flies they would introduce a sterility factor into the genetic make up of the offspring which could lead to ultimate extinction of the tsetse population. FAMILY: Muscidae, ORDER: Diptera, CLASS: Insecta, PHYLUM: Arthropoda.   M.J.P.

TUATARA *Sphenodon punctatus,* belonging to the otherwise extinct reptilian order, Rhynchocephalia. The rhynchocephalians are characterized by the presence of a 'beak-like' upper jaw, and first appeared in the Lower Triassic some 200 million years ago. The group was virtually extinct by the Lower Cretaceous about 100 million years later. The members of the group formerly had a widespread distribution, and fossils have been found from all the continents except North America. The order is now represented only by a single genus with one species, the tuatara, which is restricted to approximately 20 islands off the coast of New Zealand. The ancestry of the tuatara may be traced back to the fossil reptile *Homoeosaurus* from the Upper Jurassic and the similarities between the two forms are striking. It seems, therefore, that the structure of the tuatara has remained virtually unchanged for some 130 million years. The existence of the tuatara is just as astonishing as the discovery of a large

dinosaur would be. Perhaps even more so since the tuatara is the sole survivor of a group which reached its peak about 180 million years ago whereas the dinosaurs were at their peak about 140 million years ago in the Jurassic and Cretaceous.

The tuatara is 'lizard-like' in general appearance but is distinguished from the lizards by several skeletal features involving the skull and the ribs. The generic name *Sphenodon* means 'wedge tooth' and this refers to the chisel-like teeth on the upper and lower jaws, which are fused to the jawbone, not set into sockets. The Maori word tuatara means 'peaks on the back' and this describes the triangular folds of skin which form a conspicuous crest down the back and tail of the male. The female has only a rudimentary crest. Tuataras vary in colour from black-brown to dull green, while some may have a reddish tinge. The upper part of the body is covered with small scales that may have small yellow spots. The feet have five toes each with sharp claws and are partially webbed. A vestigial *parietal 'eye' is found on the top of the head in very young animals, but soon becomes covered over, and is invisible in adults. The presence of this 'eye' is considered to be a very primitive feature since it also occurs in the ancestors of the rhyncho-cephalians. It is usually further reduced or even absent in modern lizards. The parietal eye retains some traces of a lens and a retina, but there is doubt about its function. It may be that it acts as a register of solar radiation

and controls the amount of time the creature spends in the sunlight. This is important since the tuatara, like all reptiles, has a body temperature which is affected by the temperature of its surroundings, and is said to be ectothermic. The body temperature may therefore be controlled to some extent by basking in the sun or seeking the shade. Nevertheless, the tuatara spends most of the daytime in its burrow leaving it only occasionally to sunbathe, mainly in late winter and spring. It is therefore largely nocturnal and is active at temperatures which are much lower than those favoured by lizards. Available reports indicate that the tuatara may be active at temperatures as low as 45°F (7°C) and, further, that even in winter it only hibernates lightly. Allied to its low body temperature is the fact that it has a very low metabolic rate. This means that it requires very little energy to keep the vital body processes, such as excretion and digestion, 'ticking over'. The tuatara is reputed to grow very slowly and probably does not breed until it is 20 years old. Growth may continue until the age of 50 or beyond and the animals are said to be extremely long-lived. Estimates of the life span vary from about 100 to 300 years.

The mating habits of the tuatara are also remarkable in that the male has no copulatory organ and mating is accomplished. by the apposition of the male and female urino-genital openings (known as cloacal apposition). Pairing usually takes place in January but the sperm is stored within the female until October-December. She then scoops out a shallow nest in the ground and lays 5–15 eggs with soft white shells. These remain in the nest for a further 13–15 months before hatching, the longest incubation period known for any reptile.

At the present time the tuatara is found only on some small islands off the east coast of the North Island of New Zealand and in Cook Strait between the North and South Islands. These small islands also have large colonies of birds such as petrels and shearwaters which nest in burrows. The tuatara is capable of digging its own burrow, but seems to prefer ready-made ones, and therefore frequently shares a burrow with a seabird. The two inhabitants of the burrow have an amicable co-existence on the whole although the tuatara will occasionally eat the eggs and even the chicks of these birds. The normal diet of the tuatara is moths, beetles, crickets and other small invertebrates. It is evident that it was also found on the North and South Islands of New Zealand since the animal was so well known to the Maoris. In fact the tuatara figures very prominently in the traditional wood carvings which ornament Maori meeting houses and is a symbol of death or misfortune. This stems from the Maori myth that the tuatara, and lizards, were the close associates of the goddess of fire who originally brought death into the world by slaying her own grandson.

The reason for the survival of the tuatara in New Zealand is one of isolation. The separation of New Zealand from other land masses occurred long before the evolution of the predaceous land animals and therefore the tuatara has been able to survive in New Zealand in the absence of predators, but has been wiped out in other parts of the world.

Subfossil remains show that the tuatara was originally found in a number of parts of the North and South Islands of New Zealand, but they have long since disappeared from the mainland. This was probably due to a gradual change in climatic conditions, vegetation and perhaps also the avifauna, before and for some while after the arrival of the Maoris. There is little evidence to support the suggestion that either Europeans or introduced animals were to blame for the elimination of the tuatara from the mainland.

Although the tuatara is found on about 20 offshore islands, it appears to be maintaining a satisfactory replacement rate and age distribution on only a few of these. On many islands the population seems to consist only of adult animals, although the reasons for this are not clear. The species is very strictly protected by the New Zealand Government, and it is to be hoped that such measures will ensure the continued survival of this fascinating relic from Triassic times. FAMILY: Sphenodontidae, ORDER: Rhynchocephalia, CLASS: Reptilia.   J.R.

TUBE-MOUTH FISHES, small marine fishes with tube-like mouths found on both sides of the North Pacific and related to the sticklebacks. The term was formerly used collectively for all fishes with tube-like mouths (pipefishes, Sea horses, trumpetfishes and flutemouths) but it is preferable to restrict it to the aulorhynchids. *Aulorhynchus flavidus* from Canadian Pacific shores somewhat resembles a very slender stickleback with many spines along its back. *Aulichthys japonicus* from Japan is very similar in appearance. Like the sticklebacks, the Tube-mouth fishes build nests. The late Conrad Limbaugh, a pioneer in combining scientific observation with underwater pleasure, noticed huge shoals many yards in extent off the coast of California. The fishes build their nests amongst the roots and small fronds of the larger sea-weeds below the low water mark, the male cementing the nest together with a sticky secretion. After the female has laid eggs in the nest, the male guards them until they hatch. Spawning takes place throughout the year. FAMILY: Aulorhynchidae, ORDER: Gasterosteiformes, CLASS: Pisces.

TUBENOSES, the general term for seabirds of the order Procellariiformes, including the petrels, prions, albatrosses and shearwaters. The term has its origin in the form of the nostrils of these birds, which open through horny tubes extending forwards from the base of the bill. The significance of the tubes is unclear, though they may be to protect the nostril openings while the bird is feeding at or near the water surface.

TUBIFICIDAE, small worms 1–4 in (2–10 cm) long, slender and a bright red colour due to the respiratory blood pigment being visible through the body wall. They are exclusively aquatic, especially on soft, muddy bottoms into which they may burrow deeply. Respiration is generally carried out over the general body surface, though *Branchiura* has large tail gill filaments. The best known member of this family is *Tubifex*, used extensively for feeding aquarium fishes. Tubificids are probably world-wide, however, and although the majority are freshwater, some are estuarine or marine, the latter being most commonly found in intertidal freshwater run-offs.

Asexual reproduction is uncommon, sexual reproduction with copulation and cross fertilization being the rule. A clitellum is formed, in the region of the sex organs, only in the breeding season, on mature individuals. In one species *Tubifex costatus* at least, maturity is attained after two years and the worms die after reproducing. An indefinite number of young hatch from each cocoon, as almost perfect miniature adults. See bloodworms. FAMILY: Tubificidae, ORDER: Plesiopora plesiothecata, CLASS: Oligochaeta, PHYLUM: Annelida.   R.H.

TUCO-TUCO, a nocturnal burrowing rodent whose common name is derived from its bell-like call note. The 50 species in the genus *Ctenomys* range from tropical to subarctic regions of South America. It is stockily built, 9–13 in (23–33 cm) in total length, its fur varying from dark brown to creamy buff.

Tuco-tucos live in colonies and excavate extensive burrows. The litter of 1–5 young are born at the end of one of the long tunnels. The breeding season is usually in the wet season when food is abundant. Food consists entirely of plant material such as grass, tubers, roots and stems. FAMILY: Ctenomyidae, ORDER: Rodentia, CLASS: Mammalia.

TUFTED DEER *Elaphodus cephalophus,* a small *deer with a crest of long dense hair around the base of the antlers, ranging from Burma to southern China, including Tibet.

TUNA FISHES or tunnies, large oceanic members of the mackerel family. Almost every feature of the tunas seems to be adapted

Section through setal sacs of the worm *Tubifex*. The parietovaginal muscles regulate movements of the whole follicle, whereas the intrafollicular muscles direct the movement of individual setae.

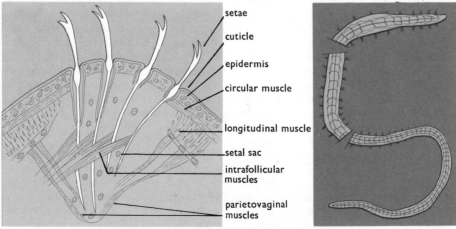

setae
cuticle
epidermis
circular muscle
longitudinal muscle
setal sac
intrafollicular muscles
parietovaginal muscles

Tuatara, the living fossil of New Zealand.

Tundra Fauna

for their life of eternal swimming. The body is powerful and torpedo-shaped, the dorsal and pectoral fins fold into grooves and the eyes are flush with the surface of the head, all of which help to reduce the drag caused by turbulent eddies as the fish cleaves the water. In addition, the scales are small and smooth and are reduced merely to a corselet round the pectoral fins. The tail is crescentic, the ideal shape for sustained fast swimming, and the finrays are closely bound to the end of the vertebral column so that the tail is no longer a flexible appendage of the body but an integral part of it. Behind the second dorsal and the anal fins are small finlets that may serve to control the formation of eddies, while the sides of the caudal peduncle, or base of the tail, bear little keels for further streamlining. A swimbladder is absent but a considerable amount of oil is present which aids in buoyancy. One remarkable feature of these large fishes is that the energy expended in fast swimming warms the blood to a few degrees above that of the surrounding water—an unusual feature for a 'cold-blooded' vertebrate. The tunas are carnivorous fishes that feed on pelagic organisms and especially on squid. They are mostly tropical in distribution but some of the larger species are found in the colder northern waters. There are six species of great tuna in the world: the albacore *Thunnus alalunga*, the yellowfin *T. albacares*, the blackfin *T. atlanticus*, the bigeye *T. obesus*, the bluefin *T. thynnus* and the longtail *T. tonggol*. Because of the size of these fishes and the difficulty of preserving specimens for comparative studies in museums, it is only recently that the confusion of names, both scientific and popular, has to some extent been resolved. Some species are world-wide in their distribution and have received a variety of common names, some of which are used for quite different species elsewhere. The names used here are those which are now generally agreed by fishery workers.

The bluefin of the Mediterranean and the Atlantic, often known merely as the tunny, is a large species that reaches 14 ft (4·3 m) and may weigh up to 1,800 lb (816 kg). The body is dark blue on the back, lighter on the flanks and silvery white with opalescent tints on the belly. The pectoral fins are short and the flesh is whitish. These fishes form the basis for an old and important fishery. The routes taken by the bluefins to their spawning grounds in special areas in the Atlantic, Mediterranean and Black Sea often pass close to the coast and such areas have been well known to the fishermen for centuries. In the Mediterranean, a system of nets, known as *madragues*, is set up to enclose a boiling mass of these powerful fishes. After spawning, the Mediterranean fishes pass into the Atlantic and migrate northwards, reaching the English Channel by about June. This was once their most

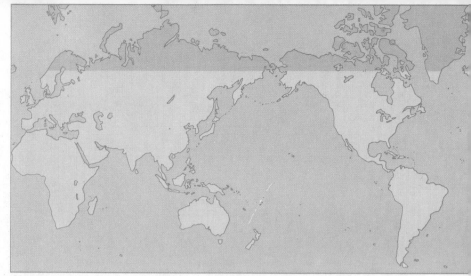

Map showing the distribution and extent of the Arctic tundra (dark area).

northerly limit, but since the 1920's they have been pressing north as far as Norway. A similar northward migration occurs along the western Atlantic coasts. Marked specimens from the Bahamas have been caught off the French coast but it is not yet known how much interchange there is between the eastern and western populations of the Atlantic. There is, indeed, much to be learned of the migrations of this important species. A subspecies of the bluefin, *Thunnus thynnus orientalis,* occurs in the Pacific.

The albacore is a smaller fish, reaching about 70 lb (32 kg) in weight. It can be immediately distinguished from the bluefin by its long sickle-shaped pectoral fins which reach as far as, or beyond, the second dorsal fin. It is world-wide in distribution, living near the surface in temperate seas but in deeper water in the tropics. Like other tunas, it is an important food fish and is especially valuable to the canning industry and, like the bluefin, it undertakes extensive migrations, specimens marked in California having been recaptured in Japan. These migrations are fairly strictly related to water temperatures and in the Atlantic the fishes migrate as far north as Iceland as water temperatures rise in the summer. The migrations of albacore in the North Pacific have been closely studied and there is reason to think that the same population inhabits the entire area.

The yellowfin is a large species that reaches a length of 8 ft (2·4 m) and can weigh up to 450 lb (204 kg). The longtail, however, is relatively small, reaching 30 lb (13·6 kg), but is important in many Indo-Pacific fisheries. The bigeye is a deep-water species. All the tunas are sporting fishes, the huge bluefin presenting a tremendous challenge to the skill of the angler. The world rod-caught record stands only a little short of 1,000 lb (454 kg). FAMILY: Scombridae, ORDER: Perciformes, CLASS: Pisces.

TUNDRA FAUNA, animal life in the Arctic grasslands (for which 'tundra' is the Lapp name) of the North American and Eurasian continents. These two areas have many species in common dating from the Bering Sea land bridge. Ecological factors limiting the numbers of species and individuals are low mean temperatures and a short growing period of only about 60 days. Nevertheless growth is rapid because of the many hours of sunlight during this period. The grassland is characterized by lichens, grasses, sedges and some dwarf woody plants. The region is one of permafrost, with the top few inches of soil unfrozen only in the growing season.

The fauna is typified by its simplicity. Northern Greenland, one of the richest tundras, has eight species of mammals: hare, lemming, musk-ox, reindeer, ermine, wolf, Polar bear and fox. By comparison, Spitzbergen has three including the fox, reindeer and Polar bear. Resident land birds are scarce; only the Rock ptarmigan being truly resident. Summer migrants, attracted to the rich seasonal growth, include many water birds—geese, ducks, swans, sandpipers and plovers. Skuas or jaegers live in the surrounding sea areas. They are specialized thieves and carrion eaters. Breeding seasons are shortened in these latitudes and, whereas a pair of robins in temperate climates will feed a brood of young to fledging in 13 days, the added daylight hours available for food gathering in the tundra, and its spasmodic superabundance, allow them to achieve this in 8–9 days. Food gathering has been observed to occur for 21 hours a day.

Reptiles and amphibians are poorly represented where they are not completely absent. Generally speaking, invertebrates are scarce, although spiders and mites are well represented, and may reach very high densities. Some classes of insects are represented, especially the Diptera, but the Hemiptera, Orthoptera, Odonata and Neuroptera are virtually absent. Lepidoptera, Coleoptera and Hymenoptera are sparse, but, although ants are scarce, bumblebees are conspicuous. Siphonaptera occur in association with the mammals and birds.

The few mammals that occur are present in large numbers, an indication of the nu-

tritious quality of the vegetation. Musk-oxen, once present in vast herds, have been constantly reduced by man until now only a few small herds are left in Arctic Canada and Greenland. Caribou in North America and reindeer in Eurasia feed exclusively on a lichen 'reindeer moss' and govern the entire way of life of the northern tribesmen. In prehistoric times the climate was more favourable, and Woolly rhinoceroses and mammoths flourished briefly until the temperatures began to fall.

The key to the energy turnover in the tundra lies with the lemming, a small hamster-like rodent. Years of high lemming density, with perhaps more than two lemmings per sq yd (sq m), are marked by the presence of large carnivorous birds such as eagles and Snowy owls and mammals such as wolverines, moving deep into the tundra lured by the abundant food. Lemming populations reach high densities every three to four years—the tundra cycle. A crash in numbers occurs when the lemmings have out-eaten their food, their predators showing a similar decline in numbers a year later. D.M.S.

TUPAIA, generic name of several species of *Tree shrew living in the forested areas of many parts of Asia, from southern China through Southeast Asia to the Philippines. It somewhat resembles a squirrel externally, but has a longer nose with no whiskers. It is diurnal, usually solitary and feeds mainly on insects with some animal food, fruit, seeds and leaves.

TUR *Capra,* two species of *ibex found in the Caucasus.

TURACOS, a family of 20 species of active and often highly-coloured arboreal birds, sometimes known as plantain-eaters or louries. They occur in Africa south of the Sahara in all habitats containing trees, from dry thornbush and gallery forest to dense evergreen forests. They are related to the cuckoos, and are fairly large, 14–18 in (35–45 cm) long, with fairly slender bodies, rather long tails and short rounded wings. The legs are rather long, with a reversible outer toe, and the birds run and leap among the branches of the trees with great agility, in contrast to the poor powers of flight. The head is often crested, the crest varying from hairy tufts or rounded domes to slender tapering structures rising to a point at the front, or to a coronet of feathers as in the Great blue turaco *Corythaeola cristata*. The bill is stout, somewhat broad, and slightly

A turaco *Tauraco livingstonii* shows the pigment that has been the cause of erroneous ideas. Unique in the animal kingdom this red pigment has been said repeatedly to be washed out by rain, which is untrue.

A turbot, large North Atlantic flatfish, swimming.

decurved and may be very deep, with a high arched culmen, and boldly coloured in yellow and red in some species, black in others. In some it extends back to form a forehead frontal shield. The nostrils may vary in shape and position from one species to another. In most species the feathers of head and breast are hairy in texture, as are those of the crest, and tend to be less glossy than wings and tail. The plumage of *Tauraco* and *Musophaga* species is usually green, violet or dark blue, and on such birds the inner webs of the flight feathers, and sometimes the crest, are vivid red, showing as a scarlet flash when the bird flies. The green and red pigments of these plumages are peculiar to the turacos. The Great blue turaco is entirely blue and green, and a group of species of the genera *Crinifer* and *Corythaixoides* (see Go-away birds) are only a sober grey ornamented with touches of black or white. In general the duller coloured species occur in the more open, drier country. The head and crest are often ornamented with patches of white, red or pink and there may be small red wattles around the large dark eyes.

The turacos are fruit-eaters, feeding the young on regurgitated fruit, but they will also eat buds and seeds and some insects and invertebrates. During sexual display the crests are raised and wings and tail flirted to show the bright colours, and males may feed their mates. The voice is sometimes a soft coo, but in some birds may consist of harsh shrieks, deeper nasal calls, loud chattering or barks. The nests are thin flat platforms of twigs and the two eggs are white or tinted blue or buff, and may be almost spherical. Both sexes incubate, for about two and a half weeks. The young have thick down and a wing-claw, and may show some precocial tendencies, being able to leave the nest and clamber about the tree long before fledging. They fledge in about a month. FAMILY: Musophagidae, ORDER: Cuculiformes, CLASS: Aves.

TURBAN SHELLS, a group of about 500 species of marine snails widely distributed in warmer seas. They are closely related to the *Top shells, important inhabitants of the same habitat on temperate beaches and they share with them a similar internal structure and function.

A typical Turban shell, for example, the Tapestry turban *Turbo petholatus,* is composed of about 6 whorls, rapidly enlarging to make a turban-like shape. All Turban shells have a thick circular stony operculum closing the shell mouth and in this species it is coloured with a bright green centre and yellowish rim and is the well-known 'cat's eye' sometimes set in 19th century jewellery. The largest member of the family is the Green turban *Turbo marmoratus,* found in the East Indies and Australia, which reaches 8 in (20 cm) in height and has an operculum which may weigh up to 1 lb (0·45 kg).

The eggs of Turban shells, as in most primitive Prosobranchia, are shed directly into the sea where they develop in the plankton. Turban shells are slow moving, herbivorous snails, grazing on algae that grow on rocks, and are often inhabitants of coral reefs. Another member of the family, the Delphinula snail *Angaria delphunis,* is confined to coral reefs in the Indo-Pacific and has a shell which is extremely variable in shape, according to the type of coral with which it is associated, sometimes being almost smooth and resembling a typical turban, at other times being fantastically ornamental with knobs and spines. FAMILY: Turbinidae, ORDER: Archaeogastropoda, CLASS: Gastropoda, PHYLUM: Mollusca.
E.M.D.

TURBELLARIA, a class of the phylum Platyhelminthes or flatworms which includes all free-living species, the best known of which are the *planarians.

TURBOT *Scophthalmus maximus,* a large flatfish from the North Atlantic. The turbot is one of the flatfish species that rests on its right side, the left side being pigmented and bearing the eyes. It is a shallow-water species found in the Mediterranean and all along European coasts. The body is diamond-shaped, with large symmetrical jaws lined with sharp teeth. There are no scales on the body but the 'eyed' side is covered by warty tubercles. The turbot is mostly found on sandy bottoms in water of 10–200 ft (3–60 m). Turbot are avid fish-eaters and tend to concentrate in areas where food is plentiful such as shallow banks near the mouths of rivers. They lie in wait for their prey and like most flatfishes are well camouflaged, the upper side being brown or grey with lighter and darker specklings.

The turbot is one of the best flavoured of British fishes. It grows to over 40 lb (18 kg) in weight and is extremely prolific, a female of 17 lb (7·5 kg) having been recorded with 9,000,000 eggs in the ovaries. FAMILY: Bothidae, ORDER: Pleuronectiformes, CLASS: Pisces.

TURKEYS, two species of large game birds. The Common turkey *Meleagris gallopavo* of North America occurs in open woodland and scrub. This is the domestic turkey. Its brown, barred plumage is glossed with bronze. The head and neck are naked and coloured red and blue, with wattles and a fleshy caruncle overhanging the bill. A tuft of bristles hangs from the breast. In display the wattles swell and the colour intensifies, the tail is erected and fanned, the body feathers ruffled and the wings drooped until the tips sweep the ground. The male's call is the noisy 'gobbling' while the female has a softer sharp note. The wild turkey is a strong flyer. It feeds on a wide variety of seeds, nuts and small creatures. It is polygamous, females laying in shallow scrapes in well-concealed situations.

The Ocellated turkey *Agriocharis ocellata*

occurs in Yucatan and Guatemala. It lives in jungles and is brighter in colour than the Common turkey. The greyish body feathers are tipped with large iridescent ocelli of green and bronze, while the head and neck are bright blue with scarlet and white caruncles. The display and behaviour are similar to that of the Common turkey but the voice is different and it flies more frequently. FAMILY: Meleagrididae, ORDER: Galliformes, CLASS: Aves.

TURNSTONES, wading birds usually found on rocky sea-shores. They are members of the subfamily Arenariinae and are normally placed in the family Scolopacidae, but sometimes in the Charadriidae. They are dumpy, short-billed and fairly short-legged birds, less than 12 in (30 cm) long, and the sexes are alike.

During most of the year, they are found chiefly on the coast, though the surfbird *Aphriza virgata* nests inland (in the Alaskan mountains). The other two species in the subfamily belong to the genus *Arenaria*: the (Ruddy) turnstone *A. interpres* has a circum-

A cock domesticated turkey, descendant of a race of the wild turkey that lives in the highlands of Mexico. It was first domesticated by the Aztecs.

Turnstones accompanied by two knots and a sanderling (greyish birds). The turnstone has red legs, the knot olive-green, and the sanderling black legs.

polar, mainly coastal, breeding distribution, chiefly to the north of the Arctic Circle, while the Black turnstone *A. melanocephala* replaces it in Alaska, on the coast of the Bering Sea. Although the turnstone is among the world's most northerly breeding birds (to at least 83°N), it also occurs in glacial or post-glacial relic populations on the Scandinavian islands and shores of the Baltic. The breeding range of the turnstone has decreased in Europe this century, possibly associated with an improved climate and higher mean summer temperatures. It no longer nests on the Baltic coast of Germany, where it was common in the 19th century. Its preferred breeding habitats are low lying stony coasts and islands adjacent to tundra, occasionally inland on moss or lichen tundra and, in the Baltic area, even on the grassy edges of conifer-clad islands.

Outside the breeding season, turnstones frequent a wide variety of coastal habitats, both rocky, pebbly and sandy. The Scandinavian populations migrate to West Africa in the northern winter, while some of the northern Greenland breeding birds winter on the coasts of the British Isles, where they moult their flight feathers after arrival in early autumn. Certain individuals have been shown by ringing to return to the same stretch of coast in successive winters. Migrant turnstones regularly reach Australasia and South America, but the breeding quarters of these populations are not known. Some individuals stay in the tropics and southern hemisphere throughout the (northern) breeding season. These are presumably immature birds, though some are in nuptial plumage and so might possibly breed, but not every year.

The turnstone is one of the few wading birds to take advantage of food provided by man. This has been recorded not only in the vicinity of expedition camps in polar regions but also in winter quarters, where garbage, potato peelings and oatmeal seem perfectly acceptable foodstuffs. The species get their name from their habit of turning over small stones and shells to search for the small insects, marine worms and shellfishes which form their normal diet. FAMILY: Scolopacidae, ORDER: Charadriiformes, CLASS: Aves.

P.R.E.

TURRET SHELLS, also known as Tower shells, marine snails closely related to the familiar periwinkles. The shell is long and tapering, with a large number of whorls, up to 19 in the European Common turret shell *Turritella communis*. Other very similar Tower species form an important part of the fauna of soft bottoms, sand, mud and gravel, in almost all seas. They are most frequently found a little below low tide level down to moderate depths, about 600 ft (200 m).

The sexes are separate and eggs are laid in stalked capsules 6–20 in each capsule in the European turret shell, the mass of several hundred capsules being fixed to a pebble by the intertwined stalks. Larvae hatch after ten days and swim in the plankton for a very short time before settling as tiny snails with only $2\frac{1}{2}$ whorls.

Turret shells are gregarious and are found buried shallowly in mud or sand. They feed rather differently from most gastropods, trapping detritus and plankton suspended in the seawater in rather the same way as *bivalve molluscs. The gill is very long with many slender filaments and it produces a sheet of mucus which entangles food carried over the gill by the action of microscopic lashing cilia. Mucus and food are then rolled into a string and passed to the mouth also by ciliary action.

Several closely-related molluscs have carried this feeding method further, namely the Worm shells, which are permanently attached to rocks, and whose shells are irregularly coiled resembling worm-tubes. For example, the Mediterranean Coiled worm shell *Serpulorbis arenarius* spins a triangular mucus net which floats in the water attached by one corner, and entangles food in the same way as a spider's web. At intervals the 'net' is drawn down to the mouth and swallowed with its catch. FAMILY: Turritellidae, ORDER: Mesogastropoda, SUB-CLASS: Prosobranchia, CLASS: Gastropoda, PHYLUM: Mollusca. E.M.D.

TURTLES, aquatic relatives of *tortoises and divisible into freshwater and marine turtles (see turtles, marine). Some of the smaller species of freshwater turtles (dealt with here) are called *terrapins and Pond tortoises. In most of them the *carapace is rather flat. In some species also it does not completely ossify when the animal gets older, so that more or less large fontanelles are left near the margin of the carapace. The legs are laterally flattened and end in free fingers and toes which are webbed at least at the base. It is only in the Soft-shelled turtles and Papuan turtles that the legs are transformed into wide flippers, from which only two or three claws protrude.

The time spent in the water by the various species varies considerably. Many of them only leave the water in order to lay their eggs or to sun themselves for a short while; others go for more or less extensive walks on land or even live there for months; the Box turtles scarcely go into the water at all. Their feeding habits also differ greatly. There are all gradations from species which are entirely carnivorous to others which are almost entirely vegetarian.

It is not always possible to tell the difference between the sexes. The tail of the male is often relatively longer than that of the female and is somewhat thickened at the base. The *plastron of the male is usually slightly concave, while that of the female is rather convex. With the exception of the terrestrial Box turtles, mating takes place in the water, usually in the spring. The female goes on land to lay her eggs and uses her hindlegs to dig a hole in the ground near the bank. She then softens the soil by evacuating the fluid contents of her anal sacs, which empty into the cloaca at the end of the intestine. Finally, she hangs her tail in the hole and then lays the eggs, one by one; she picks them up, using the hindlegs alternately and carefully allows them to slide to the ground. After depositing them she fills up the hole again and smooths the surface with her plastron until it is no longer noticeable. Finally she returns to the water and forgets about her eggs.

The eggs are incubated by the heat of the soil alone, and the young hatch out towards the end of the summer. In northern latitudes there is sometimes not enough heat to complete the development of the embryos in the same year. In that case they may hibernate in the eggs so that the young do not hatch out until the next spring. This applies to the European pond tortoise and some of the North American types.

The adult turtles of the types found in northerly areas also hibernate, digging themselves into the mud of their home waters. Since their metabolic processes are very greatly slowed down at the prevailing temperatures of 39·5°F (4°C), they do not need to come up to breathe during this period, but obtain oxygen from the water through their anal sacs.

Aestivation has been observed in some species of *Pelomedusa* and *Pelusios* in tropical Africa. When their ponds dry up, the turtles lapse into a state of rigidity. They do not stir again until the rainy season sets in and the dried up lakes and rivers fill with water.

There is little exact information available about the maximum age that turtles can reach. We do know, however, that some species can be over 100 years old. A maximum age of about 120 years has been established in the European pond tortoise.

Most freshwater turtles belong to the Snake-necked turtles, suborder Cryptodira. These hide the head or neck under the front part of the carapace retracting the neck and vertebral column in a vertical S-shaped curve; the pelvic girdle is not connate with the plastron.

The two American species of *Snapping turtles, family Chelydridae are related to the Mud turtles and Musk turtles, family Kinosternidae, which are also to be found in both the Americas, but unlike the Snapping turtles,

Head of the Narrow-bridged mud turtle *Claudius angustatus*, of Central America. The open mouth reveals the toothless gums characteristic of turtles and tortoises.

they usually remain small. They also swim very little, but wander quietly around the bottom of their usually shallow, undisturbed ponds and eat fish, small invertebrates, chiefly snails, but also vegetable matter or even carrion. The scutes of the plastron are separated from those of the carapace on both sides by a more or less complete longitudinal row of horny inframarginal plates, thus showing a really original structure of these turtles. The smooth skin of the visible soft part, which has hardly any scutes, is also characteristic.

In the Mud turtles *Kinosternon* the large plastron has an anterior and a posterior transverse hinge so that the turtles can raise the front and rear lobes of the plastron to protect their soft parts. The plastron of the other genera *Clardius* and *Staurotypus*, of Mexico and Central America, and also of the North American musk turtles of the genus *Sternotherus*, is small and cruciform. The Musk turtles get their name from the strongly odoriferous excretions which they expel from the cloaca when they are molested; for this reason Americans call them 'stinkpots'.

A complete series of inframarginal scutes on either side between the dorsal and ventral shield is also to be found in the Tabasco turtle *Dermatemys mawii* in Eastern Mexico as far as Guatemala and Honduras; it is the only species of the family Dermatemydidae. These highly aquatic turtles, up to 16 in (40 cm) long, are excellent swimmers and are entirely vegetarian.

Inframarginal scutes are also present in the Big-headed turtle *Platysternon mega-* *cephalum* of Southeast Asia, the only species of the family Platysternidae. The enormous head of this turtle ends in a downwardly hooked horny beak and is armoured with large horny scutes. It contrasts remarkably with the extremely flat dorsal carapace and cannot be retracted under it. This turtle lives in flat, stony and very cold mountain streams and its chief food is molluscs. The tail is about the same length as the carapace and covered with strong, knobby, horny scutes; with the help of the tail the turtle is an excellent climber.

The Pond turtles, Emydidae, are by far the largest family of turtles, with about 25 genera and 80 species and also a large number of subspecies. In these there are many differences in the shape of the carapace and also the living habits. There are also transitions between aquatic and terrestrial and between carnivorous and vegetarian types.

The genera *Kachuga*, *Hardella*, *Callagur* and *Batagur*, of southern Asia, stay in the water almost exclusively. They are preponderantly vegetarian and have parallel, long masticating strips on the horny jaws for chewing their food. The lungs are in bony chambers formed by the inner walls of the shield, to protect them from excessive pressures when diving in deep water. In at least some of these types the females are considerably larger than the males. The Temple turtles *Hieremys annandalei* which are looked after in their native countries in special turtle temples, are also predominantly vegetarian. *Notochelys platynota*, also indigenous to that part of the world, has similar feeding habits;

the number of vertebrals on the carapace is regularly increased by one or two.

Most species of Emydidae, however, live in the same way as the European pond tortoise *Emys orbicularis*, which usually stays in the water but occasionally comes out to sun itself and also travels short distances on land. Usually black spotted or striped with yellow, this is one of the species most widely distributed northwards; it is still found in Holland and northern Germany, near Hamburg. In the south its range extends to northwest Africa, in the east to western Asia. Its North American relative Blanding's turtle *E. blandingii* is much more terrestrial, but according to more recent findings it merits its own genus, *Emydoidea*.

In North America the turtles of this family are represented by the greatest number of species and subspecies. There, the species of *Pseudemys* are called cooters and sliders, like the Red-eared turtle *P. scripta elegans* which has a bright red stripe along the head and is often offered for sale in the pet shops. The Map turtles *Graptemys*, in which the carapace usually has a pattern like a map, are characterized by a knobby keel along the middle of the carapace. The carapace of the Painted turtles is brown and the sutures are often bordered with red. All these species have much the same way of life as *E. orbicularis*.

The North American diamondback terrapin *Malaclemys* is closely related to the Map turtles *Graptemys*. Since these terrapins lead a special kind of life and have a special significance for human beings, they are dealt with in a separate article. See terrapins.

The River turtles of the genus *Clemmys* are indigenous to North America and also Europe, northwest Africa and Asia; the old-world types have recently been assigned to the genus (or better, the subgenus) *Mauremys*. The majority of these species stay most of the time in water, like the Caspian river turtle *C. caspica* indigenous to the Mediterranean area, the East Asian ocellated turtle *C. bealei*, which has one or two pairs of yellow ocelli on the neck; or the beautiful North American spotted turtle *C. guttata*, which has bright yellow, round spots. The Wood turtle *C. insculpta* also indigenous to North America, however, leaves its watery home for months during the summer and travels on land, only returning to water to hibernate.

The species of the large genus *Geoemyda*, of Asia, Central America and northern South America, lead a different terrestrial life. Their way of life, even the shape of the carapace, may change during the lifetime of each individual. In the young of the Spiny turtle *G. spinosa*, which mainly remain on land, each marginal scute of the carapace is continued laterally in a long pointed spine; each costal scute also has a pointed spine. As the turtle

In the Spiny hill tortoise *Geomyda spinosa*, of Malaya, the whole of the margin of the shell in the young animal is saw-toothed. The serrations become reduced with age.

The European Pond tortoise spends most of its time in water.

grows the spines disappear completely and it then lives mostly in the water.

The carapace of the Asiatic box turtles is strikingly domed. These belong to the genus *Cuora,* in which the plastron is divided by a ligamentous transverse hinge into a movable front and hind flap; these truly terrestrial turtles like to eat sweet fruit. The true Box turtles *Terrapene,* of North America, have the same shell structure. *T. carolina* is the best known species, another is the Ornate box turtle *T. ornata* whose darker carapace has yellow rays on every scute, reminiscent of the Star tortoise *Testudo elegans.* These turtles remain on land and do not even go to water to breed; they feed for the most part on vegetable matter, and are alleged even to eat fungi. These Box turtles are only recognizable as members of the family of Emydidae by their free fingers and toes.

The Land tortoises of the family Testudinidae, are very closely related to the Pond tortoises family Emydidae, and some *her-petologists regard the two as subfamilies only, the Emydinae and Testudininae of the family Testudinidae.

The Soft-shelled turtles of the family Trionychidae in Africa, South and East Asia and North America form a highly aberrant group. Their carapace is not covered with horny scutes, but with a thick leathery skin which projects far beyond the edge of the bony shield beneath. The marginal plates of the bony carapace have almost or even entirely disappeared; the plastron consists only of some bony scales. The elongated head ends in a fleshy proboscis; the jaws are covered with thick lips. The legs have become paddle-shaped flippers, from which only three claws still project freely. All the Soft-shelled turtles are extremely irascible and almost entirely carnivorous. Usually they keep to freshwater, a few also go into brackish water or the sea, such as the Southeast Asian *Dogania subplana.*

Most of the species belong to the genus *Trionyx* distributed over Africa, southern Asia and North America. In the genera *Cyclanorbis* and *Cycloderma* in Africa and *Lissemys* in southern Asia there are lateral movable flaps under the hindlegs in the rear part of the plastron and the turtles can flip them up for protection.

The Papuan turtle *Carettochelys insculpta* occupies an intermediate position between the 'normal' Pond turtles and the Soft-shelled turtles, and is the only representative of the family Carettochelyidae. It lives mainly in the region of the Fly River in New Guinea, but quite recently it has also been discovered in the Northern Territory of Australia. In this species the bony part of the carapace is completely developed, but it is covered with a leathery skin and not with horny scutes. The snout terminates in a fleshy proboscis, but there are no fleshy lips to the jaws, which are fully exposed. The legs have also become paddle-shaped flippers, but each terminates in only two claws. The Papuan turtle is mainly

In the Malayan mud turtle *Trionyx cartilagineus* the shell is flattened and covered with a soft skin instead of the usual horny plates.

vegetarian and not very irascible. It is found not only in freshwater, but also in the brackish water of river mouths.

The remaining turtles belong to the second suborder the Side-necked turtles, Pleurodira. When they withdraw the head they bend the, sometimes very long, neck in a horizontal S-shaped curve. The pelvis is firmly attached to the plastron. Most of the Side-necked turtles are dark, fully aquatic species and very fierce. They are to be found only in freshwater in the southern hemisphere and are distributed over Africa, Madagascar, New Guinea, Australia and South America.

Hidden-necked turtles of the family Pelomedusidae can withdraw the head a little way into the neck before turning it sideways. The species of *Pelomedusa*, with a rigid plastron, and *Pelusios*, in which the plastron has a cross-joint, are found in Africa. There are only four claws on the hindlegs of the species of *Podocnemis*, which are mostly distributed in South America. One species, *P. madagascariensis*, also appears in the African region. The giant Arrau turtle *P. expansa* of South America is characterized by particularly large batches of eggs; the Terekay turtle *P. unifilis* is smaller and is sold in pet shops.

The second family of Side-necked turtles are the Chelidae, in Australia and South America, containing species with an extremely long neck, like the Australian snake-necked turtles of the genus *Chelodina* and the South American snake-necked turtles of the genus *Hydromedusa*, with head and neck approximately the same length as the carapace.

The peculiar *matamata *Chelys fimbriata* of South America also belongs to this group, and its extemely flat head looks triangular because of the lateral flaps of skin, and it terminates in front in a fleshy proboscis. The head and neck are decorated with long fringes of skin and the carapace has three knobby keels. It has much the same way of life as the Alligator snapper *Macroclemys temminckii* of North America. It also does not actively hunt its prey, but lies in wait for it. When a fish is lured by the skin-fringes, the matamata opens its enormous jaws at lightning speed, causing a strong rush of water which draws the prey far into the mouth.

In addition to these unusual long-necked turtles, there are also numerous species of the family Chelidae with necks of normal length, like the species of *Emydura* in Australia and

New Guinea or the *Platemys* species in South America. In these the neural plates of the bony carapace have wholly or partially disappeared, so that the pleural plates meet directly in the centre-line. ORDER: Testudines, CLASS: Reptilia.   J.H.M.

TURTLES, MARINE, tortoises adapted to life in the sea. Like the land tortoises their body is encased in a shell, which consists of a dorsal part, the carapace, and a ventral part, the plastron, joined together on either side by the bridge. From land tortoises and terrapins, they differ in the shape of the limbs, which have developed into flat flippers. These make turtles good swimmers, but make their movement on land very cumbersome. The head and neck cannot be completely withdrawn within the shell.

Seven species of turtle are known. The largest is the Leathery turtle or leatherback *Dermochelys coriacea*, the carapace of which may reach a length of 6 ft (1·8 m). The bony carapace, which is in no way joined to the vertebrae and ribs, consists of a mosaic of bony platelets covered with a leathery skin. The species is easily recognized by the presence of seven ridges, often notched, running lengthwise over the back. The plastron consists of four pairs of bony rods, arranged to form an oval ring; more superficially six rows of keeled platelets are present. The Leathery turtle is blackish above with numerous scattered, small, irregular whitish or pinkish spots; below it is white with black markings. It is found in all tropical and subtropical seas, and from there it wanders far to the north and south into temperate regions. It is a fairly regular visitor to British and French waters; in Norway it has been found up to 70°N. The food of the Leathery turtle consists mainly of jellyfish and *salps. Although it breeds all through the tropics, only a few nesting beaches are known, where large numbers of females come ashore to deposit their eggs, for example, on the east coast of Malaya and in French Guiana.

In the rest of the Sea turtles the bony shell is of a more solid construction. The carapace consists of bony plates, which are firmly joined to the vertebrae and the ribs, and of a series of smaller bones around the margin; the plastron consists of nine flat bones, which leave some openings between them. Both the carapace and the plastron are covered with horny scutes. On the carapace, the horny scutes are arranged in three longitudinal rows, one row consisting of the nuchal scute (or precentral) and a number of vertebral scutes (centrals) along the middle of the back,

with a series of costal scutes (or laterals) on either side, and with a series of small marginal scutes along the border of the shell. The number of scutes in the various series are used to identify the species.

The genus *Chelonia* contains two species: the Green turtle *Chelonia mydas,* occurring in all tropical and subtropical seas, and the Flatbacked turtle *Chelonia depressa,* which is found only along the north and east coasts of Australia. Both species have four pairs of costals, and a single pair of prefrontal shields on the snout. The Green turtle is the larger of the two; the carapace may reach a length of 55 in (1·4 m). It is this species that is in demand for preparing turtle soup; for this one uses not only the meat, but also the gelatinous cartilage ('calipee'), which fills the openings between the bones of the plastron. The *Chelonia* species are mainly vegetarian, with a preference for sea grass. However, the hatchlings are carnivorous, and adult Green turtles, in captivity, can be fed with fish. Due to the unlimited harvesting of eggs, and to a much lesser extent to the killing of adult turtles, the populations have declined. In some areas the freshly-laid eggs are taken from the nests, to be buried once more in hatcheries, where they are protected against predators. The hatchlings are kept in tanks of seawater until they have digested the remaining yolk, and until they are able to dive. Then, at night, the young turtles are released at sea

over a fairly wide area, to obviate their being taken by the large numbers of predatory fish that usually lie in wait off the nesting beaches. It is hoped that in this way the populations will regain their full strength. Important nesting beaches of the Green turtle are found on the islands of the Great Barrier Reef, small islands off Sarawak, in the Seychelles, on the island of Ascension and on the coast of Costa Rica.

The Hawksbill turtle *Eretmochelys imbricata,* like the Green turtle, has four pairs of costal scutes, but the scutes of the carapace overlap, like the tiles on a roof. The carapace may reach a length of 36 in (91 cm). Moreover, this species has two pairs of prefrontal shields on the snout. The Hawksbill is the species that yields tortoiseshell. In some areas, as in the Caribbean, it is also much appreciated as food, but in other areas, for example, New Guinea, the meat is known to be highly poisonous. The Hawksbill is carnivorous, feeding on various kinds of small marine animals. It is believed never to move far from the nesting beaches. It is found in all tropical and in some subtropical seas, for example, the Mediterranean. Those from the Indian and Pacific Oceans are more darkly coloured than those from the Atlantic.

The Loggerhead turtle *Caretta caretta* has five pairs of costal scutes; the snout is covered with two pairs of prefrontals, which often have one or more scales wedged in between

The Hawksbill turtle yields the valuable tortoiseshell of commerce.

them. Its general colour is reddish brown above, yellowish below. The Loggerhead occurs in all oceans, also in the tropics, but it is more common in the subtropics, where it breeds. It is often found far from land in mid-ocean and on its wanderings it comes to temperate seas; it is a fairly regular visitor to the Atlantic coasts of Europe, and it even has been found at Murmansk in northern Russia. The Loggerhead feeds on a variety of marine invertebrates, such as shellfish, squids, Goose barnacles and jellyfish. The carapace may reach a length of 40 in (101 cm).

The Olive Ridley *Lepidochelys olivacea* and Kemp's Ridley *Lepidochelys kempi* are characterized by minute openings (pores) on the hind borders of the scutes that cover the bridge. Both species have the snout covered by two pairs of prefrontal shields. Kemp's Ridley has five pairs of costal scutes. It is a small turtle, the carapace reaching a length of only $27\frac{1}{2}$ in (69 cm). Its only known nesting beaches are on the Gulf Coast of northern Mexico. There, the females may arrive in large 'arribadas', hundreds and sometimes thousands coming ashore at the same time. Some individuals wander through the Florida Strait into the Atlantic Ocean, going northwards along the east coast of North America, and crossing the ocean to Europe, the Azores and Madeira. In the Olive Ridley the number of scutes on the carapace is strongly variable; it usually has six to nine vertebral scutes, and six to nine costal scutes on either side (the numbers on the left and right often being different). Its carapace may attain a length of 30 in (76 cm). It has a wide distribution in the Pacific and Indian Oceans (but it has not yet been found on the east coast of Africa); in the Atlantic Ocean it is found on the west coast of Africa northward to Senegal, and on the coast of South America from the Guianas to Trinidad. As in Kemp's Ridley the females arrive at the nesting beaches in large numbers. Well known nesting beaches are found on the Pacific coast of Mexico, and in the Guianas; without doubt important nesting beaches will still be found on the west coast of Africa, and in the Indo-Pacific area. The Olive Ridley wanders far into temperate seas, for example, to Japan and to New Zealand. Both species are carnivorous.

Although turtles spend practically their whole life in the sea, the females have to go ashore to deposit their eggs, the young turtle begins its life on land, and in some areas, as in the Hawaiian Islands, Green turtles are known to leave the water to bask in the sun. Usually the eggs are laid during the night, but Kemp's Ridley prefers daylight. There are differences between the species in the way in which females move on the beach and in the way the nest is dug, but in general terms the process can be described as follows. After emerging from the surf, pausing from time to time, the female moves across the beach until

a suitable site is reached above the high water line. With alternate movements of the fore flippers a shallow pit is dug into which the body fits. This is the body pit. Then the hind flippers are used alternately to dig the egg chamber. When this is completed, the eggs are laid; in groups of two, three or more, the spherical eggs are dropped in the hole. The number of eggs in the clutch varies greatly. In Sarawak the clutches of the Green turtle were observed to vary from 3 to 184, with an average of about 104 eggs per clutch. After the eggs have been laid, the hind flippers shovel sand into the egg chamber to fill it up; the sand is firmly pressed down and the female starts to move away, and in doing so, it throws sand over the nesting site with the fore flippers; in this way the exact position of the egg chamber is obscured. During one breeding season a female will return to the beach several times, at intervals of 12–14 days, to lay new clutches. Females of the Green turtle have a breeding season once in every two or three years; the Ridleys lay every year.

It is left to the heat of the surroundings to incubate the eggs. The incubation period varies according to the species, and according to the external circumstances. In Sarawak in January to March 56–80 days may elapse before the hatchling Green turtles emerge from the nest, but from April to December this period varies from 48 to 63 days. After hatching at the bottom of the egg chamber, by joint efforts, the hatchlings move close to the surface. There they wait until night has fallen, to emerge together, to scramble to the sea, and to disappear from view. Usually they are not observed again until they are at least a year old. Very little is known as to where the young turtles spend the first year of their life, but there are indications that the young (at least of some species) move out into the open sea, to stay there far from the coasts for a year or more. Only tropical and subtropical regions have a climate that allows the eggs to develop, and it is there that the nesting beaches are found. The Loggerhead turtle apparently needs less high temperatures, and its nesting beaches are found farther away from the equator than those of any other species.

In the breeding season the turtles have to move from the areas where they find food to the nesting beaches and back, and in some instances this means migration over long distances. This migration is especially marked in the Green Turtle. This species feeds mainly on sea grass ('turtle grass') and the pastures are often far from the nesting beaches. The most remarkable migration is that of the Green turtles that cross a long stretch of open ocean, and against a fairly strong current, from Brazil to the island of Ascension. How these turtles orientate themselves, and how they navigate to pinpoint this

small island is as yet unknown. The long distance movements are demonstrated by females which were tagged on the beaches of Ascension and which were recaptured off the Brazilian coast. Females tagged on the Caribbean coast of Costa Rica have been recaptured over a wide area, extending from the south of Florida to the island of Margarita off the Venezuelan coast; the majority of the Green Turtles nesting on the beaches of Tortuguero, Costa Rica, have been recaptured on the sea grass pastures off Nicaragua. Tagging experiments have also shown that a female will nest several times in one breeding season, and that after an interval of two or three years will return once more to the same beach.

Of the distance over which other species migrate little is known. It is reasonable to suppose that the Ridleys which nest every year, do not normally move away from the nesting beaches over very great distances. Along the Atlantic coast of North America, Leathery turtles seem to migrate northward regularly to Nova Scotia and Newfoundland during summer, to pass southward once more in autumn. The long voyages across the ocean undertaken by juvenile turtles, and which are to be distinguished from the breeding migrations, are well known. Loggerheads move northward along the Atlantic coast of North America, and many of them cross the ocean to the coasts of Europe and to the Azores; a juvenile Loggerhead even got as far as Murmansk in northern Russia. Kemp's Ridley, the only known nesting beaches of which are found on the Gulf Coast of northern Mexico, occasionally passes through the Florida Strait into the Atlantic Ocean, to travel northward along the American Atlantic coast, and to cross the ocean to European shores to the Azores, and to Madeira. The Leathery turtle also seems to roam widely across the oceans.

A number of nesting beaches, which in the past were frequented by large numbers of turtles have since been deserted, due to the decline in the populations.

The dangers that threaten the nests and the hatchling turtles are many. On nesting beaches where a great number of females concentrate, the later arrivals may disturb nests that have been made earlier. Ghost crabs will burrow down into the egg chamber; stray dogs, cats and Monitor lizards will dig up the nests, and all these predators feed upon the eggs. When the hatchling turtles move across the beach, many will be taken by the same predators, and if the young turtle is still on the beach in daylight birds will take their toll. In the shallow water, just offshore, small sharks and other predatory fish are lying in wait for them. J. R. Hendrickson estimates that one female Green turtle may lay 1,800 eggs in her lifetime; of these only 405 fully develop; of the emerging hatchlings only 243

Above: female leathery turtle on her way down the beach, having laid her eggs.
Below: tracks in the sand made by a female leathery turtle going up the beach to lay.

Above: common snapping turtle laying her eggs.

Below: young snapping turtles hatching.

enter the sea, and of these only 31 will survive the first week at sea. But even adult turtles are not safe from predators. Tigers and jaguars are known to kill turtles on the beach. A Tiger shark can snap an adult Loggerhead turtle in two; there are numerous records of turtle remains found in the stomachs of Tiger sharks. Often turtles are found of which one or two flippers and part of the shell has been bitten off. Remains of a Leathery turtle have been found in the stomach of a Killer whale.

Taking into account predation on adult turtles, and death from disease and parasites, Hendrickson estimates that the 1,800 eggs laid by a female Green turtle result in only three turtles completing a full life-cycle. The great number of eggs will thus be just sufficient for the species to hold their own. However, to all the dangers must be added the havoc caused by man. In some areas turtles are used for food by the local population, and turtles are taken to prepare turtle soup for the

gourmet. If the turtles are taken at sea some damage may be done to the turtle population (and it is especially the Green turtle that suffers), but it is believed that the world population of turtles can stand this. It becomes worse when the females are killed on the nesting beaches, often before eggs have been laid. The greatest damage to the populations of all species is caused by unlimited harvesting of the eggs. All over the world millions of turtle eggs are dug up every year and used for human consumption. Even if the number laid by each female were higher than estimated by Hendrickson, and even if more turtles survived to breed, it is clear that the harvesting of eggs gives the death-blow to the turtle populations. A further danger to turtles is the new fashion of making lady's bags out of skin from the neck, shoulders and flippers of turtles killed on the beaches and skinned. This wanton destruction leads to a further decline, and much useful food for man is left unused.

In many countries measures have been taken to protect the turtles on and just off the nesting beaches, and the unlimited harvesting of the eggs is prohibited. The conservation measures often will have to aim at a compromise, allowing of a reasonable exploitation of this important source of animal protein, at the same time to try and safeguard the future of the world's turtle populations. In the Cayman Islands an attempt is made at 'ranching' turtles; eggs are imported from Costa Rica and Ascension Island and placed in hatcheries, to raise the turtles in captivity until they have reached a sufficient size to be slaughtered. Still, this means that thousands of eggs have to be taken each year from the beaches. A more adequate solution would be if one could 'farm' turtles, that is raise turtles from the egg, and to have them breed in captivity, safe from predators. In this way the heavy toll on the turtle populations in the world's seas might be lessened considerably. ORDER: Testudines, CLASS: Reptilia.   J.D.B.

TURTLE VISITANT. The Sea turtles live in warmer tropical waters but they occasionally appear in temperate regions. The Leathery turtle, in particular, finds its way into cooler waters and is sometimes seen off the British Isles. In 1959, a strange animal was seen off Soay, a small island off the coast of western Scotland, in almost the same place that a similar 'monster' was seen previously in the 19th century. The two men who saw it were completely baffled by its appearance and the Soay beast, as it was called, became another manifestation of the sea-serpent. From the detailed descriptions and sketches made by the men, Prof L. D. Brongersma, an expert on turtles, was able to identify the animal as a large Leathery turtle.

TUSK SHELLS, molluscs in many respects intermediate between snails and bivalves. The commonest Tusk shell is *Dentalium entalis,* which lives in sand at moderate to considerable depths in the sea and has a slightly curved, tubular, tapering white shell about 1½ in (38 mm) long which is often cast upon the shore. In life the shell is vertical in the sand with its narrow end projecting above the surface. From the lower wider end there projects a three-lobed foot, used for burrowing, and a bunch of ciliated feeding tentacles with sucker-like ends. The tentacles spring from the head but this bears no eyes nor other sense organs and consists mainly of a proboscis bearing the mouth surrounded by frilly lips. Water is drawn into the mantle cavity through an aperture at the top of the shell by ciliary activity and is expelled by muscular contraction. There is no true gill, neither is there any heart nor obvious blood vessels. It is thought that movements of the foot circulate the body fluids and oxygen is taken in through a series of transverse ciliated folds in the wall of the mantle cavity. There is only one gonad which discharges through the right kidney. The fertilized egg gives rise to a ciliated planktonic larva, known as a trochophore.

In some species the tentacles seize Foraminifera and draw these to the mouth. In others, such as *D. conspicuum,* cilia on the tips of the tentacles pass fine particles along their length to the head, where these collect on

Anatomy of a typical Tusk shell.

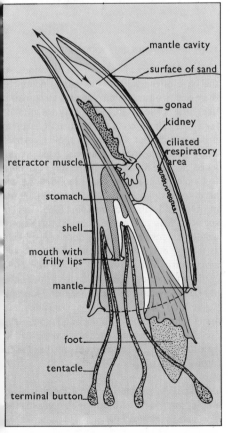

the surface of the foot in front of the mouth. There is a large ribbon-like radula, as in snails, but this only helps to pass food from the mouth to the gut, once it is taken in. CLASS: Scaphopoda, PHYLUM: Mollusca. R.C.N.

TWIG SNAKE, a species of *Thelotornis,* which appears to be most closely related to the *boomslang. These snakes are characterized by a diamond-shaped head with a large eye which has a peculiar keyhole-shaped pupil; the body is slender and the tail long. The top of the head is green, with or without black and pink markings, the body and tail are mottled grey, pink and white and resemble a lichen-covered branch or twig.

Kirtland's vine snake *T. kirtlandii* occurs in the evergreen forests of West Africa, the Congo, Uganda and northern Angola. The Cape vine snake *T. capensis* has a wide range from southeastern Kenya south to Natal and west to Angola. It usually inhabits dry savannah, but is sometimes found on the edge of evergreen forest. The largest Cape vine snake recorded is a Rhodesian specimen of 5½ ft (1·6 m) long.

The female Vine snake lays 5–13 eggs during the summer months.

The Cape vine snake is often found in bushes only a few feet above the ground. Here it remains motionless for hours until its excellent eyesight spots a lizard, frog or small snake in the vicinity. The snake then stalks its prey, climbing down very slowly and then creeping up very close to the prey before striking. The diet consists mainly of lizards, especially chameleons, small snakes, fledgling birds and birds' eggs; frogs are taken, but rarely.

The venom of the Vine snake is similar to that of the boomslang, but less toxic; it causes haemorrhage, but the bite is rarely fatal to a man. SUBFAMILY: Boiginae, FAMILY: Colubridae, ORDER: Squamata, CLASS: Reptilia. D.G.B.

TYRANNOSAURUS, the largest of the extinct reptiles belonging to the subclass *Theropoda, the carnivorous *dinosaurs. Its hindlimbs were powerful and bore three toes, with a fourth very small digit, their skeletons recalling those of birds. The forelegs were ridiculously small by comparison and ended in two tiny fingers. ORDER: Saurischia, CLASS: Reptilia.

TYRANT FLYCATCHERS, small birds of a very large and varied family restricted to the New World where they replace the Old World flycatchers or Muscicapinae. There are 350 species which have become adapted to a wider range of habitat than the Old World flycatchers. Generally they are less colourful and less capable singers. They belong to the Tyranni or non-singing division of perching

birds, whereas the Old World flycatchers belong to the Oscines or singing division.

Generally they are 3–9 in (8–23 cm) long with the exception of a few species with long tails, but are so diverse in plumage, shape of bill and other characters that it is impossible to give a general description. Few species are really brightly coloured, most being in shades of green, brown, yellow, grey, white and almost black. Red is unusual, though the Vermilion flycatcher *Pyrocephalus rubinus* is one of the best known and most widely distributed species, and blue is almost unknown. Perhaps the most striking and common character is a crown patch of yellow, orange, red or white, which is usually opened in display, and partly or entirely concealed at other times.

The family ranges from Canada to Tierra del Fuego and reaches the Galapagos Islands, but is best represented in the tropics. In higher latitudes most species migrate and almost all North American species such as kingbirds, phoebes and pewees winter in the Caribbean and northern South America. Similarly many Patagonian species move north during the southern winter.

Breeding habits are as diverse as other aspects. Most species make open cup-shaped nests, but these range from small felted cups (*Elaenia* spp) to loose untidy twig nests (*Tyrannus* spp). Some make domed nests with a side entrance (*Tolmomyias, Camptostoma*) and others nest in holes. Nests are usually placed in trees, but many open country species nest on the ground and some in reeds over water. Species of *Tolmomyias* and *Camptostoma,* and perhaps of other genera, often nest close to aggressive wasps. The eggs are generally white, cream or buff, usually spotted and blotched with dark colours and the clutch-size varies from two to four according to the latitude. Some species are known to lay at an interval of 48 hours (*Camptostoma* spp). The incubation period varies between 14 and 23 days and the nestling period between 13 and 24 days, in different species.

The diversity of the family is explained by the way in which the species have become adapted to almost every habitat from tropical rain-forest to treeless pampa between the Equator and high latitudes. Most species occur in tropical rain-forest, but where they have ranged out into temperate treeless pampa, they have become adapted to living on the ground and thus developed a variety of suitable modifications. Though most forest species are probably insectivorous, other larger species in open places take lizards, mice and small birds and some even eat fruit, so that this family has come to fill the niche of Old World shrikes and chats, as well as that of the Old World flycatchers. FAMILY: Tyrannidae, ORDER: Passeriformes, CLASS: Aves. S.M.

UAKARI *Cacajao,* two species of agile, shaggy-haired monkey living in South America and related to the sakis. See New World monkeys.

UMBRELLABIRDS, crow-sized birds living in the forests of South America. There are three species: the Bare-necked umbrellabird *Cephalopterus glabricollis* living in Panama and Costa Rica, the Long-wattled umbrellabird *Cephalopterus penduliger* found in Colombia and Ecuador and the Amazonian umbrellabird *Cephalopterus ornatus* which has the widest distribution, occurring in Guyana, Venezuela, Colombia, Ecuador, Peru, Brazil and northern Bolivia.

The Amazonian umbrellabird is the best known and is largely black with a steel blue gloss on the large tuft of feathers which forms a crest on the head and on a large pendent lappet of feathers on the throat. The sexes are alike but the female is somewhat smaller. They have a strange display in which the males spread their umbrella-like crests and the glossy lappet on the breast is dilated and waved. The call is a loud, growling trumpeting sound. One of the very few nests to be found was an open cup of sticks in a tree and contained a single egg which was incubated by the female alone. Like most cotingas the umbrellabird feeds on berries and insects. FAMILY: Cotingidae, ORDER: Passeriformes, CLASS: Aves.   F.H.

UNICORN, a mythical animal like a white horse with a single spirally twisted horn arising from its forehead. The currently popular explanation is that the myth of the unicorn was based on the one-horned Indian rhinoceros, yet Ctesias, 398 BC, the Greek historian, the first to mention it, spoke of certain asses found in India as large as or larger than horses with white bodies and dark red heads with a horn 1½ ft (45 cm) long in the centre of the forehead. Later writers tried variously to equate the unicorn with the Indian ass and the Arabian oryx, as well as the rhinoceros. Of these the oryx has a white coat, a somewhat horse-like appearance and the peculiarity that when viewed from a particular angle it appears to have only one horn.

Juvenile unicornfish lacking the 'horn' on the forehead, which develops only with maturity.

The horn of the unicorn was credited in mediaeval times with remarkable powers. It was believed to change colour in the presence of a poison, so a piece of unicorn horn was invaluable at the table for detecting whether the food presented to a person contained a poison. At the same time, a piece of the horn was thought to be a powerful antidote and the best possible protection should a poison be inadvertently swallowed. At that time also the narwhal tusk appears to have been accepted as the true unicorn horn, and small pieces of it were literally worth their weight in gold.

UNICORNFISH, members of the genus *Naso,* related to the surgeonfishes and given the name unicorn by early ichthyologists because of the curious conical horn which develops on the forehead in some members of the genus. In some species the horn may grow longer than the snout, giving the fish a most grotesque appearance. In juveniles the horn is merely a small bump but it increases in length with age. In other respects, the unicornfishes resemble the surgeonfishes in having rather compressed and oval bodies and long dorsal and anal fins armed anteriorly with spines. At the base of the tail, on the caudal peduncle there are two razor-sharp keels which project like little knife blades and may be hooked forwards. These keels are not usually present in the young but develop as the fish grows. They are dangerous weapons, used in defence, and are found also in the surgeonfishes.

Unicornfishes have small mouths and are herbivorous. The genus is widely distributed in the Indo-Pacific region. The largest species, *Naso tuberosus,* is called the Humpheaded unicorn because the horn is developed as a large bulge on the forehead. The Brown unicornfish *N. unicornis* is one of the most common species. The body is brown, the dorsal and anal fins bear lines of blue and yellow and the base of the pectoral fins and areas round the keels on the caudal peduncle are blue. This species reaches 23 in (58 cm) in length. FAMILY: Acanthuridae, ORDER: Perciformes, CLASS: Pisces.

URODELA, alternative name for the tailed amphibians or *Caudata, which contains the newts and salamanders.

V

VACUUM ACTIVITY, in German *Leer-laufreaktion,* a term first used by Konrad Lorenz to describe behaviour which an animal carries out in the absence of its appropriate eliciting stimulus.

Vacuum activities are actions which take place spontaneously. For example, Lorenz described the behaviour of a tame starling *Sturnus vulgaris* which carried out all the motions of identifying, chasing, catching, killing and swallowing a fly when there was no such insect in the room.

The Cambridge biologist Robert Hinde has described how a canary *Serinus canaria,* deprived of nest material, went through the motions of weaving non-existent material into a nest. Female Brown rats *Rattus norvegicus* have also been observed behaving in a similar fashion.

These few examples illustrate the phenomenon of vacuum activity which appears to occur under abnormal conditions. The most likely explanation for it is that the motivation of the particular behaviour is so high that it appears without being triggered off by its usual eliciting stimulus, for instance the sight of prey for the starling.

Some ethologists argue that vacuum activity results from the liberation of 'action specific energy', accumulated in the central nervous system, if the animal lacks an opportunity to carry out the behaviour

A vampire bat *Desmodus rotundus* under study in a laboratory being given its daily drink of blood.

pattern in question. If, therefore, the animal is deprived of the opportunity to perform the behaviour under a normal eliciting situation the pent-up energy finally triggers off the act from within. As the only evidence for such an accumulation of energy is circumstantial, this hypothesis is unacceptable to many biologists. See motivation. T.B.P.

VAMPIRES, bats which feed on the blood of larger mammals and birds, thus being the only parasitic mammals. They have some economic importance in certain areas because of the debilitating effect of their attacks on domestic and agricultural animals and the transmission of rabies to animals and man.

There are three species, all from South or Central America. See also bats. FAMILY: Desmodontidae, SUBORDER: Microchiroptera, ORDER: Chiroptera, CLASS: Mammalia.

VANGAS, a family of specialized shrike-like songbirds peculiar to Madagascar. The 12 species, like others endemic to Madagascar, appear to show adaptive radiation in isolation, and are sufficiently varied to be classified in eight genera. The variation in bill-shape is particularly pronounced, but in spite of this there appears to be little variation in the feeding habits. Vangas are arboreal, feeding mainly on insects and small invertebrates which they take from the branches, twigs and leaves of the trees, but the Larger-billed helmetbird *Aerocharis prevostii* and the Hook-billed vanga *Vanga curvirostris* also take small reptiles and amphibians.

The tiny Red-tailed vanga *Calicalicus madagascariensis* is like a small greyish, rufous-tailed flycatcher with a stubby bill. The vangas of the genus *Leptopterus* are finch to starling-sized, with a thrush-type bill with a small hook at the tip. Chabert's vanga *L. chabert* is white below and black, glossed with dark blue, above. The Blue vanga *L. madagascarinus* is a vivid overall sky-blue above and white below tinted with buff on the female, while the White-headed vanga *L. viridis* is white with a green-glossed black back, wings, and tail. Bernier's vanga *Oriolia bernieri* is similar in size to the last

but with a light brown plumage with fine black barring. The sicklebill *Falculea palliata* has a plumage pattern like the White-headed vanga, with white head and body and blue-glossed black on back, wings and tail, but it is half as large again and has a long slender down-curved bill about $2\frac{1}{2}$ in (6 cm) long.

The Rufous vanga *Shetba rufa* and *Xenopirostris* species have a bill of proportionally similar length to *Leptopterus* species but it is very deep along its whole length and laterally flattened, with a slight terminal hook. The former is white below and chestnut-red above and Lafresnaye's vanga *X. xenopirostris* is white and grey, both being black on the head. The Hook-billed vanga has a black, white and grey patterned plumage, and the bill has a sharp, vicious-looking hook. The Larger-billed helmetbird has a bill as big as its head, thick and with an inflated and high, curved upper mandible that rises higher than the crown of the head. The adult is black with bright chestnut on back and mid-tail, the young bird is dull brown.

Vangas are sociable birds usually occurring in small parties and sometimes associating with other species. They are confined to trees but occupy a variety of habitats within the forests and scrub of Madagascar. The calls are varied but usually include whistles and chattering notes, and sometimes harsh calls. The sicklebill has a loud 'waugh' call that is said to sound like a child at play. Remarkably little is known of the nesting of these species. The nest of the sicklebill is a shallow saucer of twigs lined with grass. The eggs of vangas may be white or green, spotted with brown, and the clutch consists of three or four eggs. FAMILY: Vangidae, ORDER: Passeriformes, CLASS: Aves.

VASE SHELLS, also known as volutes, are some of the most beautiful of all gastropods and their shells are much sought after by collectors. They are related to whelks and Cone shells. All are marine and carnivorous, crawling rapidly through the sand in search of their bivalve prey. The shell is more or less oval, smooth, often with graceful ribs and always with regular folds on the shell pillar

Velvet ant of Nigeria. These ants tend to mimic other insects, this one looking very like a local mutilid wasp.

inside the mouth. The foot is large. The colours and markings of the shell are often striking, for instance in the Music volute *Voluta musica* the markings resemble the script of mediaeval music.

Vase shells are most common in shallow tropical seas though some live in deep water and extend to polar regions. The largest numbers of species are found in Australasian and Southeast Asian waters. Eggs are laid in leathery, or sometimes calcareous, capsules produced by the foot and are attached to stones.

The related Olive shells are still more modified for life in sand, with the shell almost covered by the foot and streamlined for easy movement through the sand. In Vase shells the foot may be used in feeding by some species such as the New Zealand Bald volute *Alcithoe calva*. This suffocates small bivalves, such as Wedge shells, in the folds of its foot. Other species are probably mainly carrion-eaters. They lack the specialized feeding apparatus of other related molluscs (steno-glossans), such as boring organs or accessory salivary glands. FAMILY: Volutidae, ORDER: Stenoglossa, CLASS: Gastropoda, PHYLUM: Mollusca. E.M.D.

VEINS, blood vessels carrying blood towards the heart. In vertebrates they carry blood at lower pressures than do the arteries and hence are thinner walled and also of greater diameter since the rate of flow is less. In many invertebrates the blood vessels are not differentiated into veins and arteries and in Mollusca and arthropods veins, and capillaries, are largely or entirely absent, and blood returns to the heart through large, irregular blood spaces or sinuses.

VELVET ANTS, not ants but a family of wasps. The misnomer undoubtedly arose from the adult females being wingless and running over the ground like ants, although they are by no means as abundant as them. Inhabitants of desert and semi-desert regions, Velvet ants can often be easily identified by the thick pile of hairs covering the body and legs. In some cases, these hairs are bright red, in others white and, in any event, they contrast sharply with the background colour of the body which is black. The collector will do well to treat these insects with the greatest respect as they will sting viciously under the slightest provocation. In captivity they give the impression of being the most bad-tempered of all insects because they hum loudly and menacingly when disturbed. Some idea of the respect accorded this group can be gained from the common name given to the American *Dasymutilla occidentalis*: the Cow-killer ant. FAMILY: Mutillidae, ORDER: Hymenoptera, CLASS: Insecta, PHYLUM: Arthropoda.

VENOMS, toxic or poisonous substances produced by animals. Although the very many types of venoms make their classification difficult, it is possible to divide the animals producing them into two main groups. Actively venomous animals can inject venom using various structures to inflict wounds allowing the poison to penetrate. Passively venomous types have venom glands and ducts but lack a means of injecting the poison. In shrews, snakes and the Gila monster the venom is secreted by modified salivary glands and the teeth are also modified to allow the venom to be injected. Centipedes and spiders have the poison glands opening near to the mouth and inject venom using specialized mouthparts. All these animals have dual purpose venoms for capture of prey and for self-defence

Scorpions are unusual in having the dual purpose venom in the last body segment (tail) which can be arched far in front of the head. Female venomous Hymenoptera have venom glands and a sting in the rear part of the abdomen, used variously to kill excess numbers in the colony, to kill or paralyze insect prey, or in self-defence or defence of the colony. In amphibians, molluscs, polychaetes, caterpillars, echinoderms and coelenterates the distribution of the venom organs often has no relation to either mouth or tail.

More is known about snake venoms than other animal toxins owing to their great medical importance in the tropics and sub-tropics. Snake venom, although always highly complex in composition, is mostly non-cellular protein (90–92% dry weight) which is produced and stored in specialized salivary glands. When the snake bites or strikes, the venom is injected by hollow or grooved teeth, the bases of which press on the salivary glands. The venomous protein components are of two main types: those having toxic properties and those with enzymic properties. Many venomous snakes, such as the cobras produce a protein or series of proteins which are powerful nerve poisons (neurotoxins). These paralyze the respiratory muscles of the victim by an acute toxic effect on their nerve supply. Cobras also produce cardiotoxins which have a direct effet on heart muscle. Experiments with frogs show that high concentrations of cardiotoxins result in irreversible, violent contraction of the heart, leading to the rapid death of the victim.

A common characteristic of snake venoms is the presence of very powerful protein digesting enzymes which have an important role in the digestion of prey. These enzymes often result in rapid and very serious tissue breakdown or necrosis in human victims of snake bite. Snake venoms have complex effects on the blood of victims due to coagulant, anticoagulant and haemolytic enzymes. The latter destroy the red blood cells by causing the release of the pigment haemoglobin from the corpuscles. Several factors in snake venoms result in a rapid flow of blood into the area bitten due to extreme dilation of the blood vessels. One of the factors causes the release of the polypeptide (an amino acid chain) bradykinin, itself the vaso-dilator, from the blood of vertebrates. The enlargement of the blood vessels caused by the release of bradykinin thus facilitates rapid absorption of the lethal elements of the venom. Another of these factors is probably responsible for the delayed, sudden and fatal collapse which often occurs in cases of bites by African vipers such as the Puff adder *Bitis lachesis,* when massive blood loss from the body into the bitten limb leads to intense shock.   M.J.P.

VENUS' GIRDLE *Cestum veneris,* a relative of the *Sea gooseberries (see also Ctenophora), restricted to the Mediterranean and tropical waters. It is markedly changed from the globular shape typical of these. In Venus' girdle the median plane is very much elongated and the vertical plane very much shortened, so the animal resembles a flattened gelatinous ribbon, or a girdle, which may reach 3 ft (1 m) in length, but is usually under 32 in (80 cm). The tentacles of the typical ctenophore are reduced to a tuft of filaments and have changed from their original position to one near the mouth, which is centrally located in the ribbon. The eight comb rows (rows of fused cilia) are still present, but four are very elongated running along the aboral edge of the ribbon-like body while the other four are reduced. These comb rows are no longer used for swimming and the Venus' girdle swims by undulations of the body, rather like an eel. ORDER: Cestida, CLASS: Tentaculata, PHYLUM: Ctenophora.

VENUS SHELLS, a group of marine bivalve molluscs probably so called because of the heart shaped depression, the lunule, on the outside of the shell at the hinge end. Also included are the nearly related Carpet shells *Venerupis* and the Artemis shells *Dosina.* They have a world-wide distribution.

Most have a colourful heavy shell but have to be identified by the arrangement of the hinge teeth and the shape of the mark left by the mantle margin on the inside of the shell, the pallial line. At the posterior end of the shell this pallial line is indented (the pallial sinus) and the depth of this indentation is related to the length of the siphons, and so to the burrowing depth, of the living animal. Because of the delicacy of the hinge teeth, single eroded valves from species in this group are very difficult to identify, and so it is always best to try and find shells of recently dead animals in which the hinge ligament is intact and so is holding the two valves together.

Most of these animals are found buried in sand where they normally rest head downwards with their elongated siphons sticking up to the surface. They feed on plankton suspended in the seawater which is trapped on the mucus covering the gills.

Many species of this group are eaten as 'clams', especially the Hard shell clam *Venus mercenaria,* a native of North America where it is widely eaten. It has been introduced into Europe where it is now fished commercially. There are three main shell shapes. The Artemis shells are almost circular in outline, the Venus shells *Venus* are either circular or triangular, and the Carpet shells are mostly elongated. However, included in the group is the American piddock *Petricola pholadiformis,* which bores into soft rock, and little

crevice dwelling animals, such as *Notinus iris* and *Turtonia minuta.*

The Hard shell clam usually changes its sex from male to female once in its lifetime. This is known as consecutive hermaphroditism. Individuals normally release male gametes for the first part of the breeding season and then eggs later on, but a few individuals in a population produce both eggs and sperms throughout the breeding season. Release of both eggs and sperms in the Hard shell clam is related to changes (increases) in water temperature, this mechanism presumably allowing some sort of synchronization of breeding to occur within a population.

During the period that these animals have become fully adapted to successful life in sand they have evolved excellent methods for burrowing. The process can be observed if an animal is placed on the surface of the sand when it is just covered by the tide and then left undisturbed. The valves are opened and the foot is extended: the foot then probes the sand and the siphons close trapping water inside the mantle cavity. The foot then extends fully into the sand and its diameter increases, by a movement of internal fluids, which gives the animals a firm anchorage. Muscles connecting the foot to the shell contract, and the animal is then dragged upright. The process is then repeated, the next contraction pulling the animal further into the sand. The probing of the substrate by the foot before full extension of the foot may well be an exploitation, by the animal, of the sand's peculiar property of becoming much more easily penetrated after rhythmic mechanical agitation (a thixotropic effect). FAMILY: Veneridae, ORDER: Eulamellibranchia, CLASS: Bivalvia, PHYLUM: Mollusca.   P.F.N.

VERTEBRATA, animals with backbones, that is, with a spinal column made up of vertebrae. At one time the animal kingdom was assumed to be divisible into two subkingdoms, the *Invertebrata, without backbones and the Vertebrata. The word invertebrates is now no more than a convenient term meaning any animal not a vertebrate, and the Vertebrata represents a subphylum, or subordinate branch, of the *chordats.

VERTEBRATE GAP. Although many of the groups of animals follow each other closely so that it is possible to depict their evolution by a genealogical tree, there are several notable gaps in which hypothesis must be used to bridge the gulf. One notable gap is between the Protozoa and the rest of the animal kingdom. Another is between the invertebrates and the vertebrates. One of the biggest stumbling blocks to bridging this gap is in the anatomy of these two groups. In a typical invertebrate, as exemplified by the annelid worms, the crustaceans and the insects, the central nerve cord lies beneath the gut. That is, it is ventral to it. The main blood vessel, however, runs lengthwise through the body above the gut. That is, it is dorsal to it. In a vertebrate these positions are reversed: the nerve cord being dorsal to the gut and the main blood vessel ventral. In the early years of this century there was a great deal of discussion about how, in view of this basic difference, vertebrates could have been derived from an invertebrate ancestor. One suggestion put forward was that at some time an animal comparable to an annelid worm took to swimming on its back, so reversing the positions of the nerve cord and the main blood vessel and that this was the starting point for the evolution of the first vertebrates.

At a later stage, zoologists began to see the possibility that animals like the Acorn worm, the Sea squirts and the lancelet, formed a fairly good connecting series between an invertebrate such as an annelid worm on the one hand and the vertebrates on the other. Then came the discovery that starfishes and Sea urchins had much in common in their physiology with the vertebrates, and since these have larvae similar to those of the Acorn worm and the Sea squirt, it seemed probable that the very early vertebrate ancestor was close to the ancestor of starfishes and Sea urchins.

There is some difference of opinion on how far these various animals afford a link between the invertebrates and the vertebrates. It is even suggested that the extinct *graptolites and the recently discovered *Pogonophora belong to this complex. All can be separated from the remaining invertebrate groups by their embryology. The problem is to know how the early vertebrates became free-swimming when all these supposed prevertebrates are either fixed or bottom dwelling, so the search has been concentrated on their larvae, which are free-swimming.

Even in the adults of these animals there are similarities with the vertebrates. For example, the pharynx of Sea squirts and lancelets are very similar in structure to that of the larval lamprey, the most primitive living vertebrate. Moreover, the ventral gutter, or endostyle, of the lamprey larva gives rise to the thyroid gland of the adult (see jawless fishes) and the endostyles of the others are capable of concentrating iodine, which is a function of the thyroid. This bound iodine is then incorporated into the synthesis of thyroxine identical with the secretion of that name in vertebrates. It is probable, also, that a structure in the roof of the front part of the Sea squirt pharynx is a precursor of the pituitary, the master gland of vertebrates.

The tadpoles of the Sea squirt and the lancelet and the larva of the lamprey all agree in the detailed structure of their tails, and although this is not as advanced as that of a fish, it needs only relatively slight changes to make it so. Were the larval life of any of these to be extended and the larvae themselves become sexually mature (see neoteny, pedogenesis), we should then have something very near what the ancestral vertebrate should be, and the switch from a sedentary to a motile animal would be complete. Such a process has already been achieved, at least partially in the *Larvacea.   W.A.M.C. and M.B.

VERVET MONKEY *Cercopithecus aethiops,* or Green or Grivet monkey, a large monkey living in savannah or woodland savannah of West, East and South Africa. See guenons.

VICUÑA *Lama vicugna,* a member of the camel family living in the western High Andes, is regarded by some people as the original form of the domesticated alpaca. It is the smallest, most graceful and most agile of the four *Lama* types, having a shoulder height of $2\frac{1}{2}$ ft (75 cm). Vicuñas have a uniform, short-haired coat, reddish in colour, and a white blaze on the chest. The lower incisors, in contrast to all the others of the camel family, have an open root—as in rodents—and thus grow continuously. In captivity, for lack of wear, they often project considerably from the muzzle.

In the last few centuries the range of the vicuña has contracted and at the present time is between latitudes 10° and 30° south. The preferred habitats are the table-lands of the Central Andes, those broad, high plateaux between the chains of the Andes extending from southern Ecuador to Argentina and loosely covered with grasses, mosses, resinous bushes and cushion plants hard as stone. The vicuñas are the highest climbers of all the New World camelids, up to 16,600 ft (5,000 m) and prefer the regions just below the snow-line, in the 'bofedales' fed by rain and melting snow. The haemoglobin of their blood has a particularly high affinity to oxygen, enabling them to live at high altitudes. Vicuñas mostly drink daily and are often to be encountered standing or even lying in the water. Even in zoos they show this behaviour and water troughs or pools are provided for them. Alpacas and alpaca-vicuña crossbreeds behave in the same way. Both types also like to be sprayed, in contrast to the guanacos and llamas, which are far more afraid of water.

Vicuñas live in family groups consisting of a stallion and up to 20 mares, which occupy a fixed territory. Larger herds are also to be found—possibly the temporary joining up of several family groups. Vicuñas often mix with llama and alpaca herds. The stallion is always on the alert. If he is killed, the mares flock round him and do not run away. On the other hand, if a mare is killed, they all flee under the guidance of the stallion. Young mares intruding on the herd are usually driven off by the others.

The mare is sexually mature at the age of one year. During the rutting season from April to June there are fierce battles between the 'kings' of the herd. In addition to the fighting habits typical of all the New World Camelidae, the vicuñas have the peculiarity, not only of kicking backwards, but also sideways at the opponent. In doing this they take up an attitude crossways on to the foe, drive him broadside on into a corner and then attack him at lightning speed. This close-in position also occurs in mating. In captivity vicuña stallions are always belligerent. They not only frequently attack the females and their young, but even inanimate objects, and stallions which are kept in isolation even attack themselves! As distinct from the domestic types the preliminary mating ceremony (driving the mare and snapping at and around the legs), just as in the case of the wild guanacos, is more violent and longer than the actual mating.

The mares foal after 10 months. At the first signs of sexual activity the young stallions are driven off by the mares and join large leaderless herds. In the rutting season they each try to get a herd of their own, the size of which fluctuates all the time and which has no permanent territory.

Both in the case of vicuñas and alpacas, the dung always lies in an extremely small space, since several animals do not defaecate side by side, as in the case of guanacos and llamas, but only one after the other. Vicuñas have a remarkable ritual for this: after thoroughly sniffing the dung, they stamp and scrape in it, turn round and evacuate exactly over the heap. A similar behaviour may be observed in the Oribi antelopes, for example. It has been assumed to be marking behaviour, since oribis in this way impregnate the dung with the secretion of the glands between the toes. Vicuñas also have glands of this kind and the ritual of evacuation might therefore have the same function.

Even in the time of the Incas these animals were protected. Every 4–5 years the herds were driven to shearing and then released to roam free, except for a few animals which were slaughtered. This method is still in use at the present time, since vicuñas are almost untamable. Since the Spanish Conquest the number of herds has greatly decreased. There are now estimated to be a bare half million today.

Garments of vicuña wool, woven by priestesses of the Temple of the Sun, were reserved for the use of the Inca kings. The vicuña gives the finest wool, with a diameter of 5/10,000th of an inch. It is half the thickness of the best Australian merino wool. One animal yields little more than 18 oz (500 gm), and 10–12 animals are needed for one yard, so that vicuña wool coats are among the rarest and most expensive in the world. The

Group of vicuñas drinking at a stream.

vicuña, however, were not only hunted for their fine fleece but also for the *bezoar stones found in the stomach, which were sought after as remedies, particularly as antidotes to poisoning. The hunting and export of vicuñas has been forbidden by law for several decades. FAMILY: Camelidae, SUBORDER: Tylopoda, ORDER: Artiodactyla, CLASS: Mammalia.   H.G-P.

VINEGAROON *Mastigoproctus giganteus,* a *whipscorpion living in the southern part of the United States and Mexico. It is large for a whipscorpion, 3 in (7·5 cm) long. When attacked the vinegaroon flexes its tail forwards over the body and sprays its assailant with a fine cloud of acetic acid, which has the characteristic odour of vinegar. Vinegaroons are often encountered in human habitations and although reputed to be poisonous, at most they can inflict a sharp, but not serious, bite with their mouthparts and a mild irritation from the acid spray. ORDER: Uropygi, CLASS: Arachnida, PHYLUM: Arthropoda.

VIPERFISHES, slender-bodied deep-sea fishes belonging largely to the family Stomiatidae and related to the hatchetfishes. Under the same heading are placed certain members of other closely related families and the general name stomiatoid fishes is preferable for the whole group – a 'common' name is frequently meaningless in fishes that are not common.

Viperfishes of the family Stomiatidae are active pelagic fishes found in greatest numbers at about 6,000 ft (1,800 m); at night-time they rise to the surface waters. They have large heads and a mouth well equipped with vicious dagger-like teeth. To cope with swallowing large prey, the mouth can open to an extraordinary extent. To achieve this, the head is jerked upwards, a most unusual movement in fishes since the skull is normally very firmly attached to the anterior vertebrae. The skeleton is considerably modified to accommodate this unusual movement. In *Eustomias brevibarbatus,* for example, the first few vertebrae are widely spaced and are linked by a loop of cartilage which allows for the movement of the head.

The body in viperfishes tapers evenly from the head, the dorsal and anal fins being just in front of the tail. The pectoral and pelvic fins are reduced to a few long rays. Along the lower half of the flanks are rows of luminous organs giving the appearance of 'portholes'. There is usually a luminous gland under the eyes which is larger in the males than in the females and can be shut off by rotating it. Most of the stomiatoids have a barbel under the chin. In species such as *Melanostomias spilorhynchus* the barbel is fairly short, but in *Ultimostomias mirabilis* the barbel is no less than ten times the length of the body. In some

species the barbel ends in a slight swelling, while in others it has been described picturesquely as resembling 'a bunch of grapes', 'strings of beads' or 'branches of a tree'. The swellings usually bear luminous organs which presumably serve to lure the prey nearer the mouth. Sir Alistair Hardy has noted that the tip of the barbel in *Stomias boa* resembles very strikingly a small red copepod. Possibly the barbels serve also as means of species recognition, while the more elaborately branched barbels may have a sensory function. From the bathysphere, William Beebe noted that at the slightest disturbance of the water near the barbel the fish immediately threshed around snapping with its jaws.

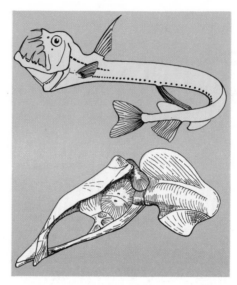

The viperfish *Chauliodus sloanei,* a deep-sea species which throws back its head when striking at its prey. A remarkable adaptation to this is the enlargement of the first vertebra (below). This vertebra, several times larger than any of the other vertebrae, serves to take the strain when the head is thrown back and also acts for attachment of the muscles required for this action.

The stomiatoids living nearer to the surface are a shining silver, while the abyssal forms tend to be dark brown or black. These fishes are found in all oceans and none has been caught much over 12 in (30 cm) in length. There may, however, be larger species since William Beebe, during the first really deep-water dive, thought that he saw one of 6 ft (1·8 m).

Closely related to the stomiatoid fishes are members of the family Idiacanthidae. At first sight these fishes are unremarkable, resembling many other deep-sea fishes in having fairly large teeth, luminous organs on the body and a small barbel under the chin. *Idiacanthus* lives as an adult in depths of about 5,000 ft (1,500 m), migrating to within a few hundred feet of the surface during the night. Lacking a swimbladder, it can make this journey without encountering difficulties

in equalizing pressure. It is known to spawn in summer but at one time nothing was known of the juvenile stages. In the early part of this century, however, numbers of delicate, transparent larvae were caught at depths of about 500 ft (150 m) off Bermuda. These larvae were quite unlike any known fish and were named *Stylophthalmus paradoxus*. The most remarkable feature was the eyes, which were located on the ends of long stalks and could be turned around by small muscles. When further specimens were later caught, it was realized that these extraordinary larvae were in fact the juveniles of *Idiacanthus*. At about $1\frac{1}{2}$ in (4 cm) the young descend into deeper water. The eye stalks withdraw, twist into loops and finally become knotted up in little capsules in front of the eye. After the eyes have retracted the sexes become differentiated and the males, which remain very much smaller than the females, retain several larval characteristics and apparently do not eat; they lack teeth, barbel and pelvic fins. FAMILIES: Stomiatidae, Idiacanthidae ORDER: Salmoniformes, CLASS: Pisces.

VIPERS, a family of snakes with a highly developed venom apparatus, comparable with that of the nearly related *Pit vipers. The true vipers are found in Africa, where they are most numerous in species, Europe and Asia. The best known species is the European viper or *adder *Vipera berus*. The smallest is Orsini's viper *V. ursini* of southern Europe, less than 1 ft (30 cm) long. The largest is the Gaboon viper *Bitis gabonica,* up to 6 ft (2 m) long and 6 in (15 cm) diameter.

Most vipers are short and stoutly built, with a short tail, and are typically terrestrial. Some, like the Mole vipers, burrow in the ground or, like the Horned vipers, burrow in sand. Few climb, although some of the Puff adders climb into bushes and the Tree vipers are arboreal and have a prehensile tail. Characteristically, vipers do not pursue their prey but lie in wait for it. They strike, wait for a while then track down the victim that has crawled away to die. Their prey is mainly lizards and small mammals. The dead prey is tracked by flickering movements of the forked tongue which picks up molecules of scent in the air, testing these by withdrawing the tongue into the mouth and placing the tips of the fork into the taste-smell organ, in the roof of the mouth, known as *Jacobson's organ.

The fangs of a viper are hollow, efficient and large, and are typically folded back when not in use. They are automatically erected as the mouth is thrown wide open for the strike. The poison flowing through the hollow fang comes from a venom gland, a modified salivary gland, at its base. This can be very large and vipers typically have broad heads to accommodate them. In some species the venom glands extend behind the head, to as

The European viper, also known as the adder.

much as one-fourth the length of the body in Night adders.

Species additional to the European viper (see adder), which rarely exceeds 2 ft (60 cm) in length, with a record of 32 in (80 cm), are the Asp viper *V. aspis*, Lataste's viper *V. latasti* and the Sand viper *V. ammodytes*, all of southern Europe, and all slightly larger than the adder. They have the dark zigzag line down the back as in the adder. In *V. palestinae,* the Palestinian viper, the zigzag has become a continuous line of dark diamond-shaped markings.

Russell's viper *V. russelli*, up to 5 ft (1·6 m) long, the most feared snake of the Indian Peninsula eastwards through Southeast Asia to Java, has a row of large oval spots along the back and a row along each flank, the spots being reddish-brown bordered with black and a white border beyond the black. Although its natural food is frogs, lizards and small birds it is a danger because of the many people who go bare-footed in this region.

The four species of Night adder living in, Africa south of the Sahara are all small, rarely exceeding 2 ft (60 cm) long. Although nocturnal the pupil of the eye is rounded, not vertically elliptical as in other nocturnal species. Their food is frogs and toads, also mice and rats, and they are generally in-offensive although one species *Causus rhombeatus* is named 'Demon adder'. This is because when aroused it coils up, blows itself out, hisses loudly, sometimes even flattens its throat cobra-fashion, and strikes.

Mole vipers of Africa are less than 2 ft (60 cm) long, slender and with only a slender head, unlike other vipers. They spend their lives underground coming out sometimes at night or after heavy rain, to feed on other small snakes, legless lizards, rats and mice.

Puff adders range in size from Peringuey's viper *Bitis peringueyi* of South Africa, less than 1 ft (30 cm) long, to the Gaboon viper 6 ft (2 m) long. They are named for the loud exhalation of air, which produces a puff rather than a hiss. Puff adders living in desert or savannah are brownish but those living in the rain-forests are beautifully coloured. The Gaboon viper is gaudy, with yellow, purple and brown patches in a geometrical pattern, yet it fails to catch the eye on its natural background of leaves on the forest floor. The Rhinoceros viper *B. nasicornis* is so called for the erectile scales at the tip of its snout. It is even more gaudy, with green triangles mar-gined with black and blue added to extensive areas of purple and blue. Puff adders are sluggish, apt to be trodden on, and with a venom almost as potent as that of a cobra or a mamba to livestock or human beings. Their venom is slow acting and may take 24 hours to cause death in a large animal or a man.

Two species of Puff adder, *B. cornuta* and

Sand viper of southern Europe.

B. caudalis, have a hornlike scale over each eye and they are *sidewinders. Species of another African genus *Cerastes* also have these hornlike scales and are known as Horned vipers. Some of them sidewind and all live in sandy deserts in northern Africa and southwest Asia. The scales along their flanks have sawlike edges. As the snake wriggles into the sand these shovel the sand aside and over the snake's back. Horned vipers do this while coiled, and their coils 'modelled' in sand are characteristic.

The counterpart of the Horned viper in the deserts of Pakistan, India and Ceylon, and also in North Africa, is the Saw-scaled viper *Echis carinatus,* less than 2 ft (60 cm) long but extremely numerous. When disturbed it goes into almost a figure of eight with its head in the centre and rubs its saw-edged scales together, making a hissing sound. The warning is appropriate since this species has the most potent venom of all vipers. FAMILY: Viperidae, ORDER: Squamata, CLASS: Reptilia.

VIREOS, 20 or so species of small nondescript perching birds, 4–7 in (10–18 cm) long, mostly grey or brown above and white or yellow below. They have rather heavy, slightly hooked bills. Most vireos are forest dwelling birds preferring the shrub level although a number are arboreal, haunting the crowns of broad-leaved trees. The Grey vireo *Vireo vicinior* lives in scrub where there are no trees and a few others inhabit thickets with little well-grown timber.

Vireos are widespread in Central and North America, occurring as far north as subarctic Canada. The northern populations are migratory, wintering in Central and South America south to Central Argentina. Only a few vireos breed in South America and these are all widely distributed in North America.

The vireos are largely replaced by the closely related greenlets *Hylophilus* in South America. Together they comprise the subfamily Vireoninae to which the name vireo can also be applied. With two other small subfamilies the Vireoninae form the family Vireonidae whose relations with other birds is not clear. There are affinities with both the shrikes Lanidae and the Wood warblers Parulidae. Within the genus *Vireo* two distinct lines of evolution are recognizable. Vireos in the subgenus *Vireo* have eye-rings and wing bars and prefer thickets, scrub or the shrub understory of the forest. Those in the subgenus *Vireosylva* lack these distinct plumage features and are more arboreal in habit.

Most vireos feed in a leisurely fashion, moving slowly through the tree or shrub and picking insects in a deliberate manner from

The only arboreal viper, the Tree viper *Atheris squamiger,* of Africa.

The Red-eyed vireo *Vireo olivaceus*, one of the commonest birds of the deciduous forests of the eastern United States.

Mountain viscachas inhabit almost the entire chain of the Andes from Peru to Patagonia and are represented by four species. They look remarkably like rabbits, except for the ears which are rather shorter and the tail which is very long and rather coarsely haired in contrast to the soft pelage of the rest of the body. They live on dry rocky mountainsides at altitudes up to 15,000 ft (5,000 m) making their nests in crevices in the rocks. They are active and agile animals in contrast to their rather lumbering relatives of the plains, but in many respects their way of life is similar: they are colonial, diurnal and vegetarian, feeding on the toughest of montane plants.

Like most caviomorph rodents, Mountain viscachas are palatable, and they are hunted both for food and for their hair which is sometimes mixed with wool for spinning. FAMILY: Chinchillidae, ORDER: Rodentia, CLASS: Mammalia. G.B.C.

VISCACHA BREEDING. The breeding of the Plains viscacha is remarkable on several counts. Like many of the South American hystricomorph rodents the gestation is very long: 155 days compared with the rabbit's 31 days. What is more remarkable, in each period of oestrus some 200–800 ova are released from the ovaries. Up to eight embryos are formed but only two survive to be born. The reason for this apparently wasteful method of reproduction is not known.

the undersides of leaves. They often hang from a branch or stretch out to search the more inaccessible places. The Black-capped vireo *Vireo atricapillus* is exceptional in this respect, moving restlessly through the branches like a warbler. It is also the only vireo with an immediately recognizable plumage that its name suggests.

During the breeding season vireos are territorial and the males are persistent but unmusical songsters. The nest is a fairly deep cup hanging from the fork of two twigs. It is normally well hidden and constructed from strips of bark, grasses and fine leaves held together with cobwebs and lined with fine grasses. The two to four eggs are white, ranging from unmarked to heavily spotted depending on the species. Both parents attend the nest for incubation, brooding and feeding. FAMILY: Vireonidae, ORDER: Passeriformes, CLASS: Aves. J.H.M.

VISCACHAS, South American rodents closely related to the chinchilla and more distantly to the Guinea pig. The two groups of viscachas, the Plains viscacha *Lagostomus maximus* and the Mountain viscachas, *Lagidium,* are superficially very different and occupy quite different habitats, as their

names indicate, but they resemble each other in many details of structure and way of life.

The single species of Plains viscacha is perhaps the most familiar rodent in Argentina. It is a large, heavily built animal, about 2 ft (60 cm) long, with a short tail about a quarter of the body length. The most striking feature is the disproportionately large head, accentuated by bold horizontal black and white lines on each cheek. The rest of the pelage is grey above and white below and the texture is coarse in contrast to the related chinchilla.

Plains viscachas are highly colonial, living in large and conspicuous colonies known as *viscacheras* on grassy plains or open scrubland. About 20 individuals may inhabit an extensive network of burrows with a number of entrances and the whole warren is made more conspicuous by the viscacha's habit of collecting any hard object it can find and depositing it outside the burrow. These accumulations may include all kinds of man-made trash as well as natural objects such as stones, twigs and bones.

Plains viscachas are crepuscular, emerging in the evening to feed on grass and other vegetation. They breed in the spring when a single litter of usually two young is produced.

VISION, the essential process of seeing: it concerns the way in which an animal receives the radiant energy of light on its eye and converts it into nervous impulses which travel to the central nervous system; it also includes the perceptual processes by which this information from the eye is used in the recognition of objects.

The initiation of the nerve impulse is the basis of all vision. All eyes contain a layer of cells sensitive to light energy, the retina. These contain pigments which undergo change when excited by light energy. The pigments are carotenoids, members, together with chlorophyll, of that group of substances which can be said to be truly essential to life as we know it, for through them the sun's energy can be trapped and used for life processes. Two main visual pigments are known both of them derived from vitamin A. This vitamin exists in nature in two chemical forms known as A_1 and A_2. It is an aldehyde of A_1 which forms $retinene_1$; $retinene_2$ is formed from A_2 in a similar manner. Retinene is combined with a protein called opsin to form the active pigment. $Retinene_1$ forms rhodopsin or visual purple, the first visual pigment discovered; $retinene_2$ is the basis of porphyropsin. The effects of light on these pigments are similar, thus, when rhodopsin absorbs a quantum of light (the smallest 'packet' of light energy), the kinked molecule is straightened out. In some way or other this causes the cell to fire off a nerve impulse and a 'dark' reaction follows, which does not require light energy and by means of which the retinene is reformed. Thus, all light cells have to have a recovery period after being stimulated before they can function again.

Rhodopsin is the pigment which has been found so far in invertebrates. It is also in the eyes of mammals, birds and most marine fishes. But freshwater fishes have predominantly porphyropsin pigments. It is interesting that Amphibia, with an aquatic larval stage and a mainly land-dwelling adult, such as the Common frog, have porphyropsin pigments up to metamorphosis when rhodopsin is laid down. It seems likely that, from an evolutionary point-of-view, the porphyropsins are primitive being superseded in most cases by rhodopsins. These latter pigments are the ones found in all animals with good image-forming eyes.

The retinal cells of most vertebrate eyes are of two kinds, rods and cones. The cones are found to predominate in the retinae of animals which are active by day, while nocturnal animals, like owls, have almost none, their retinae being made up mainly of rods. The cones are responsible for vision in higher light intensities and the rhodopsin-containing rods for seeing in low light intensities and thus for night vision. Cones are packed more closely in the retina, especially in the areas of the fovea and thus produce more acute vision. Rods tend to be on the periphery of the retinae of animals, which like man, are active by day and night.

White light is composed of light of many wavelengths but not all of them have the same effect on visual pigments. The maximum effect is brought about by light of a particular wavelength, for example, 500 μ for rhodopsin and 525 μ for porphyropsin. The pigments will, therefore, not be so responsive to light of other wavelengths. Despite this, many animals, among them honeybees, beetles, butterflies, reptiles, bony fishes of many kinds, birds and Primates have been proved to have colour vision. It seems that in insects, different retinulae cells may contain pigments responsive to different wavelengths, thus of the seven retinula cells in an ommatidium of the fly (*Calliphora*) five are green-type receptors most sensitive at 350 μ, one is a blue-type sensitive at 470 μ and the last a yellow-green-type most sensitive at 520 μ. As well as these maxima, there is another peak with all these at 350 μ, which is in the region of the ultra-violet and accounts for this insect's sensitivity in this region of the spectrum which is invisible to humans.

In humans, there appear to be three kinds of cones, blue receptors, with maximum sensitivity at 450 μ, green receptors at 525 μ and red receptors at 555 μ. Thus there is some support for a trichromatic theory of colour vision in such an eye. The light falling on the eye will then be sensed in these major bands of wavelengths, the three images being fused once again in the brain to give a fully-coloured image in the consciousness. But it must be admitted that there remains a great deal as yet unexplained about colour vision. Thus, for instance, the frog has two rod pigments (green, maximum 440 μ: red, 502 μ) and a cone pigment (maximum 560 μ) and yet these animals have a particular sensitivity to blue which does not appear to be due to any one of the receptors. The biological advantage of this sensitivity may be in escape, for if the animal jumps towards the open sky it will be jumping towards gaps in any surrounding vegetation.

When we consider the perception of images we find that some of the analysis of characteristics of the image take place in the retina. Thus there are groups of retinal cells in the frog's eye which have special functions. Some are active when the edge of a shadow moves into their area but remain active only while it continues to move, becoming quiescent when the edge is stationary. Others react only when there is a stationary edge of an image in their field. But perhaps the most dramatic results come from cells which fire when the images of small objects come into their field. Even more important, the objects to produce such responses must be fly-sized; anything much bigger does not cause impulses to pass along the nerve fibre leading from the cell group. This set of cells is, therefore, specialized to react to small images moving in relation to a fixed background. It is not surprising to find them nicknamed 'bug detectors'. Similar groups of cells seem to be found in the eyes of cats and can be thought of as 'classifiers', picking out particular parts of the visual stimulation and permitting such information to go on to the brain.

Thus, vision brings a great deal of crucial information to an animal and, with relatively rare exceptions, is the major animal sense, perhaps not unexpectedly, in a world which is filled with sunlight for at least half of the day. See also eye.   J.D.C.

VIVERRIDAE, a family of small to medium-sized carnivores intermediate between the weasel family (Mustelidae) and the cat family (Felidae) and including the mongooses, genets and civets. Its members, all in the Old World and especially in Africa, differ widely in appearance and habits but are more nearly alike in the characters of the skeleton, especially of the skull and teeth. The mongooses are long-bodied, with short legs and a long tapering tail, in appearance not unlike the otters of the family Mustelidae. The civets are cat-like but with fairly long snouts and the genets are almost like a cross between a mongoose and a tabby cat. Other members of the family are the binturong, fossa and linsang. ORDER: Carnivora, CLASS: Mammalia.

VIVIPARITY, giving birth to living young.

The birth of a new generation of any animal species presents many problems and the more complex the animal, in terms of structural organization, the greater the difficulty of establishment of the young. Among the warm-blooded animals this presents even more difficulty than in cold-blooded forms. If adequate development of the embryo to the warm-blooded state is to occur, then even in

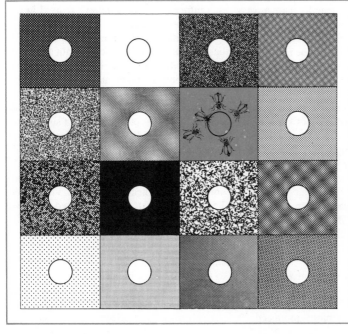

One of the experiments carried out by von Frisch. Bees which had found food regularly in a glass bowl placed on a blue background, immediately fly to a piece of blue paper (without food) in the centre of 15 other pieces of paper, coloured in shades between black and white. The experiment does not succeed with red as bees do not see this as a colour. Bees trained on yellow will also fly to yellow-green and orange-red. Bees often confuse purple and violet with blue but not blue-green.

he early stages the temperature must be maintained. This can only be achieved effectively from sources external to the embryo, until its own temperature regulating mechanism has been developed. Birds control the temperature of their young by sitting on the eggs and warming them with their own body (though a variety of some birds, for example, the *Mallee fowl, use other methods). The mammals achieve this end even more efficiently by having the embryo develop in the mother's uterus until it is capable of some degree of free life. When the young animal is born its own temperature regulating mechanism is working at something approaching adult efficiency and, given adequate food supply, the temperature will remain within the necessary narrow range especially if some external warmth, such as a community nest, is available.

Viviparity, although an essential feature of all true mammals, is by no means limited to them. The marsupials are a mammalian group showing a different form of viviparity from the Eutheria or true mammals. Marsupial young are born at a much more primitive stage of development and in most cases a temperature regulating mechanism is not fully established. Hence a marsupial at birth is not free living and must be nursed in the mother's pouch if it is to survive. It has only a short free life of sometimes as little as a few seconds or more usually minutes, during which time it climbs from the vulva to the pouch where it attaches itself to a teat.

Viviparity is not restricted to the mammals but is a feature of the higher animals which practise internal fertilization. In many of the cold-blooded species a form of viviparity is found which is not associated with formal placentation and the other features usually associated with viviparous development. The eggs are fertilized and then, instead of being laid, they are developed within an ovisac until embryonic development is complete. In such cases the process is essentially one of development of the eggs in a suitable receptacle, an incubator, in effect, which happens to be the mother. She plays a small or even no part at all in supplying it with food or oxygen. Such a form of development, which is halfway between oviparity and viviparity, is usually described as being ovoviviparous. Some salamanders and toads develop in this way and in some teleost fishes development of the young occurs within the ovarian cavity.

In the cartilaginous fishes more highly developed viviparity is found, as in sharks and skates. The ovisac is quite highly developed and gives metabolic support. For example, in some of these there are outgrowths from the wall to which the yolk sac of the embryo becomes attached rather like a mammalian placentation.

Although most of the reptiles are oviparous a number are viviparous, for example,

Most voles are small, but the Water vole of Europe is as large as the Common rat.

vipers and many lizards, and in some of these quite high forms of placental development may be found, matching that of many mammals.   K.M.B.

VOLES, mostly small mouse-sized rodents with short tails and blunt snouts which, with the lemmings, constitute a very distinctive subfamily, Microtinae. This is usually placed in the family Cricetidae, with the hamsters, gerbils and American mice, although some taxonomists include all these in the family Muridae with the Old World mice.

In outward appearance voles are generally distinguished from mice by their shorter tails, less-pointed snouts and long, dense coats, but one of the most important differences is not so easily visible and concerns the molar teeth. These number three in each row, as in the majority of mice, but in most species of voles, molars, like the incisors of all rodents, grow throughout life without developing roots. The sharp ridges of enamel that traverse the flat grinding surface extend through the whole column of the tooth and the column is continually renewed at the base as it is worn away at the top.

Voles are therefore well equipped to deal with tough herbage, and they are one of the dominant groups of herbivorous animals throughout the northern hemisphere. There are about a hundred species, and one or more species can be found, often in great

Volvox

abundance, in almost any piece of grass-land, marsh, heath or woodland with dense ground vegetation, from the northernmost tundra south to North Africa, the Himalayas and the mountains of Mexico. The ubiquity and abundance of voles can be explained by their adaptation to feed on the dominant vegetation, and, therefore, if the vegetation is dense enough to give protection from their many predators, especially birds, they thrive with an abundance of food.

Voles are prolific breeders. They are capable of breeding at the age of about two months, and since the females can become pregnant while still suckling and the gestation period is only about three weeks, several litters, often of about five or six young, can be produced during one summer. In most areas breeding ceases in winter, but in the Mediterranean region, where the main growth of fresh vegetation is during this season, the local vole, *Microtus guentheri*, breeds then and has its off-season during the dry summer.

Especially in the northern parts of Eurasia and America, voles tend to undergo periods of abundance and scarcity, usually with a remarkably regular cycle of four years. A great deal of research has been devoted to these cycles, but no simple explanation has emerged. However, it is likely that the two major factors are the slower breeding of the predators, e.g. the owls and weasels, and a physiological reaction in the voles themselves, the stresses caused by high population density inhibiting breeding. When the population is declining due to these physiological factors the predators accelerate the process by concentrating the same attention on fewer and fewer voles, and it is not until the voles themselves are really scarce that the predators suffer a decline. This in turn allows the vole population to recover, and the slower breeding of the predators means that at this stage of the cycle they are too scarce to stop the increase of the voles.

The Bank voles or Red-backed voles, genus *Clethrionomys,* are rather unspecialized members of the group. Their molar teeth start like those of other voles, but when the animal is only a few months old the teeth begin to develop roots and therefore cease to grow. Correlated with this, these voles feed on soft leaves, berries and some insects and live especially in the shrubby undergrowth in woodland. The two best known species are the Bank vole *Clethrionomys glareolus,* in Eurasia, including Britain, and the Red-backed vole *Clethrionomys gapperi,* in North America.

The Field voles and Meadow voles, genus *Microtus,* are more specialized grassland species, and are the ones that most often reach plague densities. *Microtus arvalis* is the most common species in Europe, making conspicuous burrows in meadows. The only

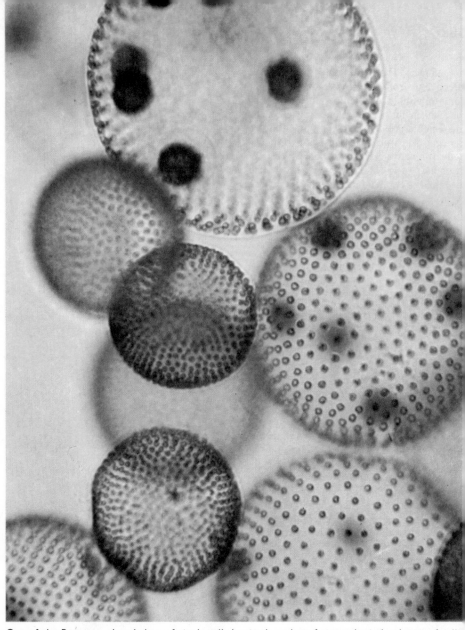

One of the Protozoa, the phylum of single-celled animals, volvox forms spherical colonies of cells in freshwater.

species in Britain, the Field vole *Microtus agrestis* lives in longer grass and burrows less. It can cause serious damage by barking young trees in plantations. The Meadow vole *Microtus pennsylvanicus* is the most common species in North America and is scarcely distinguishable from *M. agrestis.*

The Water vole *Arvicola terrestris* is larger than most voles, being about the size of a Brown rat. Water voles are confined to Eurasia and as the name implies live especially on the banks of rivers and lakes where there is an abundance of waterside vegetation. Some races, however, e.g. in the Alps, live a subterranean, mole-like existence in grassland far from water. In North America the Water vole is represented by the even larger musk-rat or musquash *Ondatra zibethicus,* which is more strictly aquatic and is trapped for its fur. FAMILY: Cricetidae, ORDER: Rodentia, CLASS: Mammalia.
G.B.C.

VOLVOX, colonial *phytoflagellate consisting of hundreds of cells arranged in a single layer at the surface of a watery mucilaginous sphere. Each cell bears two flagella and one species, *Volvox globator,* has 1,000–20,000 cells in a single colony. Each colony is a green ball, rotating in freshwater ponds and lakes, visible to the naked eye. *Volvox* has been known and studied for at least 300 years. Most species have a world-wide distribution.

In asexual reproduction, a few cells divide by splitting longitudinally and these form miniature colonies. At first the daughter cells—those resulting from the splitting—form a hollow sphere with the front ends of the cells directed inwards but, when division is completed, the daughter colony turns inside out through a small pore. After this 'inversion' the flagella lie on the outside of the daughter colony which becomes motile within the parent and is eventually released by the death of the latter.

Sexes are separate in some species, together in others. In sexual reproduction a few cells divide longitudinally numerous times to form hollow spheres (which invert) or flat plates of narrow, pointed, biflagellate spermatozoids. Other cells swell each to form a single ovum. The sperm bundles are released and swim to the ova, attracted by a female sex substance. One sperm fuses with the egg and a spiny resting zygote is formed which subsequently divides to produce a hollow sphere of cells which inverts to form a new colony. *Meiosis occurs at the first division of the zygote nucleus. There is a notable division of labour in *Volvox,* with a few cells acting as reproductive cells, asexual or sexual, and the rest acting as vegetative or body cells destined to die. ORDER: Volvocida, CLASS: Phytomastigophorea, PHYLUM: Protozoa.   G.F.L.

VORTICELLA, a very common and conspicuous freshwater ciliate protozoan consisting of an inverted bell—*Vorticella* used to be called Bell animalcule—and a contractile stalk by which the animal is attached to the water plants. The mouth is surrounded by a triple circle of cilia which beat and create a vortex into which minute food particles are drawn and pass into the mouth. When the animal is disturbed, by vibrations or other causes, it suddenly contracts, its stalk drawn down like a spring, and after a few seconds it expands again and the cilia resume their rapid beating. The macronucleus is very large and elongate while the micronucleus is small and round (see nucleus). The dispersal stage of *Vorticella,* called a telotroch, is a cylindrical free-swimming larva formed from the whole of the bell part of the ciliate which breaks free from the stalk. Alternatively, under unfavourable conditions, a cyst forms on the stalk and eventually this drops off to hatch and give rise to new stalked individuals. Under normal circumstances *Vorticella* divides asexually by

Body of *Vorticella* (the whole animal with its stalk is shown on right).

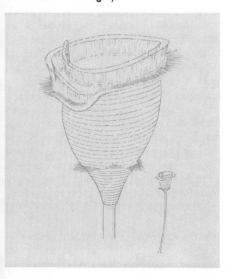

unequal division in such a way that one daughter retains the stalk while the other swims away as a telotroch. *Vorticella* also reproduces sexually by producing a free-swimming equivalent of a male organism and a fixed female which resembles the normal feeding form but which has the ability to attract males to it. The two partners fuse to form a single individual which soon afterwards gives rise to a number of telotrochs. ORDER: Peritrichida, CLASS: Ciliata, PHYLUM: Protozoa.   F.E.G.C.

VORTICELLA DESCRIBED. Vorticella were discovered by the early Dutch microscopist van *Leeuwenhoek in 1675, as can be seen from his description of 'wretched little creatures' found in a water butt. 'The bodies consisted of 5, 6, 7, or 8 very clear globules, but without being able to discern any membrane or skin that held those globules together . . . When these animalcules bestirred themselves, they sometimes stuck out two little horns, which were continuously moved, after the fashion of a horse's ears. The part between these little ears was flat, their body else being roundish, save only that it ran somewhat to a point at the hind end; at which pointed end it had a tail . . . looking as thick, when viewed through my microscope, as a spiders web'.

VULTURES, comprise two groups of large diurnal birds of prey (Falconiformes), not closely related to each other. The New World vultures, found only in the Americas, are a primitive family, the Cathartidae. The Old World vultures of the warmer parts of Europe, Asia and Africa, are one branch of the large family Accipitridae, their closest true relatives being some species of eagle.

All vultures share several features, presumably through convergent evolution. Their heads and necks are partly or wholly naked, probably because they feed on and inside dead animals, those that feed mainly on large carcasses having longer, more naked necks. Since, with few exceptions, they do not kill their own prey, they lack powerful grasping feet. The claws are short and blunt, more adapted to walking than to killing. Several have specialized tongues, to feed rapidly on soft flesh or perhaps extract bone marrow. All are large birds, adapted for soaring. New World vultures include condors, the largest flying birds, but some of the Old World species are nearly as large, weighing more than 15 lb (6½ kg) and spanning 8 ft (2½ m). The smallest, but not the weakest, is the Egyptian vulture *Neophron percnopterus.*

New World vultures differ from the Old World species in having 'pervious' nostrils, opening through the bill at the point. The hind toe is rudimentary, placed above the three front toes on the leg. They have large

Young Hooded vultures *Necrosyrtes monachus* on the Serengeti in Tanzania. The red skin on the face can range from very pale to deep red according to the bird's mood.

olfactory chambers and, apparently, some sense of smell, though this is not used to locate prey. In America leaks in gas pipe-lines are sometimes located by circling vultures, attracted by a small amount of vile smelling chemical added to the gas.

The seven species of New World vultures include the two huge condors, *Vultur* and *Gymnogyps*, the extraordinary King vulture *Sarcorhamphus papa*, brown and white in adult plumage, with brilliant orange, red, blue and purple bare skin on head and neck, the Turkey vulture *Cathartes aura*, widespread in North America, two other *Cathartes* species and the rather small, but locally abundant, Black vulture *Coragyps atratus*. All eat flesh, but the Black vulture is also said to eat decaying or over-ripe vegetable matter.

Old World vultures include 13 species in eight genera, all but one being monotypic. Two species, the Egyptian vulture and the lammergeier *Gypaetus barbatus,* have more

heavily feathered heads and more powerful feet than is typical. Both are remarkable, specialized birds, the Egyptian vulture being a tool-user and the lammergeier, the avian equivalent of the hyaena, feeding largely on bones. The Hooded vulture *Necrosyrtes monachus*, common in most of Africa south of the Sahara, is relatively small, but still a large bird. It is a scavenger, especially around human dwellings, and is the only African vulture found much inside forests. The typical, gregarious, carrion-feeding vultures of the genus *Gyps* include seven species occurring in open, or mountainous country throughout southern Europe, Asia and Africa. They were formerly placed in two genera, *Pseudogyps* (two species) and *Gyps* (five species). However, the Indian Griffon vulture *Gyps indicus* has intermediate habits, so it is preferable to group them all in one genus. They are collectively known as White-backed vultures and griffons. Finally, there

are four very large, more specialized vultures, of more solitary habits: the European Black vulture *Aegypius monachus,* the largest bird of prey in the Old World, almost as big as a condor; the African Lappet-faced and White-headed vultures, *Torgos tracheliotus* and *Trigonoceps occipitalis*; and the Asian Black vulture *Sarcogyps calvus*, black with a bright red head and neck.

The feeding habits of New World vultures are less fully described than those of the Old World. All, however, find their prey mainly or exclusively by sight, not smell. Their eyesight is probably acute, but not so acute as that of some raptors that feed upon small, moving animals. Vultures can see a large carcass, or each other, from several miles. They also observe other birds, and even lions and hyaenas, in their search for a meal. Since they locate prey by sight they cannot find it in heavy woodland or forest and, since they have little sense of smell, a covering of branches or grass will usually conceal a dead animal, even in open country. Normally they are exclusively diurnal feeders, but in India both Black vultures and White-backed vultures *Gyps bengalensis* have been known to feed by moonlight on tiger kills.

Where several species occur together, as in Africa and India, they fall into three main ecological types: the large, gregarious vultures (griffons and White-backed vultures) that feed, up to 100 together, on a dead animal; the large, powerful, solitary vultures (*Aegypius, Torgos, Sarcogyps*); and the small, weak-billed types such as Egyptian and Hooded vultures. The feeding habits of each are sufficiently distinct to enable all to survive together. The large gregarious vultures can also be ecologically subdivided into White-backed vultures (formerly *Pseudogyps* spp), regularly breeding in trees, and the true griffons (*Gyps*), normally colonial rock-breeders; the Indian griffon, however, also breeds in trees. Usually only one species each of rock and tree-breeding griffons occur together, but in northern India three species of rock-breeding griffons (*G. himalayensis, G. fulvus* and *G. indicus*) may be seen at the same carcass and two even breed together.

The large solitary vultures hunt and usually roost singly or in pairs and seldom are more than ten seen together. They are suspected of killing some small live animals and certainly kill flamingo chicks and even adults. At a carcass they are very aggressive, snatching portions of flesh from other vultures (Lappet-faced and European Black vultures) and able to force their way to meat through a throng of griffons. Their heavy powerful bills also enable them to tear hide and sinews. On the other hand, griffons and

Left: the King vulture of tropical America.

Opposite: Griffon vultures around a carcass.

White-backed vultures feed on soft flesh and intestines. Their tongues have backward pointing processes and a tubular form, enabling them to pull flesh into the throat, and their necks and bills are long and thin, so that they can reach into openings, or right into a body cavity. The New World condors are perhaps rather similar in this respect. The weak-billed Egyptian and Hooded vultures cannot compete at a carcass with any of the larger species, but pick up discarded scraps. Their thin bills also enable them to pick up shreds of flesh which other heavier-billed vultures cannot reach.

At a carcass gregarious griffons establish a dominance hierarchy. The hungriest vultures thrust their way to the food with bounding, wing-spreading or foot-stretching threat displays. They dominate very briefly and ability to gulp food rapidly is an advantage here. Other vultures wait their chance to replace the dominants and there are usually one or two groups of fully-fed birds resting close by. Up to a hundred vultures often feed on one carcass, and they may travel 100 miles (160 km) to reach food. They do not maintain any individual or group feeding territory.

The lammergeiers and the Egyptian vultures may be quite closely allied, but both are very different from other vultures and each other. The lammergeier feeds on bones and is known as the 'bone-breaker' in much of its range. It carries the bones to a height, approaches downwind to drop them on a chosen slab and alights upwind to pick up the fragments. It also eats carrion and perhaps live animals. The Egyptian vulture, besides being a common town scavenger, is one of the few known avian tool-users. It hurls stones at ostrich eggs in order to break them. It also picks up and smashes smaller eggs by dropping them on rocks and kills and eats the fledglings of such colonial birds as pelicans and flamingos.

All Old World vultures make nests, in trees or on rock ledges. No New World vulture makes any nest at all, breeding in caves, hollow trees, or on the ground. Of Old World vultures, lammergeiers and Egyptian vultures nest in caves or holes in cliffs and the large solitary vultures singly in trees, as also does the Hooded vulture, White-backed vultures breed colonially in trees and the true griffons, apart from the Indian griffon, colonially on cliffs, sometimes hundreds together.

All vultures lay one or two eggs, the larger birds, normally one. Incubation and fledging periods are all long, or very long. Eggs hatch in 46 days (Hooded vulture), 38–41 days in the Turkey vulture and in over 50 days for larger species. The young, of at least Old World species, remain in the nest for three and a half to four and a half months. Like chicks of other diurnal birds of prey, at first downy and helpless, they acquire feathers in about two months, but remain longer in the nest thereafter than, for instance, eagles of similar size. Species nesting in temperate climates (European and Himalayan griffons) start breeding very early in the year, sometimes when snow is still on the ground. Their young are thus flying and able to compete with adults by the early autumn. Presumably young vultures are able to feed themselves as soon as they can fly to a carcass, but it is likely that adults are more aggressive, so that where dead animals are scarce the young would probably have difficulty in obtaining food.

Despite their rather unattractive habits, all vultures are beneficial to man, eating noxious dead animals or scavenging potential sources of such pests as blowflies. They are, nevertheless, persecuted by some ranchers and sheep-farmers for alleged killing of calves or lambs. A few such reports, where carrion is scarce owing to good management, may be true, but the majority are certainly incorrect. Even if vultures do attack an occasional lamb, they are on balance beneficial, deserving protection. See also condor. FAMILIES: Cathartidae and Accipitridae, ORDER: Falconiformes, CLASS: Aves. L.M.B

Adult Egyptian vulture gliding down to land beside two juveniles and two eggs.

W

WADERS, birds including both small and medium sized species, often with long legs and bills which enable them respectively to walk in shallow water and feed in soft ground or mud. This group of birds forms the suborder Charadrii, one of three suborders of the Charadriiformes, together with the Lari (gulls and terns) and Alcae (auks). The waders are the so-called 'shorebirds' of North America, and are usually found in open habitats near water, though not necessarily near salt water as the American name implies. Indeed, during the breeding season, many more species are found inland than by the sea and a few even in woodland, e.g. the woodcock *Scolopax rusticola*. The females of most species (except, notably the ruff *Philomachus pugnax*) are slightly larger than their respective mates. The breeding plumages of many waders are much brighter than their winter plumages, though some species (chiefly those associated with freshwater marshland habitats) keep cryptic plumages throughout the year. Almost all the members of this suborder are fast flyers and many can also run fast over short distances. Their songs are not elaborate and their simple call- or alarm-notes are often easier means of identification than their plumages or silhouettes. Most of the waders frequenting the sea-shore, and many of the less cryptic freshwater species, are gregarious. Many undertake long migrations between breeding and 'winter' quarters, journeys of over several thousands of miles; such wader species were aptly termed 'globe-spanners' by Abel Chapman.

Most of the species in the Charadrii belong either to the family Charadriidae (plovers) or Scolopacidae (sandpipers). ORDER: Charadriiformes, CLASS: Aves.   P.R.E.

WAGTAILS, small birds deriving their name from their habit of wagging their long tails rapidly up and down (or side to side in one species—the Forest wagtail *Dendronanthus indicus*) as they stand or walk. They belong to the genera *Motacilla* and *Dendronanthus* of the family Motacillidae which also includes the pipits.

The White wagtail *Motacilla alba* (and the British race of this, the Pied wagtail) has

The Yellow wagtail, like other wagtails, eats almost entirely insects and mainly two-winged flies.

A Pied wagtail in the typical habitat of its family, which is open country near water.

a boldly patterned black and white plumage, as do the African and Indian Pied wagtails. The six or more other species have much yellow in the plumage, particularly on the underparts. The beak is finely pointed in all wagtails.

The wagtails are an Old World group, though one race of the Yellow wagtail extends across the Bering Strait, into Alaska. One or two species are resident in the tropics and some of the Palearctic breeding species migrate into Africa and tropical Asia (some individuals even reach Australia) in winter.

The most intriguing feature of the group is the perplexing geographical variation some species exhibit. This reaches such a complexity in one species, *Motacilla flava,* that taxonomists differ widely in the number of species they recognize. Some treat each form

as a geographical race (i.e. a subspecies) while others give them species rank. Many of the 20 or so different races (as they will be termed here) are markedly different from one another in appearance and therefore in their vernacular names, which refer to the males in breeding dress. The race confined to Britain, and a few small areas across the English Channel, is the Yellow wagtail *Motacilla flava flavissima* which is yellow all over. On the European continent there are several other races in which the male's head is distinctively coloured: the Blue-headed wagtail *M. f. flava* in France, Germany and adjacent areas; the Grey-headed wagtail *M. f. thunbergi* in northwest Europe; the Black-headed wagtail *M. f. feldegg* in the Balkans, and several others. In Asia, too, there are many races, one of which, the White-headed

wagtail *M. f. leucocephala* of Central Asia, is particularly striking. The main reason for treating such morphologically distinct populations as geographical races, and not as distinct species, is the frequency of interbreeding where the races come into contact with one another. A second reason is the tendency for aberrant birds to appear in the breeding range of a particular race, the aberrant individuals having the characteristics of a different race. In the winter quarters in tropical Africa and Asia, individuals belonging to several races may live together in mixed flocks and show few, if any, differences in their general behaviour. However, when spring comes, they finally separate, the individuals belonging to races breeding in warmer parts of the breeding range setting out on their northward migration first, leaving the rest behind. The last to leave are generally those belonging to the most northerly races, the breeding grounds of which do not offer suitable conditions for nesting until early summer.

The nest is an open cup of grass sometimes placed among grass and herbage but often in cavities in walls, banks or trees. The clutch is of four to six eggs, generally incubated by the female alone. Incubation lasts two weeks and the young leave the nest two weeks later, but are fed by the parents for a few more days.

They are generally to be found in open country, usually close to water. A few species such as the African Mountain wagtail *Motacilla clara* are at home in densely forested country where, however, they keep to the torrents and rivers. The food of all wagtails comprises small insects which are actively hunted on the ground. They have a somewhat jerky walk, but often make short, rapid runs to capture flying insects they have flushed. Flocks of Yellow wagtails, of many races, are often seen feeding on the ground where a herd of large mammals is grazing. They may be cows in a European meadow, or 'big game' in the winter quarters. Several wagtails, *Motacilla flava* in particular, have benefitted from the clearing of forests by man. For example, large flocks of them now over-winter on golf-courses, lawns, airports and other open spaces in equatorial areas, such as southern Nigeria, and Singapore, which were, until recently, covered with dense rain-forest where these birds could not previously have found a winter home. FAMILY: Motacillidae, ORDER: Passeriformes, CLASS: Aves.   P.W.

WAHOO or peto, the common name given to *Acanthocybium solandri*, a fast-swimming oceanic fish that is related to the tunnies and mackerels. The species was named after the Swedish naturalist Dr Daniel Solander who accompanied Captain Cook on his first voyage around the world. The wahoo is found mostly in tropical seas but is nowhere abundant. It has a streamlined, cigar-shaped body, a moderately long and low first dorsal fin; a short and pointed second dorsal fin and a row of small finlets between the latter and the tail. The jaws give a rather beak-like appearance. The body is deep blue along the back and silvery below, the two areas being separated by a broad green band. Along the flanks are 20–30 green vertical bands or loops; the fins are blue to black. It feeds on squids and other fishes and is eagerly sought by anglers because it takes the bait very willingly and will put up a hard fight. A large wahoo may weigh up to 120 lb (55 kg) and the flesh makes excellent eating. FAMILY: Scombridae, ORDER: Perciformes, CLASS: Pisces.

Female wallaby with young in pouch.

WALIA *Capra walie,* or Abyssinian *ibex occurring only in the Simien mountains of Ethiopia.

WALLABIES, a large and diverse assemblage of about 30 species of kangaroo-like marsupials of generally smaller size than the true kangaroos, of the subfamily Macropodinae of the family Macropodidae which also includes the kangaroos. The wallabies have large hindfeet, strong hindlimbs and a long tapered or untapered tail. They are herbivorous and adopt a bipedal method of locomotion when moving quickly.

The Dorcopsis wallabies, two species of

Dorcopsis and two of *Dorcopsulus*, are ground dwelling but show more resemblances to the Tree kangaroos than to the remaining wallabies. They have a tapered tail which is prop-like. Behind the body it extends parallel to the ground for about one-third of its length then bends downwards to touch the ground at its tip. The Dorcopsis wallabies have functional canine teeth in the upper jaw as do the Tree kangaroos. The larger species weigh 12–15 lb (5·5–7 kg) but the smallest species *Dorcopsulus vanheurni* weighs 4·5–6·5 lb (2–3 kg).

The Hare wallabies *Lagorchestes* (3 species) are small, swift wallabies of slender

build weighing up to 9 lb (4 kg). The Banded hare wallaby *Lagostrophus fasciatus* differs from other Hare wallabies, and from all remaining kangaroos and wallabies, in the structure of its incisor teeth and in the mode of union at the front of left and right halves of the lower jaw. These differences apparently reflect different feeding habits to those of other Hare wallabies. The reproductive system resembles that of *kangaroo 'rats' rather than that of true kangaroos. The chromosome number is 24, two more than in any other wallaby. The Nail-tailed wallabies *Onychogalea* (3 species) are a little larger than the Hare wallabies and differ from them in possessing a minute horny spur (the nail) at the end of the tail tip.

The pademelons *Thylogale* (4 species) and Rock wallabies *Petrogale* (about 6 species) are a group which have, or are derived from forms with, 22 chromosomes. They are medium to small sized wallabies weighing 10–25 lb (4·5–11 kg). The pademelons have a tapered tail whereas the Rock wallabies have an untapered tail. The hindfeet of Rock wallabies are equipped with pads and granulations and the claws are short, adaptations to rock haunting habits which are absent in the forest dwelling pademelons. The *quokka Setonix brachyurus* also has 22 chromosomes but these are of different shapes from those of Rock wallabies and pademelons. The quokka is a stockily built grey-brown wallaby with a short tail and weighs 5–10 lb (2–4·5 kg). The Little rock wallaby *Peradorcas concinna* is unique amongst wallabies and kangaroos in having more than four molars. Up to nine erupt; the anterior ones being successively shed from the front so that seldom more than four are present at one time.

The Scrub wallabies are a group of larger wallabies with 16 chromosomes weighing up to 40 lb (18 kg). The Agile wallaby *Macropus agilis* is of sandy-brown colour with a distinct white stripe across the thigh (hip stripe) and short ears. Bennett's wallaby *Macropus rufogriseus fruticus* is a large grey wallaby with a reddish tinge in the fur on shoulders and rump, an indistinct white cheek stripe and naked muzzle. It is confined to Tasmania and may prove to be specifically distinct from the Red-necked wallaby *Macropus rufogriseus banksianus* of coastal eastern Australia. The Black-striped wallaby *Macropus dorsalis* has a pronounced black stripe down the mid-line of its back and a distinct white hip stripe. It may not be specifically distinct from the much smaller Parma wallaby *Macropus parma* which may lack the hip stripe and, at best, have an abbreviated back stripe. The Black-gloved wallaby or Brush kangaroo *Macropus irma* is character-

Red-necked wallaby, one of several species killed for its fur.

ized by a general bluish-grey fur, the hands and feet being black. The tail has a crest of long hairs (the brush) on its upper surface. The most beautiful of the Scrub wallabies is the whiptail or Pretty-face wallaby *Macropus elegans* a grey animal of slender form with a very long tapering tail. It has a distinct white face stripe from muzzle to beneath the eye. It is perhaps the most closely related of all the wallabies to the Grey kangaroo with which it will cross yielding a viable but sterile hybrid. The smallest 16-chromosome wallaby is the Tammar or Dama wallaby *Macropus eugenii* weighing 10–19 lb (4·5–8·5 kg).

The Swamp or Black-tailed wallaby *Wallabia bicolor* is derived from the 16-chromosome group of wallabies but has the lowest chromosome number known in marsupials and perhaps the lowest chromosome number of any vertebrate animal. There are eight autosomes and two X sex chromosomes in female animals and eight autosomes, one X sex chromosome and two Y sex chromosomes in males. The X chromosomes are compound structures consisting of an autosome fused to an original X chromosome. The eight autosomes of the Swamp wallaby result from union of some of the separate

chromosomes of its 16-chromosome relatives into single structures. The Swamp wallaby is a sturdily built animal with coarse dark grey fur and an indistinct grey face stripe.

The Dorcopsis wallabies are confined to New Guinea. The Brown hare wallaby *Lagorchestes leporides* formerly inhabited dry open grassland and saltbush plains in inland southeastern Australia and may now be extinct. The remaining species survive in parts of central and northern Australia and on three small islands off the coast of Western Australia. The Banded hare wallaby formerly had a wide distribution in Western Australia but is now mainly confined to the offshore islands of Shark Bay. The Nail-tailed wallabies have also greatly diminished in numbers since European occupation of Australia but one species is still moderately abundant in tropical areas near the Gulf of Carpentaria, and in the northern parts of the Northern Territory and Western Australia.

The pademelons inhabit forest country in eastern coastal Australia from Tasmania north to Cape York. One of the Australian species is also found in New Guinea and a further species is indigenous to New Guinea. The Rock wallabies are found throughout continental Australia wherever suitable rocky outcrops and mountains occur. They are absent from Tasmania and from New Guinea. The quokka is a southwestern Australian wallaby now rare on the mainland but surviving in large numbers on Rottnest and Bald Islands. It was seen by the Dutch navigator Samuel Volckerson on Rottnest Island in 1658 and again by the Dutchman Willem de Vlamingh in 1696 who called the island 'Rottnest' because of the abundance of a kind of rat as big as a common cat, whose dung is found in abundance all over the island'. The 'rats' were marsupials—the quokkas. Two Australian marsupials, one of which may have been a wallaby, the other definitely a wallaby, were earlier seen by European explorers. The animal collected and eaten during Torres' 1606 expedition through what is now called Torres Strait, between New Guinea and Australia, was either a cuscus or a pademelon. The animal described by the Dutch merchant Pelsaert, from Houtman's Abrolhos off the Western Australian coast where his ship was wrecked in 1629 was the Tammar wallaby. It remains abundant on the Wallabi Group of Islands in the Abrolhos to this day.

The Scrub wallabies are widely distributed in coastal Australia sometimes being found several hundred miles inland. The Agile wallaby, of wide northern Australian tropical distribution, is also found in southern New Guinea.

The wallabies all produce but one young at a time. Their methods of reproduction are essentially like those of the *kangaroos. All so far investigated exhibit embryonic diapause

—the prolonged storage of a dormant but viable embryo in the female reproductive tract during suckling of a young in the pouch. In the tammar, which has seasonal breeding from January to about June on Kangaroo Island, South Australia, embryonic diapause initially occurs during pouch suckling but the embryo remains dormant in the non-breeding season after the young has left the pouch. The dormant embryos begin development at the start of the new breeding season each January after a total resting period of about 11 months. Young animals breeding for the first time at the end of the breeding season may enter diapause without a young being present in the pouch. The Swamp wallaby is unique in that the mating giving rise to the dormant embryo occurs just before the first young is born, instead of just after as in other wallabies and kangaroos.

The Scrub wallabies contribute significantly to the Australian fur trade. Up to 45,000 skins of Agile, Red-necked, Swamp and Whiptail wallabies have been sold each year since 1954 from the State of Queensland. Over two million Bennett's wallaby skins were sold from Tasmania during the period 1923 to 1955. The pademelons are not generally exploited for the fur trade except in Tasmania where two and a half million skins were sold during the period 1923 to 1955. Shooting for skins does not, however, appear to have caused a decline in numbers of the exploited species. These remain relatively abundant whereas a number of species which have never been extensively hunted are now extremely rare. FAMILY: Macropodidae, ORDER: Marsupialia, CLASS: Mammalia.

G.B.S.

WALLABY'S RETURN. Among the many exotic animals which were introduced to New Zealand, such as Red deer and chamois, there were about 12 species of wallaby. The exact number is not known because those responsible did not always bother to identify the animals they let go. In 1958 it was found that some wallaby skins from Kawan Island, some 30 miles (45 km) north of Auckland, were of the Parma wallaby. This species had once been common in New South Wales but had been extinct in Australia since the 1930's. It is now being threatened again by control measures in New Zealand to protect pine plantations.

WALLACE, A. R., 1823–1913, English naturalist and co-founder of the theory of evolution by natural selection. He also made important contributions to the study of animal colouration and mimicry, island biology, the species concept and, particularly, zoogeography. With no formal education in biology or indeed in any science, Wallace became one of the foremost naturalists of the

19th or any other century. Overshadowed by the weighty evolutionary publications of Charles Darwin his contribution to biological science has been generally neglected. From the age of 14 he had to support himself, but was never in official employment, earning his living after reaching manhood by collecting natural history specimens and later by writing.

In 1848 Wallace journeyed to the Amazon with H. W. Bates (1825–1892), exploring and collecting, returning in 1852. Then in 1854 he set off on his very important journey to Malaysia where he stayed for eight years, during which time he travelled 14,000 miles (22,000 km) and collected over 125,000 specimens. In 1855 he published an important paper 'The law which has regulated the introduction of new species', in which he noted that every species has come into existence coincident both in time and space with a pre-existing closely allied species. Then in 1858, while ill with fever, he recalled Malthus' *Essay on Population,* with its comments on the natural checks to population increase, and over the next three evenings he drew up an essay 'On the tendency of varieties to depart indefinitely from the original type' and sent it to Darwin. Wallace's theory was essentially the same as Darwin's and the latter, with his customary humility, felt he should give Wallace precedence. However, mutual friends prevailed against this course and in July 1858 Wallace's essay and an extract of Darwin's were read to a meeting of the Linnaean Society. This stimulated Darwin to complete a shortened version of his great work, and *The Origin of Species* was, as a result, published in 1859.

In 1864 Wallace considered the evolution of man and suggested that his physical evolution preceded that of his mind, and that he evolved in Africa. Unfortunately he later retracted these ideas when he developed an interest in spiritualism.

Wallace's contribution to an understanding of the development of species was considerable. For example, he noted that contact between similar forms without intermixture was a good test of specific difference. He also recognized geographical isolation as an important mechanism in species evolution. And he pointed to the reality of convergent evolution by showing that the very similar sunbirds and hummingbirds are not closely related.

Wallace's most important work outside evolution was his foundation of zoogeography, significant contributions being made by his publications *The Malay Archipelago* (1869), *The Geographical Distribution of Animals* (1876), and *Island Life* (1880). We are reminded of his contribution by *Wallace's Line' which divides the very different faunas of the Australian and Malayan regions.

Another biological area significantly advanced by Wallace's work was that of animal colouration. He focused attention on warning, deflecting, alluring and recognition colours, and contributed to our knowledge of mimicry and polymorphism.

Honoured in his own time—he was elected Fellow of the Royal Society in 1892 and received the Order of Merit in 1910—Wallace has been sadly neglected by subsequent generations of biologists whose science he helped to establish.   P.M.D.

WALLACE'S LINE, WEBER'S LINE, WALLACEA,

three terms connected with the faunas of the islands which lie between Southeast Asia and Australia.

Most of the boundaries between the major zoogeographic regions of the world are comparatively sharp, since these are separated either by major stretches of ocean, such as the Atlantic between North America and Eurasia, by a narrow land bridge such as the Panama Isthmus between North and South America, or by a climatic barrier such as the deserts and mountain ranges which separate the Ethiopian and Oriental regions from Eurasia. The fauna of the Oriental zoogeographic region and that of the Australian region are instead separated by a complex island pattern, including the Greater and Lesser Sunda Islands, the Philippines, the Celebes and the Moluccas. Their two faunas are very different from one another, especially in their mammals, since the Oriental fauna contains only placentals while that of the Australian region originally contained only marsupials; the reptile and bird faunas of the two regions also differ. These two faunas have colonized the intervening islands from both east and west, and the resulting overlap of the faunas shows many interesting features.

That same Wallace who, with Charles Darwin, proposed the theory of evolution by natural selection, was also the first to realize that the change between the Australian fauna and the Oriental fauna was not a series of gradual and more or less equal steps. In his many travels in the area in the mid-19th century, Wallace noticed there was instead a rather sudden, sharp change in the faunal balance along one particular line, which has since become known as Wallace's Line. The northern course of this line was later altered by T. H. Huxley so as to leave all the Philippine islands (except Palawan) to the eastward. This line defines an eastward limit to which most elements of the Oriental fauna have penetrated, but beyond which a far smaller number are to be found. For example on the island of Bali nearly 94% of the reptiles and 87% of the birds are of Oriental origin but on neighbouring Lombok, the next island to the east of it, these figures have droppped to 85% and 72·5% respectively. Though many Oriental mammals reach Java and a smaller number reach Bali, none except rats and mice and bats occur naturally farther east (though a number have been carried from island to island by man).

It may be significant that all of the islands west of Wallace's Line (as amended by Huxley), which have an overwhelmingly Oriental fauna, are on the continental shelf of Southeast Asia. At several times during the Pleistocene the sea-level was lower than today, so that these islands may all have been linked by dry land. It is therefore possible that they may have been colonized by the Oriental fauna at this time. Further east, the point beyond which the fauna becomes overwhelmingly Australian, is similarly along the continental shelf of Australasia, which includes New Guinea and a few small offshore islands. The whole area between this line and Wallace's Line, within which the transition between the Oriental and the Australian faunas takes place, is sometimes called Wallacea. It is possible to draw a line within Wallacea along the zone of approximate faunal balance. To the west of this line known as Weber's Line, over half of the fauna is of Oriental origin. The Oriental fauna has been more successful than the Australian at colonizing Wallacea. As a result, Weber's Line lies east of the geographical centre line of Wallacea.   G.B.C

WALL LIZARD,

name used for several European species of typical *lizards, the best known being *Lacerta muralis*. Their natural habitat is among rocks but when living in gardens they use walls instead. FAMILY Lacertidae, ORDER: Squamata, CLASS: Reptilia.

WALRUS,

similar to a sealion in appearance but heavier, more wrinkled and having distinctive tusks. It belongs to the family Odobenidae in the order Pinnipedia. The two families Odobenidae and Otariidae (sea lions and Fur seals) are grouped together in the superfamily Otarioidea. Walruses are like otariids in that their hindflippers can be brought forwards underneath the body, but resemble true seals in lacking a visible external ear: Studies of chromosomes have

Opposite: walrus bulls hauled out on a beach.

Malayan Archipelago, showing position of Wallace's Line, as well as Weber's Line.

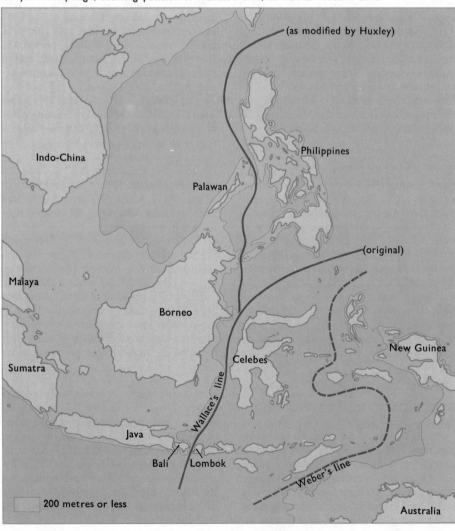

Indo-China

(as modified by Huxley)

Philippines

Palawan

Malaya

Borneo

(original)

Sumatra

Celebes

New Guinea

Java

Wallace's line

Bali   Lombok

Weber's line

200 metres or less

Australia

shown that those of walruses are similar in some respects to those of both otariids and true seals. There is one species of walrus *Odobenus rosmarus,* with two subspecies, the Atlantic walrus *O. r. rosmarus* and the Pacific walrus *O. r. divergens.* The differences between them are not great, the Atlantic walrus having shorter tusks and a narrower facial part of the skull.

Walruses prefer the shallow water round the circumpolar arctic coasts. The Atlantic walrus occurs in two main areas: in Baffin Bay roughly between Ellesmere Island and Davis Strait, in Foxe Basin, Hudson Strait and the northern and eastern parts of Hudson Bay and also in the Barents and Kara Seas, round the shores of Novaya Zemlya, Franz Josef Land and Spitsbergen, and occasionally off Iceland. The Pacific walrus occurs on both sides of the Bering Sea from the Gulf of Anadyr northwards, and along the northern coast of USSR, in the Chukchi, East Siberian and Laptev Seas. There are occasional records of walruses reaching far south of their usual range. William Caxton for instance recorded a walrus taken in the River Thames in 1456, and there are 21 records of walruses off the Scottish coasts between 1815 and 1954, and ten records of them off Norwegian coasts between 1902 and 1954. An early stranding of a walrus about 1500, probably in Dutch waters, is of interest, as it was sent as a gift to the Pope in Rome. Probably the head and skin were sent, preserved in a barrel of salt, and during his travels the artist Albrecht Dürer must have seen this head and made his well-known drawing of it. The slightly distorted appearance of the drawing could be accounted for if Dürer saw only the preserved head. Although not all walruses migrate each year, a large proportion of them follow the edge of the ice as it moves north in summer and south in winter.

It is not known exactly where walruses originated but it is thought that the primitive walrus ancestors occurred in the North Pacific and that they later moved into the Atlantic. The earliest walrus fossil known is a jaw, about 15 million years old, from Miocene levels in Virginia, USA, but Pliocene walrus remains have mostly been recorded from Europe, though there are two records from California. Later, from the Pleistocene, fossil walrus remains are present in Florida and South Carolina, and in Suffolk, England.

Walruses are perhaps one of the most spectacular and best known of all the pinnipeds, and their heavy wrinkled bodies and whiskery, tusked faces are easily recognizable. Adult males are about 12 ft (3·6 m) in length and weigh up to 3,000 lb (1,360 kg), while females are slightly smaller, about 10 ft (3 m) in length and 1,800 lb (816 kg) in weight. The head looks rather square in side

view and has small bloodshot eyes, rows of thick whiskers and long tusks that are present in both sexes. These tusks, which are formed from the upper canine teeth, erupt when the animal is about four months old, have grown to about 4 in (10 cm) long at two years, about 1 ft (30 cm) by 5–6 years, and may reach a length of over 3 ft (1 m). The skin is rough and wrinkled and adult males have many warty tubercles about their necks and shoulders. The thickness of the skin increases with age and in an adult animal may reach over 1 in (2·5 cm) on the body and about $2\frac{1}{2}$ in (7 cm) on the neck. Under the skin is a thick layer of blubber which may also be $2\frac{1}{2}$ in (7 cm) thick and weigh over 900 lb (408 kg). The hide is a light grey, but when basking in the sun the blood vessels dilate and the animals appear rust red. Young animals have a scanty coat of reddish hair, but old animals have a practically naked skin.

A peculiarity of walruses is the pharyngeal pouches that may occur in the adults of both sexes but not in every individual. The lateral walls of the pharynx are extremely elastic and are expanded into a pair of pouches, with a capacity of up to 11 gallons (50 lt), that extend backwards between the muscles of the neck as far as the scapula, and sometimes even to the posterior end of the thoracic cavity. There are muscles round the openings of these pouches into the pharynx, so that they can be inflated with air and give buoyancy. Many walruses sleep in an upright position in the water and these air sacs help to keep them afloat. During mating activities walruses make a bell-like sound and the pouches also act as resonators amplifying this.

A single pup is born in April or May after a gestation period of almost a year, but in any one year only about half the adult females produce pups. The newborn pups are about 4 ft (1·2 m) in length, 100 lb (45·3 kg) in weight and greyish in colour, though they soon moult to become a reddish colour. They are suckled by their mothers for over a year, but become more independent during the second year, supplementing the milk with small invertebrates. Even after weaning they remain with their mothers for another year or so, possibly because with their very short tusks they are unable to dig up enough food for themselves and have to rely to a large extent on animals stirred up by their mothers. Mating is believed to take place shortly after the birth of the pups, but as this happens far out on the ice floes it is difficult to get reliable information.

Walruses have few enemies, man, Killer whales and Polar bears being their only predators. Walruses are found chiefly in shallow waters of 40 fathoms (72 m) or less, where there is abundant gravel which supports a large fauna of molluscs. Bivalve

molluscs form the greater part of the food eaten, although echinoderms and fish are also taken. A full stomach of a bull walrus has been shown to contain about 85 lb (38 kg) of mollusc feet. Such stomachs, full of the feet of the mollusc *Cardium,* are considered a great delicacy by the Eskimos. The long tusks of the walrus are used to stir up the gravel and the lips and whiskers sort out the food material and convey it to the mouth. It is a curious fact that although molluscs form the main food, it is only very rarely that pieces of mollusc shell are found in a walrus stomach. Mussel shells are frequently found in quantities near walrus breathing holes and it has been suggested that the walrus may hold the mussel on the ground with its whiskers and then suck the fleshy parts out of the shell. Certainly the mollusc feet and siphons that are found in walrus stomachs are entire, and not crushed, so it is very probable that they feed in this way. Occasionally walruses will eat young Bearded and Ringed seals, and even young walruses, but they do this only when other food is scarce, though an occasional rogue walrus is seen with tusks and skin stained with grease from habitual seal eating.

The numbers of walruses have been declining since the introduction of rifles among the Eskimos has made hunting easier. Some areas have now been declared sanctuaries, and with the education of the Eskimos and Alaskans to the proper conservation of these resources, there has been some improvement in walrus numbers, and they have been reappearing in areas where they had not been seen for many years. Walruses still provide much of the meat eaten by an Eskimo, his family and his dogs, and walrus skin is an extremely useful product, making the strongest harpoon and boat lines, being stretched to cover umiaks, and still being found in other societies irreplaceable for buffing silver. Use of the intestines for making rainproof clothing and the ivory for making harpoon points has been largely superseded now by modern products, but the ivory tusks still provide the Eskimo with an occupation and an income. Eskimo carvings of walrus tusks are beautiful and unique. It is a pity now that so many of these carvings are losing their artistic merit and are being debased into tourist souvenirs. FAMILY: Odobenidae, ORDER: Pinnipedia, CLASS: Mammalia.   J.E.K.

WAPITI *Cervus elephas,* the counterpart in North America of the European *Red deer.

WARBLE FLIES, known in North America as grubs, lay their eggs in the skin of cattle, the larvae from these causing swollen skin-boils or warbles. The flies look like small bumblebees but have only one pair of wings, so are true flies.

All *Hypoderma* species and several other oestrids look rather like small bumblebees (Hymenoptera), but of course have only one pair of wings, as they are in the order Diptera. The mouthparts of the adult are rudimentary and non-functional, hence the mature insect has to rely for its energy reserves on food ingested during its three larval stages.

The two cattle Warble flies, *Hypoderma lineatum* and *H. bovis,* are common throughout the temperate zone of the northern hemisphere, but do not occur further south. They are usually very host-specific, but serious conditions occasionally arise in other animals, and in man, for example, eye infection with a maggot, following chance contact with egg-laying flies. During summer the adult *Hypoderma* females irritate cattle by flying round them and darting down to lay their eggs on the legs and underside of the body. This can cause entire herds of cattle to panic and run, known as 'gadding' (hence the alternative name of gadfly for the Warble fly). The eggs are attached to the hair, rather like lice eggs, although they are placed well down in the coat and so not usually very obvious. The name *lineatum* refers to the lines of 5–12 eggs laid on individual hairs by this species.

The eggs hatch in 3–4 days and the $\frac{1}{25}$ in (0·75–1·00 mm) first stage larva crawls down the hair to the skin, which it penetrates by means of digestive juices and its two tiny cutting mouth-hooks. It then travels along underneath the skin until, in the case of *H. lineatum,* it is near the diaphragm, which it crosses and so finds and enters the oesophagus (gullet). The larvae, which are now $\frac{1}{12}-\frac{1}{5}$ in (2–5 mm), rest and grow in the tissues of the oesophagus during the autumn-winter. Larvae of *H. bovis,* on the other hand, find the ends of nerves and track along them until they reach the spinal cord. They then pass into the fat which surrounds the cord, coming to rest within the spinal canal itself. As with *H. lineatum,* the larvae rest during the winter months.

In early spring (about February for *H. lineatum,* March-April for *H. bovis)* larvae of *H. lineatum* leave the oesophagus via the diaphragm and pass up to the skin of the back, while larvae of *H. bovis* move upwards from the spinal canal through one of the nerve openings directly to the nearby overlying skin. The larvae, now about $\frac{2}{3}$ in (15–17 mm) long, first slowly cut and digest their way through this last barrier, but then fully retract and moult underneath the skin to the second stage. They are unable to cut through the skin in the second stage, as by then they retain only vestigial mouth-hooks; each larva next pushes backwards up into the hole, breathing from the air through its two posterior spiracles. The parasites continue to feed and grow in the subdermal tissues of the host. The

tissues of infected animals gradually surround each parasite with a cyst wall, and as the cysts and their enclosed white grubs enlarge and become obvious the swellings are called 'warbles'. In 1–2 weeks' time a further moult occurs and the final, third stage, larva is produced. Each swollen cyst (and there may be twenty in the animal's back) now contains large numbers of dead host cells and bacteria, and the farmer can fairly easily squeeze out the larvae and pus from the warble swellings.

After 4–6 weeks the third stage larva has become dark brown and is mature, measuring about 1 in (25 mm). One morning it squeezes itself through the rather small hole of the swelling and falls on to the soil, where within 24 hours the larval skin hardens to form a strong black puparial case. Inside this protective coat the pupa develops for 3–4 weeks and then a triangular cap lifts off at the front end to release the new Warble fly. Females mate within 1–2 days of emergence and then fly off to lay their eggs on cattle.

Economic losses and control. Cattle plagued with Warble flies gad even more than those attacked by Horse flies and clegs (family Tabanidae). They put on less weight than uninfested stock and milk yields also suffer. Internally the migrating larvae cause yellow gelatinous lesions ('butchers' jelly') and haemorrhages, and they may produce posterior paralysis while moving and feeding near the spinal cord. Their principal economic effect is by the damage they cause to cattle skin, which downgrades the hide and makes it poor (or quite useless) for leather manufacture.

Warble flies are best controlled in the larval stage, either in the spring by putting insecticides on the back after the third stage larvae have reached (and damaged) it, or during the autumn-winter by dressing the back with special systemically active organophosphorus insecticides. These diffuse into and through the skin and circulate around the body in the blood-stream, killing any young larvae they meet. Both techniques have been used in suitably geographically isolated areas to eradicate cattle Warble flies, for example, in Cyprus by derris dressings and recently in Ireland by organo-phosphorus systemically active insecticides, but the modern systemic technique is the better of the two and is now being used in several countries.

The name Warble fly usually refers to the two species of *Hypoderma* which attack cattle, *H. lineatum* and *H. bovis.* Cattle warbles are known in North America as 'grubs'. A third British *Hypoderma* species, *H. diana,* infests Red deer in Scotland, while the three remaining species occur through the mainland continents of Europe and northern Asia: these are *H. actaeon* (Red deer), *H. moschiferi* (Musk deer) and *H. capreola* (Roe deer). Some related types of Warble flies were formerly considered to be species of *Hypo-*

derma, but they have now been transferred to the genera *Przhevalskiana* (on gazelles) and *Oedemagena* (very common on reindeer throughout Lapland and the USSR). Still other genera include Warble flies of rodents.

Larvae of species closely related to *Hypoderma* parasitize the stomach (*Gasterophilus* in horses) or nasal passages (*Oestrus* in sheep). FAMILY: Oestridae, ORDER: Diptera, CLASS: Insecta, PHYLUM: Arthropoda.

W.N.B.

WARBLERS, small, perching birds, comprising the Sylviinae, a subfamily of the Muscicapidae. Their closest affinities are with the thrushes (Turdinae) and flycatchers (Muscicapinae) both of which, however, unlike the warblers, have spotted juvenile plumage differing from that of the adults. Almost all warblers have thin, pointed bills (though there are exceptions, such as the Thick-billed warbler *Phragmaticola aedon*) and are mainly insectivorous. They have ten primaries (flight feathers) and, with a few exceptions, for example Rüppell's warbler *Sylvia rüppelli,* the sexes have similar or identical plumages. Where there is a sexual difference, the male is the more conspicuously coloured and, in these cases, the juvenile plumage resembles that of the female. The plumage is usually similar at all seasons, with no special breeding plumage.

The English name (warbler) refers to the pleasant and melodious song of many of the species, especially some of those best known in western Europe. The blackcap *Sylvia atricapilla,* a common woodland warbler, for instance, has a rich warbling song rivalling, in many people's opinions, that of the blackbird *Turdus merula* and nightingale *Luscinia megarhynchos.* Other species, such as the Grasshopper warbler *Locustella naevia,* however, have monotonous and relatively unmusical songs and some species even have harsh and unpleasing songs (e.g. whitethroat *Sylvia communis*).

Whilst some (mainly tropical) species are brightly coloured, most are various shades of brown, green or grey and identification is often not easy, and frequently depends on behavioural differences. Tail-cocking, for instance, may help to distinguish difficult species (e.g. Moustached warbler *Lusciniola melanopogon,* Upcher's warbler *Hippolais languida*). The warblers include many examples of sibling species in which separation of species pairs is frequently more easily made by means of song or call-note than by plumage differences. Examples of this amongst west European species are the Willow warbler *Phylloscopus trochilus* the chiffchaff *Ph. collybita,* the Greenish warbler *Ph. trochiloides* and the Arctic warbler *Ph. borealis,* the Melodious warbler *Hippolais polyglotta* and the Icterine warbler *H. icterina.* There are cases where identification

Warblers

is sometimes impossible even when a bird is caught and examined in the hand (e.g. first-year Reed and Marsh warblers *Acrocephalus scirpaceus* and *A. palustris*). This challenge of identification makes the group a particularly attractive one to ornithologists.

The subfamily (Sylviinae) is virtually confined to the Old World and, hence, they are often referred to as the Old World warblers to distinguish them from the American wood warblers which have nine primaries. Most species are to be found in Africa (150 odd species) but the group also extends throughout Europe, Asia and Australia. Some species have a very restricted geographical range whilst others have very wide distributions. The two extremes are exemplified by Marmora's warbler *Sylvia sarda,* confined to the Mediterranean islands and parts of coastal Spain and Tunisia, and the Arctic warbler, with a breeding range extending from Norway east to Alaska and south to Korea and Japan.

Whilst some species are virtually sedentary (although even some of the non-migratory species undertake altitudinal movements with the seasons), others undertake vast annual migrations. These biennial journeys are prodigious considering the tiny size of the birds, the smallest being only $3\frac{1}{2}$ in ($8\frac{1}{2}$ cm) long, and some of the largest weight changes in birds are exhibited by warblers, which may almost double their weight in the few days immediately prior to undertaking a long migration. Two examples of long migrations are those of the Arctic warbler which travels 7,000–8,000 miles (11,250–12,900 km) twice a year between its breeding area in northwest Europe and its wintering area in Southeast Asia, and the East Siberian race of the Willow warbler *Phylloscopus trochilus yakutensis* which winters in East Africa, some 6,000–7,000 miles (9,700–11,250 km) from its breeding area. The westernmost populations of some of these migratory northern species move eastwards in autumn before going south to winter in Asia. A proportion of the population sometimes moves in the opposite direction to that followed by the majority and this 'reversed migration' is thought to explain the occurrence in Britain, in autumn, of such species as the Barred warbler *Sylvia nisoria* and Pallas's warbler *Phylloscopus proregulus,* which would normally be moving away from Britain in that season. Different populations of the same species (even the same race) often winter in quite different areas, providing 'migratory divides'. An example of this is the blackcap, with the British and other populations breeding west of longitude 11°E migrating southwest to winter in Iberia, Morocco and Algeria and most of the Scandinavian and the European populations

Wood warbler *Phylloscopus sibilatrix*, of Europe.

breeding east of 11°E migrating southeast to winter in the Lebanon, Egypt and northeast Africa. This phenomenon can only be shown by ringing large numbers of birds and is probably more widespread than the relatively few known examples. It is probably the result of unification of populations that were isolated during glaciation in Europe.

Of the 300 odd species of warbler in the world, only about 45 are known in Europe, some 34 breeding regularly and the others merely occurring as vagrants. 13 species breed regularly in Britain and a further 26 or 27 have occurred as migrants or vagrants, the latest addition being a Spectacled warbler *Sylvia conspicillata* trapped at Spurn Head, Yorkshire in 1968. Apart from the mainly resident Dartford warbler *S. undata,* only two species of warbler, the blackcap and chiffchaff, regularly over-winter in Britain but even these do so only in very small numbers. The habit has been increasingly noted, however, and may be becoming more frequent. Hard winters in Britain severely affect these populations and the New Forest population of the Dartford warbler was drastically reduced in the winters of 1961/62 and 1962/63. Mid-winter snows often bring the normally retiring blackcaps to garden bird-tables in search of food. Though normally insectivorous, diet is clearly modified under conditions of stress. For instance, the habit of feeding on berries (particularly blackberries and elderberries) seems to be particularly evident in migrants.

Whilst the breeding range of some species is contracting, others have spread markedly in recent years. The Greenish warbler has recently extended its range northwestwards in Europe and this has resulted in increasing numbers being seen, as vagrants, in Britain. The population of the mainly sedentary Cetti's warbler *Cettia cetti* of southern Europe has also expanded in recent years and there have been several records in Britain (including birds in summer) and one even as far west as western Ireland (Cape Clear Island, Co. Cork in 1968). An extraordinary, but isolated, case of breeding in Britain was that of a pair of Moustached warblers which nested at Cambridge in 1946. This species normally nests no nearer to Britain than the Mediterranean countries and has only occurred as a vagrant on two occasions. Savi's warbler *Locustella luscinioides* became extinct in Britain in the mid-19th century, with the draining of the East Anglian fens, but has recently recolonized, a small population being discovered in Kent in 1960.

Most species of warbler build their nests at or close to ground level, in grass, reeds or low bushes. The nest varies from a shallow cup to a domed nest or even, in the case of some of

Marsh warbler, one of many species of small birds so alike that it is hard to tell one from the other.

the grass-warblers (*Cisticola* spp), a bottle-shaped nest. In some species, such as the blackcap, the male may build several 'cock's nests' of which only one is eventually used. Various species lay from three to ten eggs, but most of the familiar western European species lay from four to six. These are usually pale-coloured, often with faint spots or streaks. In some species, for example the whitethroat, both sexes may incubate, whereas in others the female incubates alone (e.g. chiffchaff), but both usually share the task of feeding the young. Most species breed in isolated pairs, but some (e.g. Reed warbler) form loose colonies.

Being mainly insectivorous, warblers are almost constantly on the move, searching for food. Leaf warblers of the genus *Phylloscopus* frequently flick their wings and have 'nervous' actions. Some, like the Dusky warbler *Ph. fuscatus,* are mainly ground feeders whilst others, like the chiffchaff, are more typical of the tree tops. The Reed warblers (mostly *Acrocephalus* spp) are, as their name suggests, on the whole birds of the reed beds and sedges, though often extending into bushy areas adjoining reed beds and sometimes even into quite dry habitats. Warblers of the genera *Sylvia* and *Hippolais* are more typical of dry habitats, from woodland to scrub, and the skulking *Locustella* warblers are usually associated with damp habitats. The Grass warblers (*Cisticola* and *Megalurus* spp) have a mainly African, Asian and Australian distribution and vary in habitat from dry scrub to damp sedge and grass. *Cisticola* is the largest genus of warbler, including some 75 species and providing taxonomists with many problems of classification. The only species in this large genus which is found in Europe is the Fan-tailed warbler *C. juncidis,* of the Mediterranean region but also extending as far south as northern Australia. The relatively nondescript *Phylloscopus* warblers of the north are largely replaced in tropical Asia and Africa by a number of genera of more brightly coloured warblers (*Abroscopus, Apalis, Eremomela, Seicercus* and *Sylvietta*), tailor-birds (*Orthotomus*) and Wren warblers (*Prinia*). The kinglets (Regulidae) are usually included with the warblers but are here dealt with separately under goldcrest. FAMILY: Muscicapidae, ORDER: Passeriformes, CLASS: Aves. J.T.R.S.

WARM-BLOODED ANIMALS. The animal body may be compared with an extremely complex chemical laboratory. All chemical reactions are directly linked with temperature and, in general, the higher the temperature the quicker the reaction. This is only partly true for biochemical reactions, for most of these are particularly efficient at a certain temperature, the rate of reaction falling away both above and below that level.

Cold-blooded (poikilothermic) animals are very much linked to the environment and, up to their level of maximal biochemical efficiency, the warmer the conditions the more rapid their activity. Except in a few areas the temperature rarely exceeds that of maximal efficiency so that the fall off above that point is only of local importance.

Obviously an animal which could be free of this linkage between rate of activity and temperature would have enormous advantages; it would be able to operate at maximum efficiency at all times. Mammals and birds have evolved to a body heated by its own chemical reactions and maintained at an efficient working level. That is, they are warm-blooded or homoiothermic. The blood circulating around the animal maintains the temperature level in all parts even though the heat producing chemical reactions may take place mainly in the liver or muscles. Mammals and birds can therefore be as active on a cold day as on a warm one.

The price of warm-bloodedness is high, both in food, the fuel which has to be 'burned' to produce heat, and oxygen, which is needed for the 'burning' process. Warm-blooded animals therefore need a plentiful supply of food at all times, particularly when it is cold, and also have to be air breathers.

As so often happens in biological systems, specialization leads to further specialization. In warm-blooded animals the enzyme

systems responsible for the biochemical activities have in many cases become more closely linked to temperature than in cold blooded forms, giving greater efficiency a optimum body temperature but a more rapid fall away both above and below this point. Many mammalian enzyme systems are only really efficient over a range of 3–4°C. Sperm production in mammalian testes illustrate this point most dramatically. In many mammals the testes are carried outside the body in scrotum where the temperature is a few degrees lower than the body, when sperm production enzyme systems work at optimal efficiency; if the testes approach body temperature sperm production ceases.

A warm-blooded animal must be capable not only of producing the heat for a steady warm, body temperature but also have defensive mechanisms to prevent over cooling or over-heating. Fur, feather and fat act as insulators; blood vessels carried near or farther from the skin, panting and sweating allow variable amounts of heat loss. Some warm-blooded animals find the cold winter dangerous and so have evolved the defensive mechanism of *hibernation, returning to a warm-blooded state when the prevailing conditions are suitable. K.M.B

WARTHOG *Phacochoerus aethiopicus,* a large grey-brown African hog with smooth or rough hide sparsely covered with hair

Warthog foraging in a forest edge in Africa.

except around the neck and on the back. As the name suggests it has warty bumps on the face beside the eyes and on the sides of the face. The dental formula is: incisors $\frac{1}{3}$; canines $\frac{1}{1}$; premolars $\frac{3}{2}$; molars $\frac{3}{3} \times 2 = 34$. The lower canines are highly developed, curving to the top of the snout and being up to 24 in (61 cm) long in some specimens. The feet are typical of the hog family with four toes on each foot. The length of the head and body of 12 males measured, averaged 52·3 in (133 cm). The same number of females averaged 46·3 in (117 cm). The height at the shoulder of the males averaged 30·5 in (77 cm) and the females 26·4 in (67 cm). The tail length of the 12 males averaged 18 in (46 cm) while that of the females was 15·7 in (40 cm). Males are heavier than females, the average weight of the 12 adult males studied being 191·4 lb (87 kg) while that of the females was 132 lb (60 kg).

The warthog is found over almost the entire continent of Africa, but principally south of the Sahara.

The breeding season varies with the locality but birth of young generally coincides with the rainy season. Mating in southern Africa occurs in June and July and young are born in late October and November after a gestation period of 171–175 days. There are usually four in each litter.

Warthogs inhabit savannahs, open plains and bushy edges. They are not found in dense forest. Usually they form small groups but they may sometimes be solitary. They are almost entirely diurnal, spending the nights in burrows, usually those made by antbears or porcupines. When retreating into burrows they back in, presumably in order to face any enemy. They run with tails erect and can reach speeds of 20–30 mph (32–48 kph).

They are vegetarian, feeding largely on roots and rhizomes of grasses and other plants. The warthog is a frequent visitor to waterholes or 'pans' and is fond of mud wallows. The body temperature is about 102°F (38·9°C) but may vary by 7°F. The animal cannot withstand low temperatures, especially when young. Warthogs are hosts of the protozoan *trypanosomes which cause sleeping sickness in cattle. For this reason they have been eliminated in some parts of Africa where cattle are reared. FAMILY: Suidae, SUBORDER: Suiformes, ORDER: Artiodactyla, CLASS: Mammalia. L.K.S.

WART SNAKES, are unique in being covered with a skin that is like sandpaper to the touch. The two species are the Elephant's trunk snake *Acrochordus javanicus* and the File snake *Chersydrus granulatus*. Both are harmless and highly specialized for aquatic life. They differ from other snakes in a number of features. Both the right and the left carotid arteries are present. The left lung is

absent but the right is highly developed and extends the length of the body. Adaptations to aquatic life include a small head with nostrils facing upwards and tiny eyes. The nostrils can be closed when the snake is submerged by a flap of cartilage in the roof of the mouth. There are no enlarged belly scales and the skin consists of small almost uniform granules. The scales do not overlap each other as is usual in snakes but instead lie side by side, sometimes with skin showing between them. Each body granule is wart-like and has a central tubercle which gives the snake a granular appearance and abrasive texture. The skin of the Elephant's trunk snake is flabby, and this and the snake's girth account for its common name. Occasionally the Elephant's trunk snake grows to 6 ft (1·8 m) long, with a girth of 1 ft (30 cm). The File snake grows to only half this size and has a shorter and more compressed, rudder-like tail. Its eyes are more lateral and its nostrils more dorsal than those of the Elephant's trunk snake. Wart snakes are the only primitive snakes so well adapted to aquatic habits.

The Elephant's trunk snake occurs in Southeast Asia from Cochin-China to new Guinea and also in northeastern Australia. It is found in streams, pools, canals and estuaries. The File snake is almost entirely marine and more widespread; it is found round coasts and estuaries from Ceylon and India across southern Asia as far as the Solomon Islands.

Along the belly from throat to vent is a longitudinal row of slightly fringed scales which may act like a fin and increase the File snake's swimming ability.

Both species produce their young alive and in the Elephant's trunk snake litter sizes from 25 to 32 have been recorded whereas the File snake produces only 6–8 young at a time. The Elephant's trunk snake is sluggish, mostly nocturnal, and feeds on fish. It can remain underwater for over half an hour and swims slowly but well. On land it is practically helpless due to the fact that, lacking large belly scales, it is unable to gain much purchase on the ground. If provoked it may deliver fierce slashing sideways bites.

Wart snake skins with their non-overlapping scales are suitable for leather, which is known as karung. They are used in their native countries for drum skins but are also exported for use in ladies' shoes and handbags. In some years no less than 300,000 skins have been used. The skins can be bleached, tanned, and then crushed smooth to give a highly polished end product with a pleasant mottled appearance. FAMILY: Acrochordidae, ORDER: Squamata, CLASS: Reptilia. J.S.

WASPS, typically stinging insects, banded black and yellow, related to bees and ants.

The majority are solitary. That is, male and female come together only for mating, after which the female alone provides for her offspring. A small minority are social, which means they live in a colony of thousands of individuals, the workers, with a 'queen' that devotes most of her active life to laying eggs.

The most primitive wasps are known as *Velvet ants. The females are wingless and they look like hairy ants. They parasitize bumblebee and beetle larvae, laying their eggs in them but exercising no parental care for the offspring, in which they differ hardly at all from the parasitic Ichneumon flies. The female Spider-hunting wasp (Pompiloidea) excavates small cavities in the ground to store the paralyzed spiders she captures. She lays an egg on this inert prey then seals the entrance to the cavity scattering the disturbed soil to disguise the nest site. In the more specialized Sand wasps (Sphecoidea), a nest cell is prepared in sandy soil or decayed wood, and one or more paralyzed insects or spiders is placed in it before the egg is laid, to serve as 'living meat' for the larva when it hatches. Although most sphecoid wasps seal the nest cell after laying, some species, for example *Ammophila pubescens,* add further prey to the cell during development of the larva, thereby allowing some contact between the mother wasp and her offspring. Occasionally, several cells, with larvae at different stages of development, are maintained by one female at the same time. Under the circumstances the wasp exercises considerable abilities in determining the individual requirements of each cell in her charge, by providing the correct size or number of prey for each larva.

In the Vespoidea, which include the familiar social wasps, several specializations can be seen in which this is taken a step further, including the progressive feeding of the larva, the tending adult chewing the prey before giving it to the larva, and, with a prolongation of adult life, the daughter wasps—all workers being sterile females, as in bees and ants—have the opportunity to co-operate in a colonial establishment with their parent and sisters. But some vespoids, such as the Heath potter wasp *Eumenes coarctata* are strictly solitary, constructing small cells of mud in which paralyzed prey are stored, the egg is laid, and the cell sealed, with no social contact between generations.

In one wasp, the eumenid *Synagris spiniventris* from Africa, which normally mass-provisions the larval cell, lack of prey due to bad weather will cause the female to switch to progressive feeding—an interesting link in the evolution from the solitary to the social way of life. The more primitive social wasps (Polybiinae) are found mainly in Africa and South America where they construct complex nests of 'wasp-paper' and, rarely, mud. Several hundred wasps may be found in such

colonies, generally with several egg-laying females which are difficult to distinguish from the non-laying worker wasps. An important social wasp, of Europe and North America, is *Polistes* which constructs a nest consisting of a single comb of cells, suspended by a central pillar and without any protective envelopes. Finally, the peak of social life is reached in those wasps which are such a familiar, if unwelcome, visitor to the picnic or dining-table.

In Britain, there are seven species of social wasp including the hornet and the two most common species, *Vespula vulgaris* and *V. germanica*. These produce populous colonies, founded by a single queen and having an annual life-cycle and two female castes: a queen, the larger, egg-laying female, and workers, smaller, sterile females.

During the long winter months, queen wasps produced during the previous summer undergo a period of hibernation for which they are well supplied with fat, and with a low metabolic rate, so are able to survive their six months' sleep. Hibernation sites are generally in well insulated places such as outhouses, dense leaf-litter and crevices in bark and wood, but large aggregations of queens have also been observed hibernating in the original wasp nest.

When the queens leave their winter quarters in April they begin searching for nesting sites. These are often the disused burrows of small mammals, but almost any cavity will do, including attics, roofs and cavity walls of houses, disused beehives or even old card-board boxes. In the search for limited nest sites, fighting between competing queens often occurs, sometimes resulting in the death of one or both combatants. The nest begins as a blob of wasp-paper fixed to the roof of the nest site from which small umbrellas of paper are built. These 'envelopes', which surround the first comb of cells, insulate the nest and permit a high and constant temperature to be maintained. The initial comb is composed of 30–40 hexagonal cells in which the queen lays her eggs and the larvae develop. Throughout this period, the queen behaves in the same way as the solitary wasp which practises progressive-provisioning, but with the emergence of the first daughter wasps—the workers—the queen becomes more restricted to egg-laying activities, and soon ceases to leave the nest as the workers take over foraging duties.

The larvae are fed on protein which is collected in the form of insect prey (including flies, caterpillars and bees), carrion and even meat and fish from shops and markets. When the prey is caught the wasp normally kills it by biting it in the neck—the sting is used principally for defence. The wasp then cuts off the head, legs and wings before carrying the carcass back to the colony. The adults feed themselves on carbohydrate, such as nectar, honey-dew of aphids and other sources such as jam. This is stored in the wasp's crop and, on the return to the colony, is distributed to the adult occupants.

Nest building is one of the major duties performed by the workers and involves the collection of massive quantities of chewed-up wood fibres—scraped from fences, posts and dead trees. The wood is mixed with saliva to form a thick paste which is drawn through the mandibles and applied to the nest in a strip. When the load of pulp is used up, the completed strip is allowed to dry—a process essentially similar to the paper-making techniques of man. Each strip represents a single load and the different colours illustrate the source of wood pulp.

The typical mature wasp nest has the size and shape of a football—a sphere representing the most economical shape for building—although the site can impose severe restrictions on nest construction and influence its ultimate shape and size. As development proceeds, more combs are added below the original queen-built comb, and existing combs widened. Each comb is supported by a large number of stout pillars made of wasp-paper, and separated from each other to afford sufficient space for adult wasps to crawl between them. By the end of

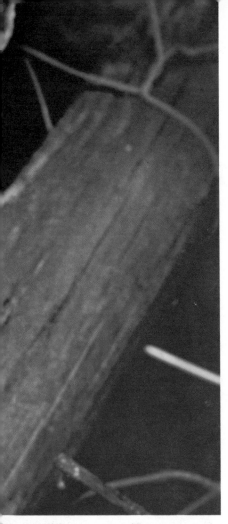

Workers of Common wasp of Europe on outside of nest.

Part of comb in nests of Common wasp of Europe. In the open cells an egg can be seen near the base of each.

Part of comb of Common wasp with larvae in some of the cells. The cells closed at the top contain pupae.

the season, most nests have 8-9 combs. Surrounding the combs, the original envelopes of the embryo nest are replaced by a thick, cellular wall with excellent insulation properties. The temperature in wasp nests is remarkably constant, especially in mature colonies with their thick walls and large populations. Heat is produced through the activity of adults and larvae, and if the temperature rises above the optimum, wasps in the nest entrance fan vigorously with their wings to produce a stream of cooling air. If the temperature continues to rise, water is brought to the nest and allowed to evaporate on the combs and walls.

Building accounts for much of the activity of workers until early August, when colonies of 10,000 cells or more can be found. As each cell is completed or vacated by an emerging adult, the queen lays an egg in it. The queen, whose ovaries enlarge so that the abdomen is almost entirely filled with eggs, attains an oviposition rate of 300 eggs per day at the height of the season.

With the recruitment of emerging workers to the population, the number of adults increases, reaching a peak towards the end of August of up to 5,000. By the end of the season, colonies produce up to 40,000 workers. All cells in a colony are used at least once and about 70 per cent of them used to produce a second generation by the end of the season. The re-use of cells makes possible the high rate of productivity in the wasp colony.

The interrelationships between adults and larvae, and among the adults, help to explain some of the mysteries of colonial life, and the social integration of its members. When workers feed the larvae on chewed-up prey, the larvae often produce a drop of 'saliva' which is swallowed by the tending adult, an exchange called trophallaxis. Larvae also secrete this watery-looking fluid when gently nipped by an adult which is not supplying food. This saliva is possibly a method of maintaining water balance, whereby excess water is 'excreted' through salivary glands. But there is another important role served by this secretion. Some of the protein given to the larvae is converted into sugars which are then passed on to the adults in the saliva. The larvae can therefore be considered as miniature food-converting factories which act as reservoirs of energy-providing food. It has been noted that during weather unsuitable for foraging the larvae are 'milked' by the workers until a visible shrinking occurs. The saliva also acts as a dietary supplement for the newly emerged wasps and the nest-bound queen, and forms the major part of the diet of males. The saliva also contains break-down products of protein digestion—amino acids, and enzymes necessary for protein digestion. It is interesting to note that the sugar and protein content of wasp larval saliva is in the same proportions as those found in human milk.

The exchange and circulation of food between adults and larvae and among adults can be compared to the circulatory system of man which is used to carry oxygenated blood, food supplies and hormone messages to all parts of the body. The transfer of food in social wasps involves the transmission of social signals, and with the complicated rituals involved, serves to establish a social order in the community. This is particularly true of the more primitive social wasps such as *Polistes*. During food transfer between adults, one wasp, the donor, assumes a subordinate attitude with its head tilted to one side while the acceptor strokes the mouth parts of the donor with its antennae until the

Cell in comb opened to show wasp pupa inside.

Queen Tree wasp at entrance to nest.

Opposite: a small colony of Tree wasps on their nest, on the island of Curacao, off the coast of Venezuela.

Queen wasp *Polistes* of North America. *Polistes* wasps are remarkable for their very narrow waist.

donor responds by regurgitating food from its crop. The transfer of food from submissive workers to dominant individuals provides the means of social co-operation; the submissive worker offers food to the wasp immediately above it in the dominance scale which in turn offers food to its immediate superior. Thus, a social hierarchy is established that permits the most economical organization of the available workers without constant squabbling for the food brought into the colony. It is interesting to note that males, because of their longer antennae, are unable to stimulate workers to regurgitate food and have to rely on larval saliva, or 'stealing' food during the trophallactic transfer between two workers.

Within the colony dead larvae and adults accumulate at the bottom of the nest cavity, and the larvae of several species of hoverflies

develop in this refuse. The female flies, which have body markings and colouration similar to the wasps, are able to enter colonies unmolested and lay their eggs. The parasite *Metoecus paradoxus* is another insect encountered in wasp colonies. The adult parasite lays eggs on or near flower heads and the larvae wait for passing wasps which they use to transport them to the colony. *M. paradoxus* attacks the wasp larvae. After a larva has spun its pupal cocoon it is devoured. The parasite is found in very small numbers and undoubtedly plays an insignificant part in controlling wasp populations. Other foreign insects, including wasps of the same species but from different colonies, rarely gain access to a wasp colony due to the efforts of the guard wasps, which can be seen on the alert just inside the entrance tunnel to the colony.

The guards, which are few in number, are on duty day and night, but in the case of a general emergency, such as an attack by a badger, or unprepared and unwise entomologist, the majority of mature adult workers will be mobilized for the defence of the colony. Wasps, though normally not aggressive, will vigorously defend their colony. There is another wasp, *Vespula austriaca,* which enters the nests of some wasps with impunity and parasitizes the colony by killing the original queen and laying eggs in the queen cells. The developing larvae of the usurper are tended by the workers of the original queen and emerge as queens. This parasitic or 'cuckoo' wasp has no worker caste of its own.

When the colony is approaching its peak, in early August, male pupae are found. Males are produced from unfertilized eggs and their sporadic distribution in the combs and low number suggests that the queen, at the peak of her egg-laying activity, lays eggs that fail to be fertilized. Some workers develop ovaries and they also contribute to male production, particularly in the later stages of colony development. At the time of male pupal production, the nest building activities of the workers undergo a profound change: they begin to construct the queen cells. Unlike the primitive social wasps, *Vespula* species have specialized queen cells, similar in shape and length to worker cells, but 30 per cent wider. Queen cell construction begins in early August and continues until the end of September with up to 4,000 cells constructed.

Queen brood production coincides with the most favourable period during colony development; food resources are more plentiful in August and September, with a large number of wasps available for foraging due to the recruitment of new workers and the decrease in nest building activities. Also, the size of workers, which increases throughout the season allied to a decrease in the wing loading factor (weight/wing length), permit a greatly increased weight of food per forager to be brought back to the colony. The large number of workers per colony throughout the queen rearing period also permits a more efficient division of labour with the segregation of a 'brood-nurse' force. The increase in the number of workers reduces the number of larvae each worker has to tend, from eight larvae per worker to one. This reduction in the larva/worker ratio is perhaps the most significant change associated with queen rearing. With better attention from more workers, coupled with increased food intake at optimum nest temperatures, the female larvae in the larger cells develop into queens.

When the queens emerge they spend some time in the colony before departure. Males leave the colony during this period and mating occurs around the nest entrance and elsewhere—probably near flower heads, where males and queens can often be seen feeding in the early autumn. With the dispersal of the young queens, and death or physiological disintegration of the old foundress queen, the social organization of the colony declines. Larvae fail to be fed or are ejected from the nest, foraging activities are reduced, and many workers form independent aggregations away from the original colony. These aggregations often construct abortive nests, but no cells are built, despite the development of the ovaries of these workers. Eventually the frosts of autumn overcome the few remaining workers and males, leaving the new queens to find places for their winter sleep, to continue the species in the forthcoming season. ORDER: Hymenoptera, CLASS: Insecta, PHYLUM: Arthropoda.

J.P.S.

WASP STINGS. The stings of wasps and bees are modified ovipositors. The difference between the two is that a wasp's sting can be withdrawn but that of a bee is barbed like a harpoon so that when, after stinging, the bee tries to tug itself clear the sting and poison glands are torn out of its body and the bee dies. In the solitary wasps the sting is used to paralyze prey but in social species the workers use their stings for defence. The venom of wasps contains a mixture of histamine, the enzyme hyaluronidase and other toxic substances. Hyaluronidase breaks down the cement that binds the body cells together, so speeding the diffusion of the venom, and histamine causes the weal, inflammation and itching that is characteristic of wasp, bee and nettle stings. Bee venom does not contain histamine but an enzyme present causes the liberation of histamine by the victim's own tissues.

WATER BALANCE. Water accounts for about 80% of the composition of living cells and a relatively constant water content of this order of magnitude must be maintained if the biochemical functions of the protoplasm are to be performed.

In multicellular animals the extra-cellular fluid volume (blood and interstitial fluid) must also be maintained to ensure circulatory function. Consequently mechanisms controlling water content are normally present at two levels: regulating cell fluid volume and regulating extra-cellular fluid volume.

Cellular water balance. The total concentration of the cells of most animals is similar to that of the fluid surrounding them but special steps to prevent the osmotic movement of water are required. This can be explained by considering what happens when an artificial cell, composed of organic molecules enclosed by a membrane permeable to ions but not to the organic compounds, is placed in an isotonic salt solution. Sodium and chloride ions tend to diffuse in down the concentration gradient. Ionic balance will be reached when

$$\frac{Na_i}{Na_o} = \frac{Cl_o}{Cl_i}$$

Where Na_i and Cl_i are the sodium and chloride concentration inside the cell and Na_o and Cl_o are the concentrations outside. However, since organic compounds are also present in the artificial cell the osmotic concentration inside will exceed that in the medium even when ionic equilibrium has been reached and water will continue to enter the cell under the influence of the osmotic gradient.

Theoretically a number of solutions are available to a living cell to prevent net water intake. 1 The water can be physically extruded as fast as it enters; 2 the cell wall can be made sufficiently strong to resist an internal hydrostatic pressure large enough to counteract the difference in osmotic pressure between cell and medium; and 3 metabolic processes may be used to create an ion imbalance across the cell membrane so that the osmotic pressure inside and out can be matched. It is this last method which is the prime one used by animal cells though some marine and all freshwater protozoans extrude water by means of contractile vacuoles and many plant cells are capable of supporting large internal hydrostatic pressures by virtue of their cellulose cell walls.

The ionic regulatory mechanism is based on the universal ability of animal cells to extrude sodium. In essence it operates as follows. Sodium ions are secreted from the cells by the cell membrane as fast as they enter. The extrusion of a positively charged ion in this way is balanced by the uptake of potassium ions into the cell. The intercellular potassium concentration maintained by this process is greatly in excess of that in the extra-cellular media and consequently there is a tendency for potassium to diffuse out down its concentration gradient. Loss of potassium ions is prevented by the development of a potential difference across the cell membrane (outside positive to inside) of sufficient magnitude to balance the tendency for potassium to escape. This potential may be produced in one of two ways: by the action of an electrogenic sodium extrusion mechanism or by the separation of charge when potassium ions escape from the cell unaccompanied by the organic anions with which they are associated. The relative roles of these two mechanisms in creating the membrane potential is still subject to considerable discussion but irrespective of how it is created the membrane potential not only restricts the net loss of potassium from the cell but also controls the distribution of chloride ions across the cell membrane so that

$$E = RT\ln\frac{(Cl_o)}{(Cl_i)}$$

where R is the gas constant, T the absolute temperature, E is membrane potential in volts) and (Cl_i) and (Cl_o) are the internal and external chloride concentrations.

As a result of the action of the sodium pump, therefore, restraints are placed on the net diffusion of both sodium and chloride ions and a dynamic balance is maintained between the internal and external osmotic concentrations. Interference with the action of the sodium extrusion mechanism disturbs this osmotic balance and results in an increase in cell water content. For example, when vertebrate red blood cells are cooled the action of the sodium extrusion mechanism is slowed. The sodium content of the cells rises, the potassium content falls and the cell volume increases. When the cells are rewarmed to 98·6°F (37°C) in the presence of a metabolite these processes are reversed and the cells replace the lost potassium and lose the excess sodium and water.

Most marine invertebrates have cells and body fluids with the same osmotic concentration as seawater. About one-third of the osmotic concentration of the cells of species such as the Shore crab (*Carcinus*) are accounted for by potassium and other inorganic ions; the remainder is largely due to free amino acids. If the blood concentration varies when the concentration of the medium is charged as happens in many forms living in brackish water (see osmoregulation) a corresponding adjustment is required in cell osmotic concentration to prevent water shifts between blood and cells. This is achieved by a reduction in both the inorganic ion and free amino acid concentration of the cells when the blood concentration is reduced. Conversely increase of both components occurs on a rise in blood concentration. As a result of these changes the variation in water content of the cells is limited to a few percent over a wide range of blood concentration.

Extra-cellular volume regulation. In species which lack wide powers of regulating cell osmotic pressure, water is distributed between the intra- and extra-cellular compartments according to their respective solute concentrations. Increase in the concentration of the extra-cellular fluids draws water from the cells and decrease in extracellular concentration results in cellular swelling. The maintenance of the volume of the various fluid compartments is thus dependent on the constancy of the blood concentration and hence on regulation of the Na and Cl input and output from the body since these are the principal ions in the blood.

Variation of the water content of the body by dehydration or hydration without a change in blood solutes tends to cause shrinking or swelling, respectively, of both cellular and extra-cellular compartments, whilst uptake of saline of the same concentration as the blood or loss of blood by haemorrhage affects the blood volume independently of cell volume. In order to regulate both total water content of the body and its relative distribution between cellular and extra-cellular compartments it is, therefore, necessary that an animal should be able to monitor both its blood concentration and volume. When changes occur in either factor appropriate alterations in the rate of ion or water input and output must be made to restore the normal situation.

The blood monitoring systems are best known in mammals. Sensors which detect variations in the concentration of the blood are present in the hypothalamus of the brain. Increase in the concentration of the blood reaching the receptor cells results in the release of the antidiuretic hormone (ADH) from the ends of the nerve axons in the pituitary gland. ADH then passes in the blood to the kidney where it acts to decrease the volume and increase the concentration of urine excreted (see excretion). Coupled with the response to thirst which arises (in man) when the body has been dehydrated by 0·5–1% this action tends to restore the blood concentration to normal. Dilution of the blood below the normal level results in a decreased release of ADH by the pituitary and the kidney then produces a copious flow of more dilute urine. Complete cessation of ADH output, as occurs in diabetes insipidus, causes urine volume in man to rise to $17\frac{1}{2}$–35 pt (10–20 lt) a day instead of the normal $1\frac{3}{4}$ pt (1·5 lt).

Regulation of the sodium loss rate from the body is independent of the ADH control of water output. Sodium loss is governed by hormones, particularly aldosterone, originating from the cortex of the adrenal glands. Increase in the amount of aldosterone in the blood supply to the kidneys decreases the rate of sodium loss in the urine. Conversely, complete absence of aldosterone results in an increase in the sodium loss in the urine to 10% of the initial filtrate instead of 1–2% as normal.

The adrenal cortex is not innervated but the concentration of sodium in the blood directly affects the rate of aldosterone production. Other factors known to increase the release of aldosterone are raised blood potassium, the adrenocorticotrophic hormone (ACTH) which is released from the pituitary under the influence of the corticotrophic releasing factor (CRF) produced in the hypothalamus and conveyed to the pituitary gland in the blood and another hormone, angiotensin, formed by interaction of renin from the kidney with a blood protein.

Detection of blood volume changes is mediated by stretch receptors in the heart and other parts of the central circulation. Abnormal stretching of the walls of the auricles such as might arise if the volume of the circulatory blood was larger than normal initiates responses in the vagus nerve receptors. Both ADH and aldosterone released into the blood decline after stimulus of the cardiac stretch receptors, thus permitting an increase in the rate of loss of water and sodium from the blood. In cases of severe haemorrhage and associated shock all the physiological stops are pulled out to preserve water and salt; kidney filtration is decreased, ADH limits renal water output further, whilst ACTH and angiotensin cause aldosterone release from the adrenal glands which in turn conserves sodium.

Water balance in relation to environment. The nature of the water balance problem encountered by animals (over or under hydration, sodium excess or lack) varies with the environment inhabited.

Most marine invertebrates have blood which has a total concentration similar to that of the medium (isosmotic) and so have no overt problem in maintaining water balance. Forms which live in dilute media and which maintain the blood at a higher concentration than that of the medium (hypertonic) tend to gain water by osmosis whilst marine teleost fishes, prawns, some mysids and isopods, which regulate the blood concentration at a lower level than seawater (hypotonic), lose water by osmosis to the medium.

Hypertonic regulators eliminate excess water by the copius production of urine and the volume of urine is usually proportional to the gradient maintained between blood and media over a wide range of salinities.

During the course of their evolution brackish and freshwater animals have decreased the permeability of their body surface to minimize the rate of water entry and loss of salt. Thus the permeability of the surface to water in the marine crab *Macropipus (Portunus) depurator* is three times greater than that of *Carcinus* which can live in brackish water, whilst the freshwater crayfish *Austropotamobius* is more than three times less permeable than *Carcinus*. Most freshwater species of invertebrates and all vertebrates conserve salt by the production of urine more dilute than the blood. Freshwater invertebrates, fishes and amphibians replace salt loss by actively taking up sodium and chloride ions from the media across the body surface.

Marine species, the blood of which is less concentrated than seawater, drink the medium to replace water lost by osmosis and in the urine. Salt and water are taken up from the gut and the excess salt is secreted out across the gills. Air-breathing forms, such as marine reptiles, birds and mammals, have highly impermeable body surfaces and lose little water by osmosis. Water loss does occur in the respired air, however. Birds and reptiles drink the media to replace this loss and eliminate excess salt by means of nasal and orbital glands respectively. Marine mammals normally depend on their food for their water intake and their kidneys remove excess salt by forming urine more concentrated than the blood. They do not usually drink seawater.

Some of the most interesting responses to the problem of water balance maintenance are found in terrestrial species. Three main categories are involved: 1 tolerance of water loss; 2 behavioural responses to restrict loss;

and 3 structural and physiological devices to restrict water loss.

Tolerance of water loss. In general, terrestrial animals are more tolerant of water loss than aquatic forms and those which live in regions where they are liable to suffer from lack of water tend to be particularly tolerant. Various species of Amphibia illustrate this point; toads from dry habitats, for example, survive a larger degree of water loss than aquatic frogs.

Species	% body water loss required to kill	Habitat of adult
Scaphiopus holbrookii	60·2	Dry terrestrial
Bufo terrestris	54·9	Terrestrial
Rana pipiens	44·9	Semi-aquatic
Rana grylio	38	Aquatic

The extraordinary complexity of the sensory and hormonal systems involved in the regulation of the water and salt balance in mammals.

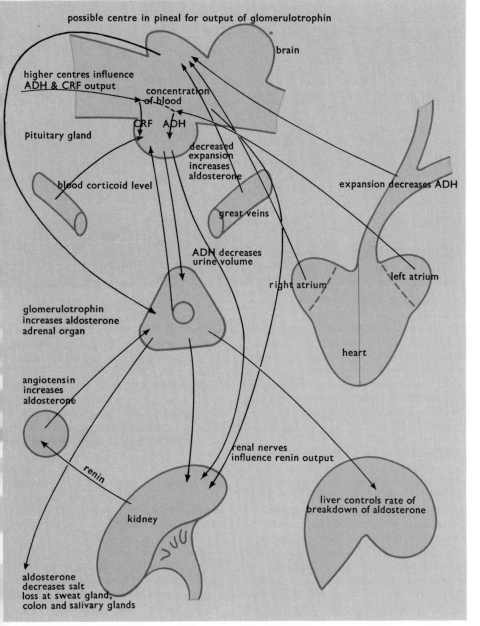

possible centre in pineal for output of glomerulotrophin

brain

higher centres influence ADH & CRF output

concentration of blood

CRF ADH

pituitary gland

decreased expansion increases aldosterone

expansion decreases ADH

blood corticoid level

great veins

ADH decreases urine volume

right atrium

left atrium

glomerulotrophin increases aldosterone adrenal organ

heart

angiotensin increases aldosterone

renal nerves influence renin output

renin

liver controls rate of breakdown of aldosterone

kidney

aldosterone decreases salt loss at sweat gland, colon and salivary glands

Other animals which tolerate extensive water loss include earthworms, such as *Lumbricus*, and many slugs and snails. *Lumbricus* will survive loss of 70% of its water, but the most spectacular tolerance of water loss is that shown by the larvae of an African midge, *Polypedilium vanderplankii*. The midge lays its eggs in small temporary pools which are liable to dry out. If this happens before the larvae complete their development they may suffer total dehydration and pass into a state of suspended animation. However, when put into water they will rehydrate and resume normal activity.

Behavioural responses. The behaviour of many terrestrial forms aids the restriction of water loss. Woodlice display hygrokinetic responses which tend to keep them in areas of high humidity by day. Terrestrial snails become inactive in dry weather, remaining in the shell and sealing the entrance with a secreted epiphragma to restrict water loss, whilst earthworms, such as *Lumbricus* and *Eutyphaesus*, burrow downwards when the upper layers of soil dry out. Many of the smaller animals from desert and semi-arid regions are crepuscular or nocturnal and spend the day in humid burrows emerging only when the risk of rapid evaporative water loss lessens.

One of the features developed by terrestrial species of crab is the ability to select the medium with a salinity that will restore their blood volume and concentration to normal after they have suffered desiccation or salt loss. A range of behaviour exists from that shown by the Rocky-shore crab *Pachygrapsus*, which always prefers seawater when given a choice of media, to the more fully terrestrial *Coenobita perlatus*, which selects the most appropriate media. Another factor which contributes to the ability of *Coenobita* to remain out of water for extended periods is that it fills the snail shell which it carries, like other Hermit crabs, with brackish water. This water comes into osmotic equilibrium with the blood and can therefore be regarded as an extension of the haemolymph.

Various insects, including the Fruit fly *Drosophila* select a low humidity when they are hydrated and a high humidity after partial desiccation. Behavioural responses can therefore be altered by the physiological state.

Structural and physiological mechanisms restricting water loss. Structural modifications render the skin less permeable to water in animal groups which are primarily terrestrial by comparison with those which are mainly aquatic or semi-terrestrial. Thus the evaporative loss rate from reptiles is only about $\frac{1}{40}$ of that of amphibians of comparable size and similarly the loss through the cuticle of insects is very much lower than that from crustaceans. The principal permeability barrier to water in the insect cuticle lies in the epi-cuticle and there is evidence that impermeability is largely dependent on the integrity of an organized monolayer of grease or wax molecules no more than 0·0001–0·0003 mm thick. Removal of this layer increases water loss up to 100–300 times. Some mites and insects, such as the Flour beetle *Tenebrio* and flea, can compensate for such slow rate of evaporation as occurs by taking up water from humid air even when no liquid water is present.

One of the principal physiological means adopted by terrestrial animals to conserve water is the modification of the form of the nitrogenous excretory products. The major nitrogenous waste of aquatic animals is ammonia but this highly toxic substance requires considerable volumes of water for its removal. As an alternative terrestrial forms excrete mainly the less toxic compounds urea and uric acid which can be eliminated from the body with less associated water loss.

Uric acid, the main nitrogenous excretory product of snails, insects, most reptiles and birds, is highly insoluble and so can be eliminated in the form of a sludge with a minimal water loss. Urea, although more soluble, can be highly concentrated in the urine of mammals.

Respiratory water loss forms an important part of the total water loss in warm-blooded forms with high metabolic rates, such as birds and mammals. Birds, particularly small birds, must normally remain relatively close to a source of water. However, a novel feature found in some hummingbirds is the ability to drop the metabolic rate and become 'cold-blooded' at night and, by thus reducing the respiratory rate, conserve both water and metabolites.

Desert rodents such as *Dipodomys* and *Psammomys* are among the few vertebrates which do not require to drink to replace water loss. Both produce very highly concentrated urine and so can eliminate waste nitrogen with minimal water loss. They also remain in humid burrows by day thus limiting respiratory loss. These two factors combined keep the total water losses at a level equal to the water gained on metabolization of the food. Thus, provided they can eat, they remain in water balance.

The two principal factors which differentiate camels from most mammals and which contribute largely to their legendary ability to survive without drinking are the tolerance of changes in body temperature and the tolerance of variation in body water content. When fully hydrated a camel sweats if its temperature is raised, but when short of water sweating is restricted and a rise of body temperature of up to 49°F (9·4°C) is tolerated. Furthermore, the animals open the skin capillaries and lower body temperature in the early morning and, during the day, the thick coat of fur insulates the body and slows the rise in body temperature in the sun. Loss of body water equivalent to $\frac{1}{3}$ of the body weight is tolerated and the camel, being a rapid drinker, can replace water loss very rapidly when given the chance. One camel after loss of 181 pts (103 lt) took in this amount in ten minutes!

It is, of course, an old wives' tale that the camel stores water in its hump, but water storage is not unknown even amongst vertebrates. Many Amphibia do this, perhaps the best example being the toad *Bufo cognatus* which lives in arid and semi-arid regions of Mexico. When water is available *Bufo* produces a copious supply of dilute urine which

Female Great diving beetle *Dytiscus marginalis*.

is stored in the exceptionally large bladder (up to 30% of body weight when full). During periods of water shortage the bladder wall can be rendered semi-permeable and water is taken back into the body fluids by osmosis until the limit is reached when blood and urine are isosmotic. See also osmoregulation.   A.P.M.L.

WATER BEETLES. Several beetle families have aquatic members but the two most important are the Dytiscidae and the Hydrophilidae, both widely distributed in the freshwaters of the world. The dytiscids are mainly predators, they swim strongly with synchronous oar-like movements of the hindlegs, and catch small aquatic invertebrates as food. The largest species, of the genus *Dytiscus,* will even attack small fish. The larvae of this family are also fierce predators with hollow needle-like jaws that pierce the prey and act

as ducts through which digestive juices are passed into the prey, and through which the liquified contents of the prey are sucked into the gut.

The adult hydrophilids are in the main herbivorous, although a few of the larger forms are predators. They are generally more feeble swimmers than the dytiscids and use the hindlegs alternately. A few of the smaller species are found in salt marshes and even in rock pools on the seashore. The larvae of hydrophilids are carnivorous and deal with their prey in a similar way to the dytiscid larvae. FAMILIES: Dytiscidae, Hydrophilidae, ORDER: Coleoptera, CLASS: Insecta, PHYLUM: Arthropoda.

WATERBOATMEN, aquatic bugs of two distinct families. Due to the confusion of common names given to the two families it is best if the carnivorous and predatory Notonectidae are known as *backswimmers, although they are also called waterboatmen, and the plant feeding Corixidae are called waterboatmen, although they are often called Lesser waterboatmen to distinguish them. The Corixidae tend to be smaller than the Notonectidae and the common British species *Corixa punctata* is only ½ in (12–13 mm) long.

The Corixidae have been found to resemble the colour of the floor of ponds in which they live. E. J. Popham noticed that immature corixids or young adults retain the colour of their background after moulting and that a pale floor inhibited the formation of dark pigment in their bodies. Popham also discovered that corixids, if given a choice, generally came to rest on a background with which they merged. In a series of experiments, Popham showed the advantage of this camouflage. In a laboratory experiment small fish (rudd) destroyed about three times the number of corixids that were not well camouflaged compared with those which were. Popham also observed that the proportion of corixids living in fish-less ponds that matched their background significantly increased if minnows were then introduced. FAMILIES: Notonectidae, Corixidae, ORDER: Hemiptera. CLASS: Insecta, PHYLUM: Arthropoda.   M.J.P.

WATERBUCK, large African antelope related to the reedbuck but larger, with more spreading horns, and lacking the bare patch below the ear. All of the antelope which are loosely described as waterbuck belong to the genus *Kobus,* but the five species involved fall into three subgenera: *Kobus* for the true waterbuck, *Adenota* for the kob and puku, and *Hydrotragus* for the lechwe. Like reedbuck, in waterbuck only the males have horns.

The true waterbuck all belong to one species *K. ellipsiprymnus.* This is the largest species in the genus, 48–53 in (120–133 cm) high and weighing 475 lb (216 kg). There are no inguinal glands (in the groin), unlike the other species, and the face glands are also absent. The coat is long and wiry, forming a mane on the neck. The general colour is brownish, and there is a white ring or patch on the rump. The horns are long, simply divergent and forwardly concave—like very elongated reedbuck horns. Waterbuck are heavily built, adult males developing a thick neck and haunches.

For a long time waterbuck with a white ring round the buttocks, and those with a white buttock patch, were considered to be distinct species, called respectively the Common waterbuck *K. ellipsiprymnus* and the Northern, Defassa or Singsing waterbuck *K. defassa.* In general the former type, the ring-type, occupies the southern and eastern parts of the range (northeast, eastern and

northern Transvaal, southern Botswana, north to Caprivi, southern Barotseland, the Luangwa valley, East Africa east of the Rift valley, as far north as the Juba and Webi Shebeli rivers in Somalia); while the latter, the patch-type, lives in the western areas (Angola, western Zambia, the Okavango district, Angola, southern Gabon, northeastern Zambia. East Africa west of the Rift valley,

the Sudan north to the Atbara river, Lake Chad, west to Senegal). More recently it has become apparent that the two forms are only geographic variants of one and the same species. While in Zambia they are separated by the Muchinga escarpment and by tracts of unsuitable country, in the Rift valley there are intermediates between the two: in the Nairobi National Park, for example, every

Waterboatman *Notonecta glauca* hanging from the surface film.

type between the ring and the patch is found.

Waterbuck are inhabitants of savannah. While sometimes living in fairly arid country, they normally keep down by the banks of rivers, spending the night in the thick riverine cover, and emerging at 8–10 am onto the grassland where they remain all day, going back to the river at dusk. Where they are heavily hunted, for example in Somalia, the rhythm is reversed, and waterbuck have become more or less nocturnal. Each male has a territory, of $\frac{1}{4}$–1 sq mile (0·7–2·7 sq km) in extent. Its boundaries are stable and well-marked on the river side, but inland the areas are less fiercely contested. The male's daily movement to and from the river is confined within his territory. The length of frontage on the river is taken as an indication of rank among the males. A proportion of males have no territory, but belong to a peripheral herd. They are usually young males, less than two and a half years old and without the muscular shoulders of the adults.

At night, the females keep in groups of three or four with their young but by day they gather in herds of up to 30 on their home ranges. These home ranges are of approximately the same extent as the males' territories, but there is free movement, and the females, which more or less 'belong' to one male, may constantly stray into another male's territory. When this happens, their own male tries to herd them, running and standing in front of them with his head up and forefeet together. He may also make butting motions as he runs, or chase the females. When a group of females is moving around in a male's territory, grazing towards the edge of it, the neighbouring male moves to the boundary, ready to herd them as soon as they enter his territory. Females with young emerge from the cover later, and go back earlier in the day; the calf itself begins to come out after three or four weeks. Male calves are chased out of the territory, into the peripheral herd, at puberty.

When a female is in oestrus, she grazes for a longer time, and moves a greater distance, visiting other males. Normally a male greets a female by smelling and licking her vulva and tail. He then draws back his mouth in the 'flehmen' chemoreception gesture, and performs the 'laufschlag' (leg-beat) motion, after which he mounts the female but without erection. The greeting ceremony is often restricted to a smelling of the vulva, after which the male begins to graze, and makes contact with other females. When the female is in oestrus, the same greeting ritual obtains, but there is much rubbing of the female with the face, and the base of the horns; often the male puts his horns on either side of the female's rump and

Male waterbuck of the type known as defassa.

Young male waterbuck with white ring round buttocks, the Common waterbuck.

pushes slightly. After this act, the male's penis erects and he rests his head on the female's back, pressing downward. There is a series of laufschlag and mounting, and eventually copulation is achieved. The sequence may be gone through more than once during a single day with the same couple, but omitting some of the preliminaries.

Both sexes of waterbuck have a depression on the forehead and in this is a foramen carrying a branch of the trigeminal nerve. Kiley-Worthington suggests that the rubbing sequence may be a stimulation of this nerve.

The second subgenus *Adenota* contains animals with a short coat and no mane. The horns are rather short, somewhat lyrate, and face-glands and inguinal glands are present.

The kob *K. kob* is found from southwestern Kenya through the savannah zone west to Senegal and on the Bijagos islands. A male kob stands 34–36 in high (85–90 cm) and weighs 200–220 lb (90–100 kg); a female weighs only 137–145 lb (62–66 kg). The colour varies geographically from reddish orange to nearly black, with white round the eye and base of the ears. There is a black line down the front of the forelegs, and the muzzle, lips, underside, insides of the thighs and a band above the hoofs are white. The smaller puku *K. vardoni* is found in the Chobe district, eastern Caprivi, the Kwango region, Zambia, Central Malawi, southern Tanzania and part of Katanga. It stands 32–35 in (80–88 cm) high. The male weighs 150–170 lb (68–77 kg) and the fe-

male 125–140 lb (57–64 kg). The puku has no black on the forelegs, no white hoof-band, and a narrower white eye-ring. The coat is longer and rougher and the inguinal glands open forwards instead of backwards as in the kob.

The behaviour of the Uganda kob *K. k. thomasi* is well-known from the study by Buechner, which stands as a classic in bovid behaviour. Within the Toro Game Reserve, where 15,000 kob occupy an area of 158 sq miles (425 sq km), there are 13 territorial breeding grounds, each situated on a ridge or knoll with good grazing, good visibility and watering places. Within each breeding ground are an inner area where the stronger, more dominant males have their territories, and an outer area where others have territories. Those males who cannot obtain territories live in a bachelor band on the periphery. The inner area, 200 yd (183 m) across, has 12–15 territories, usually with common boundaries but not always. Each male's activity is concentrated on the centre of his territory, where the grass is closely cropped and the ground heavily trampled. The outer area, 1–200 yd (91–183 m) wide all round, will have as many as 30 territories. A territory may change hands, by a male galloping in from the periphery, engaging one of the incumbents in combat, and wresting the territory from him. The challenger seems always to head for one particular territory, perhaps one that he has possessed before. Incumbents sometimes have to leave their territories to drink, and another male may have taken possession by the time the original one has returned. Nonetheless, the rights of occupancy seem very strong; a challenger rarely ousts an incumbent, and is usually forced to beat a hasty retreat through the surrounding territories, being chased or threatened in turn by each of the occupants. Buechner captured a number of males and released them 2 miles (3·2 km) from their areas and one-third of them returned to their old territories.

Males display to one another at the edge of their territories, walking towards the boundaries with lowered ears and making feints with their horns. They display to females, who wander through the territories, by prancing. Often this display carries a male outside his boundaries, and he is then chased back again by his neighbour. Oestrus in females lasts for a day only and when it is over the female rejoins the herd on the periphery of the breeding-ground. Breeding occurs all year.

Puku have territories up to 20 times the size of those of the kob, and somewhat less rigid; neighbouring males often wander into a territory the owner of which has gone to water. Because of their larger size, the puku's territories are not close-cropped in the centre. The puku's display also differs. There is no laying back of the ears, but instead the tail is rapidly wagged, and males may chase each other as they display. But the general pattern of territorial breeding males, a bachelor band of males always contesting for territories, and females which wander through the territorial ground when in oestrus, being covered by a number of males, is the same.

The third and last subgenus, *Hydrotragus*, contains two species which are both known as lechwe. They have a coarse, long coat like true waterbuck, but no mane and long slender lyrate horns with, however, a double curve, up and then back, somewhat gazelle-like. There are no face-glands, but rudimentary inguinal glands. The Nile lechwe or Mrs Gray's waterbuck *K. megaceros* has

horns with a longer, more pronounced backward curve. The adult male is nearly black with a large white patch in front of the withers (usually), joined via a white line up the back of the neck to a pair of white eye-rings. The chin, lips, belly, inner surfaces of hindlegs, and a hoofring are also white. Females and young are yellow-brown, with white on the head, but not on the neck or shoulders. Both sexes are 35–40 in (88–102 cm) high. This species lives in the swamps of the Nile, Bahr-el-Ghazal and Sobat, and between the Baro and Ghilo rivers in adjacent parts of Ethiopia. Little is known of its habits or social organization. Herds are said, however, to contain about equal proportions of males and females.

The true lechwe *K. leche* is found from northern Botswana, north of Lake Ngami, to eastern Angola, the upper Zambesi, Kafue, Chambeshi and Luapula rivers, and the southeastern Congo to 6°S. It is 40 in (1 m) high, with long coarse hair. The horns are shorter, and not swept back so far. The white eye-ring is present but not the white shoulder- and neck-markings. Females are more or less reddish coloured with white below. In the males the colouration differs in three very well-defined subspecies: (1) Red lechwe *K. l. leche*, from the upper Zambesi and its tributaries; light reddish-tawny with a black line on the fronts of the forelegs and hindshanks. A big race; males weigh 220–260 lb (100–120 kg). (2) Kafue Flats lechwe *K. l. kafuensis*, from the swamps of the middle Kafue; equally large but with longer horns, up to 32 in (80 cm) long, and the black line on the forelegs expanding onto the shoulder to form a conspicuous patch. (3) Black lechwe *K. l. smithemani*, from Lake Bangweulu and Lake Mweru into the Congo; smaller, only 150–200 lb (68–90 kg), the size of the females of other races; black covers the whole head, upperparts, and fronts of limbs.

Lechwe are semi-aquatic, the most water-loving of all antelopes except the sitatunga. They live on the water margins and in the shallows. The sexes tend to live in separate herds for most of the year. The rainy season extends from November to March, flooding the marshes around the rivers and lakes where lechwe make their homes. Towards the end of the rains, when the floods are at their height, lechwe are confined to a very narrow belt on either side of the water, and they have to feed mainly on dry land grasses, and their condition becomes poor. In June and July the floods recede, and hundreds of square miles of fresh new grass are uncovered, and the lechwe become sleek and fat.

The rut takes place mainly from late October till early January. The bucks make a staccato grunting challenge, audible $\frac{1}{4}$ mile (400 m) away, and fight very viciously,

sometimes until one is killed. Harems are gathered, but apparently there are no territories as such. 40% of one-year-old does breed, as against 95% of older does. However, females are not quite full-sized until three years. Males may breed at three years, but do not reach full size until four, when the horns reach their maximum size and the leg-stripe develops. Gestation lasts seven to eight months and most calves are dropped from mid-July to late August, and remain hidden in tall grass, often on high ground surrounded by flood patches, for three or four weeks before they and their mothers

Domestic Water buffalo at a mud wallow.

rejoin the herds. The young are weaned at three to four months, by which time half of the season's crop are lost, either from predation (hyena, crocodile, python, eagles, shoebill) or by drowning during stampedes. At 12–14 months, yearlings undergo a further depletion with a warble infestation. About 33% of the adults are males.

In the present century lechwe numbers have been sharply reduced; only 8,000 Black and 25,000 Kafue Flats lechwe remain.

The personal interest of President Kaunda has undoubtedly saved the lechwe from complete extinction. FAMILY: Bovidae, ORDER:

Artiodactyla, CLASS: Mammalia.   C.P.G.

WATER BUFFALO *Bubalus (Bubalus) arnee,* the largest species of Asiatic buffalo, genus *Bubalus,* domesticated over very large areas of the tropics and subtropics and in the Mediterranean region. The domestic Water buffalo from Italy was first described by Linnaeus in 1758 as *Bos bubalis,* but wild buffalo from India were not described until 1791, when Kerr named them *Bos arnee.* The Asiatic buffaloes can be divided into those with expanding horns, subgenus *Bubalus,* and those with straight horns, subgenus

Anoa. To the first group belong the Water buffalo and the *tamarao, while to the second group belong the two species of *Anoa. The two groups differ in their skulls and teeth as well as their horns. Asiatic buffaloes differ from African buffaloes in their skulls, and in having reversed hair along the back.

Water buffalo have horns which face backwards and outwards in their basal part, and gradually turn inwards so that the tips face each other. They are triangular in section and irregularly ridged. Unlike true cattle, genus *Bos,* Water buffalo have a straight back with no hump on the shoulders, a sparsely haired grey skin, a smooth tongue. a small scrotum and large hoofs. They are leanly built, taller than an ox of equal weight with a longer body and a low head.

Wild buffalo are found in northern India, from the Ganges and Brahmaputra plains to part of Orissa and southeastern Madhya Pradesh, and Nepal and from northern Burma into Indo-China, and also in Ceylon In most parts of their range they are slaty black, with the legs white from just above the knees and hocks to the hoofs, and a white crescent on the throat. The newborn calf is very light, almost yellowish in colour. The horns either curve up in a semicircle, with the tips close together, or else spread out horizontally going slightly up and in at the tips.

Indian wild buffalo *Bubalus arnee arnee* are 5½ ft–6½ ft (1·7–2 m) high and some bulls may weigh 2,600 lb (1,170 kg). The horns may be as much as 6 ft (1·8 m) long round the curve, and 4½ ft (1·4 m) is not unusual. The Ceylon wild buffalo *B. a. migona* is much smaller, only 5 ft (1·5 m) high, with horns not exceeding 39 in (1 m) in length. Similar small buffaloes are recorded from Vietnam. The buffalo found in the Mishmi Hills of Assam is said to be a separate, dun-coloured form. *B. a. fulvus*. A population of wild buffaloes exists in Sarawak, but these are almost certainly feral domestic stock.

Domestic buffalo are smaller than Indian wild buffalo, and have differently shaped, shorter and thicker horns, the tips of which are less inturned. They have been transported over most of the tropical and subtropical latitudes, and are the staple beasts of burden or milk and meat providers for much of the world's human population. There are about 78 million domestic buffalo in the world, of which 45 million are in India.

Two basic breeds of domestic buffalo have been developed, the Swamp and River buffaloes. The Swamp buffalo can work in marsh and jungle, is heavily built and highly dependent on water. It suffers if exposed to too much sun and recovers by wallowing. This breed is used in the rice-fields of Malaysia, Indo-China, southern China and the Philippines. In the latter country it is known as the carabao and in Indonesia as kerabau, which is the same word. It was domesticated in the ancient Khmer Empire, and is an excellent working breed.

The River buffalo differs more from the wild buffalo. It is more sparsely built and prefers dry pastures. It bathes in clear rivers and canals, is very docile, and is used more as a milk produeer than as a draught animal. It is the common domestic type of India and Pakistan and is gradually replacing the swamp breed in Malaysia.

Water buffalo have a particularly long history in India and China. The River buffalo was domesticated in India about 2,500 BC. The Swamp buffalo was domesticated in China about 1,500 BC. From these two centres they have been taken around the world, most of this spread having taken place in comparatively recent times.

Domestic buffalo of the River type are used in Iraq, Syria, Turkey, Transcaucasia, Azerbaijan, Greece, Bulgaria, Hungary, Rumania and Yugoslavia. It is also found in Egypt, where it was introduced about 900 AD; in Eritrea, where it has been recently introduced from Egypt; and in central Italy, where it was introduced in the 6th century AD from Hungary, but has been steadily decreasing in numbers since the draining of the Pontine marshes. From Italy, domestic buffalo have been introduced into Andalusia in southern Spain, Guyana, Cayenne, Trinidad, Marajo island at the mouth of the Amazon and the lower Congo.

The 40,000 buffaloes in Italy supply the milk used in making mozzarella cheese. The ranchers on the Marajo island rate the buffalo more productive than any other cattle in an environment which includes widespread flooding and marshy conditions. There are some 2,000 small, sturdy Water buffaloes in Hong Kong for general use. Added to this thousands are imported yearly from China, and other countries of the Far East, mainly for slaughter. These examples illustrate their range of utility.

In 1825, some buffalo were imported from Timor (Indonesia) to Melville Island, North Australia, for food for colonists and aborigines. Three were introduced in 1825, a further 15 in 1827 and 16 more in 1829. From these small beginnings the buffalo increased and in 1885 there were 6,000 but just how many there are now is not known. In 1838 some buffaloes were introduced to the vicinity of Port Essington (mainly from a shipwreck) and they spread south and west from there, increasing in numbers, and now there are 60,000 on the Australian mainland.

The basic characteristic of Water buffalo which must have contributed largely to their original domestication is that they are tractable. They cannot be easily driven or herded but they can be led. They seldom use their horns or hoofs in attack and in southern Asia it is a commonplace to see one of these huge beasts, with its massive horns, being led by a child. Children ride them lying on their broad backs to wallows, even entering the water to wash them down and carefully clean their ears, eyes and nostrils.

The buffalo with its slow plodding walk is ideal for work in the paddy fields. Its sureness of foot enables it to step over the low mud walls bounding the paddy fields without disturbing them. In any work in which speed is not essential they serve well. In rice-growing areas they are used to plough, using the wooden plough unchanged for centuries. They can harrow and puddle the sticky. lumpy earth to the correct consistency for planting rice, working with as much ease in liquid mud as on dry land helped by the unusual flexibility of the joints above the hoof.

A further example of their versatility is that Water buffalo are widely employed in threshing rice. Sheaves are laid on a rattan mat over a hard mud floor and two or more buffaloes plod in a tight circle trampling out the grain.

Wild buffalo live in tall grass jungles and reed brakes near swamps. In the southern parts of their range, they live on rather harder ground. They form small herds of 10–20, which sometimes combine to form larger grazing groups. They graze in the early morning and again in the evening, avoiding the heat of the sun and have been known to feed at night. The members of the herd communicate by grunting; bulls occasionally bellow like a domestic bull. It is unfortunate that wild buffalo are fond of cultivated plants and this fact, together with their competition with tame buffalo for grazing, has caused a reduction in their numbers. It is probable that there are under 2,000 remaining in the wild, of which 400 are in Kaziranga, Assam.

Buffalo cows come into oestrus every three weeks. The rut takes place at the end of the rains and calves are usually born from March to May, although they have been seen at other times of the year. Young adult bulls, unable to mate with wild cows because of the aggressiveness of the older and stronger bulls, may mate with domestic cows. This is not usually welcomed by the herdsmen, although in fact it probably improves the breed. Gestation lasts 310 days and maturity is reached at three and a half to four years. Where there is access to plentiful food, for example in Hungary, the animals will mature more quickly, while in poor countries. like India, a buffalo may be five years old before it is fully developed.

The continual need of Water buffalo to bathe or wallow is a distinct drawback to their usefulness to man. They plaster themselves with mud, and create an impenetrable layer over their skins: this and their love of submerging up to their noses rids them of many of their ectoparasites and helps them escape from insects, and in this respect they have an advantage over ordinary cattle. Although their milk yield is less than many cows and their meat is probably less nutritious, their great strength and their ability to remain healthy under conditions in which cattle would perish, ensure that Water buffalo will find a place in the economy of many countries for many years to come. FAMILY: Bovidae, ORDER: Artiodactyla, CLASS: Mammalia.   C.P.G.

WATER DEER *Hydropotes inermis*, a small *deer of the reed swamps and grasslands close to rivers of eastern and Central China and Korea.